AF408590

Also by Shane Almgren

The Trumpland Diary
A Journal of Bigly Proportions

Conspiracy Christianity
*The 7 Evangelical Training Principles that Promote Wild Propaganda, Dangerous
Misinformation & Outlandish Conspiracy Theories*

DESPERADOS

The Insane True Story of Undercover Missionaries, Counterfeit Rock Stars & the Music Hoax of the Century

SHANE ALMGREN

Book Cover and interior design by Shane Almgren

First edition 2024

ISBN 9798218513139 (Paperback)

For Mum, who got the tire over the fence.

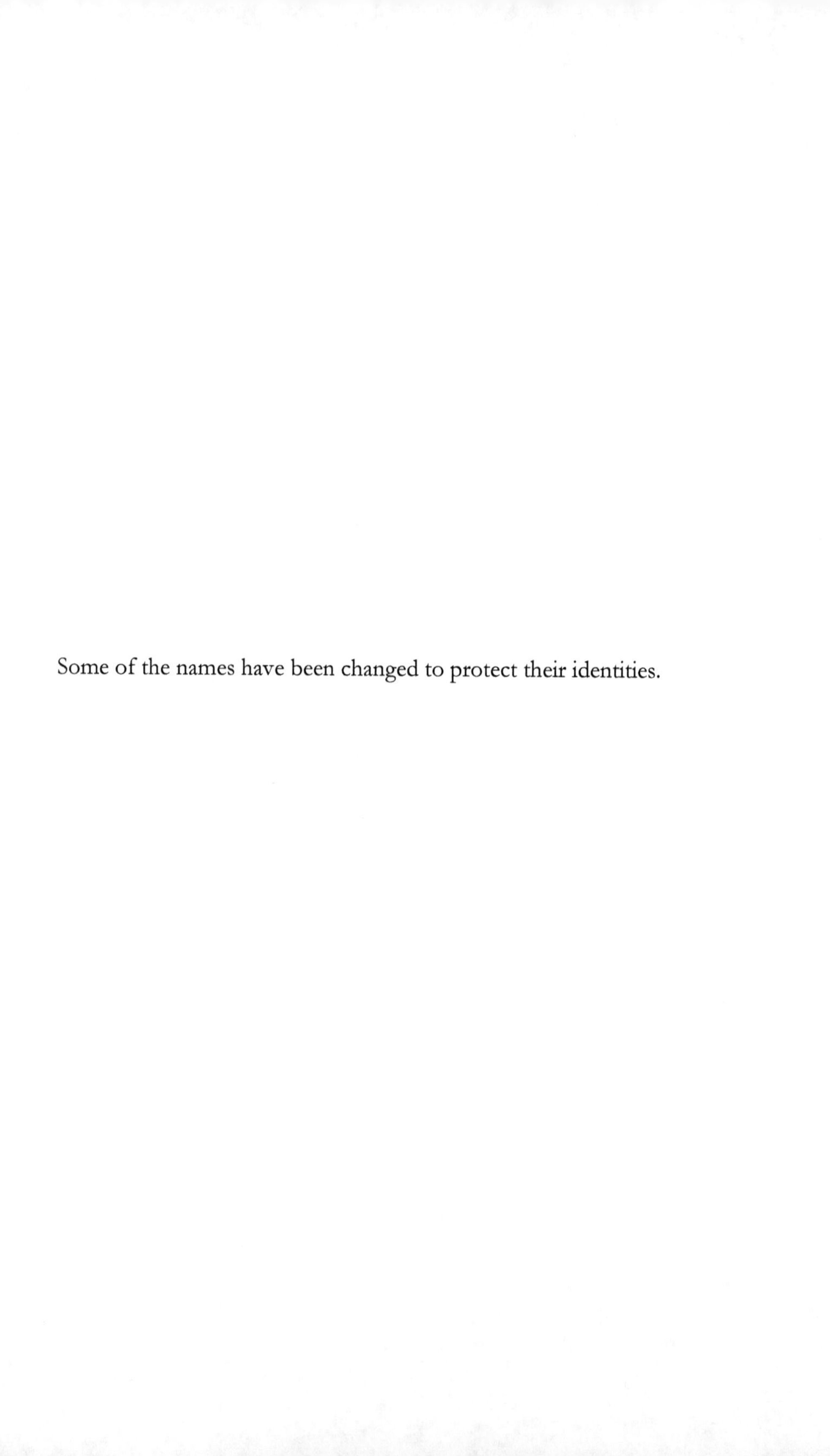

Some of the names have been changed to protect their identities.

Contents

DESPERADOS

Here's to the crazy ones, the misfits, the rebels, the troublemakers, the round pegs in the square holes, the ones who see things differently.

They're not fond of rules, and they have no respect for the status quo. You can quote them, disagree with them, glorify or vilify them. About the only thing you can't do is ignore them – because they change things. They push the human race forward. While some may see them as the crazy ones, we see genius.

Because the people who are crazy enough to think that they can change the world, are the ones who do.

– Steve Jobs

Some of the world's greatest feats were accomplished by people not smart enough to know they were impossible.
– Doug Larson

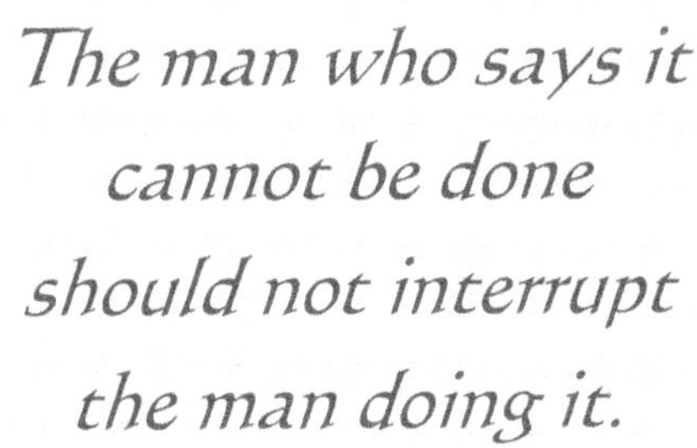

The man who says it
cannot be done
should not interrupt
the man doing it.

– Ancient Chinese Proverb

介绍

Introduction

A Brief History of Western Music in China

n August 1966, Communist Party leader Mao Zedong launched the Cultural Revolution in China in an effort to strengthen his authority over the nation and steer it back in the "right direction," as he estimated it. The production of politicized artwork—nearly all of it featuring Mao as its centerpiece—exploded across the country.

Art in all its forms, including music, painting, sculpture, and theater, was now required to fulfill a political purpose. They were to be propaganda mouthpieces extolling the virtues of Communism and the Motherland. Art for the sake of joy, pleasure, or beauty was heavily discouraged or outright condemned. Finding joy in any creative outlet that glorified anything other than the Communist Party was looked at as "bourgeois." Institutes of learning, cultural and religious traditions, historical artifacts, and untold amounts of art were mindlessly destroyed in an attempt to eradicate any vestiges of non-conformism to Mao's Communist ideals. Public beatings and humiliations, torture, and killing were the Red Guard's primary methods of enforcement.

After Mao's death in 1976, Deng Xiaoping assumed leadership, reversing a number of policies Mao had put into place, and acknowledging the abysmal failure that had been the Cultural Revolution. Deng believed the people should be entitled to greater freedoms than his predecessor, and his amicable interactions with the West paved the way for the West's cultural influence to begin gradually making its way back into China.

In the early 1980s, John Denver and Karen Carpenter became the first artists sanctioned to play in China. Not to perform there, mind you, just to legally have their music imported and played over loudspeakers. Since they were the only Western artists China's population was aware of, they became instant sensations, with Carpenter's 1973 hit "Yesterday Once More" quickly becoming the biggest song in the country.

By the time the mid-80s rolled around, the Chinese government was ready to show both the world and its own people precisely how "open" they'd become: it was time to roll out the red carpet and welcome a Western musical act into China for the first time in their history. It was time for . . .

(drumroll, please)

George . . . Michael?

Wait, what?

Okay, that was out of left field. Allow me to explain.

In the West, the pop charts were being dominated by Duran Duran, Culture Club, and Wham! (the duo of George Michael and Andrew Ridgeley). Wham! had aspirations for global domination and was looking for ways to cement themselves as The Biggest Group in the World.

As detailed in [Wham! manager] Simon Napier-Bell's book, *I'm Coming to Take You to Lunch*, the idea to play China was hatched by Wham!'s co-manager, Jazz Summers, as a half-joke: If Wham! truly wanted to become the biggest group in the world, what better way to do it than to be the first act to play Communist China?

George Michael instantly loved the idea, and it fell to Napier-Bell to figure out a way to make it happen.

With his marching orders in place, Napier-Bell set out for China and holed himself up in a Beijing Holiday Inn. With precisely zero connections—and not the slightest clue who to reach out to try to make any—he simply went through the phone book and called every government ministry he could locate a number for. If anyone answered who happened to speak English, he'd leave a message saying, "Tell them Simon Napier-Bell has called to take them to lunch."

The first person to return his call was a minister of energy who thought Napier-Bell was a coal buyer. According to Napier-Bell, "It was two years of lunches—I fed the whole government [including the confused energy minister], 143 people three times each."

After 18 months of buying lunch for random Communist officials, Napier-Bell tried a different approach: he convinced them that their best opportunity to secure foreign investments was by demonstrating to the outside world that they were serious about opening up to foreigners and that there was no better way to do so than by bringing over a British pop group.

To make it look like he wasn't solely there to push Wham! (which he absolutely was), Napier-Bell had brochures made up of both Wham! and Queen (who, along with The Rolling Stones, were angling to be the first to play China), offering the Chinese a choice between the two acts.

The Wham! brochure was designed to make the band and its fans look as wholesome as possible. The Queen version featured a leather-clad Freddie Mercury in as many provocative poses as Napier-Bell could find photos of. The ultra-conservative Chinese chose Wham!. Two weeks later, the group was on their way to Beijing as the first-ever Western performing act in China's 5,000-year history.

The concert itself was seen as more of a symbolic success than an actual musical one. To put it bluntly, it was *weird*. Held in a Beijing gymnasium on April 7, 1985, a break dancer came out to open the show and warm up the crowd before a loud voice squawked over the PA system that dancing was strictly forbidden.

The concertgoers had no idea what to make of the colorful outfits, bizarre hairdos, flamboyant stage presence (Chinese acts typically dressed in drab colors and stood perfectly still while they performed), and the sheer *loudness* of it all. Terrified of the repercussions of acting out of turn, the attendees sat rigidly in their seats the entire time, convinced that the film crew on hand to document the show were actually the Secret Police. Not even Michael relentlessly imploring the audience to clap along was able to coax out more than a few tepid and sporadic gold claps. The few people who ignored the PA voice and got up to dance anyway were taken away by the real police.

George Michael later called it "the hardest performance I've ever given in my life."

Despite the bizarre nature of the entire affair, it was seen as a win-win for both parties. Wham! was heralded as an international ambassador between the Western world and China. China, in turn, got to present itself to the outside world as being far more "open-minded" than anyone was inclined to give it credit for, and no one "out there" was really buying anyway.

China also didn't do themselves any favors in their follow-up attempt to show the world they were indeed modernizing, hosting Jan and Dean in 1986 for a three-stop "Friendship Tour" that included Beijing, Shanghai, and Guangzhou. Internally, the Chinese were touting the performances as a "cultural exchange program," and since Jan and Dean were singing mostly doo-wop hits from the 60s, the international community just rolled their eyes. Going from 80's chart-toppers to essentially oldies music wasn't anybody's idea of "progress."

Somewhat humiliated, China decided to take its ball and go home. It slammed its doors to outsiders, vowing no more Western bands would play there again.

And so no Western band did.[1]

Until 1999.

---

[1] While staunchly resistant to the Western pop charts, China's censors did develop a strange fascination with Muzak and other offerings generally reserved for elevators, hotel lobbies, and answering services. Jazz crooner Harry Connick Jr. was invited to perform one show in Shanghai in 1995, and Greek composer Yanni recorded a live concert at the Forbidden City in 1997.

Basically, if you go
looking for trouble,
it'll come find you.

— Estelle

Enter The Dragon

BEIJING, OCTOBER 26, 1999

"You!"

Gavin and I popped our heads up from our chess match like meerkats on the savannah, peeking over the wall of the little café we were anxiously camped out at in the middle of the Beijing airport. We craned our necks for a glimpse of whatever poor unfortunate soul happened to be garnering such an aggressive salutation in this country whose entire population was programmed from birth to fly under the radar. Nobody was sprinting through the terminal, or causing a scene, or doing anything else noteworthy enough to merit such attention. We turned back to our game.

"You!" Louder and closer this time.

We looked up again, this time spotting three angry-looking security guards armed with submachine guns bearing down on our table and pointing at someone who—based on the direction one of them was indicating with the business end of his rifle—I judged to be sitting directly behind my sternum.

I'm very good at perceiving angles like that.

I turned and glanced over my shoulder at the tables behind us. They were either completely vacant or totally occupied by warring factions of ninjas who had achieved mastery over the metaphysical art of invisibility. As an aspiring ninja myself, and someone who definitely knew a thing or two about their invisibility capabilities, the latter couldn't be ruled out.

Leave it to the Chinese to train their police officers so rigorously and thoroughly as to be able to detect invisible ninjas, despite a pair of rarely-spotted-but-easily-noticed foreigners directly blocking their line of sight.

"*You! You are Americans?*"

I wasn't sure why these guys were still yelling. All three of them were standing directly over us now, staring down over the ferns at our chess game rather than over at the invisible anarchist ninjas and their blatant-yet-imperceptible throwing-star battle that was definitely probably happening. Maybe.

I was nearly certain they were inquiring about us now.

That scenario would also be plausible, possibly even more likely. After all, we were currently in a country we weren't supposed to be in, pretending to be people we definitely *weren't*, had infringed on God-knows-how-many copyright laws to get here, and were only here in the first place for the singular purpose of doing something incredibly illegal. So, yeah, I suppose I could kinda/sorta see them wanting to have a chat with a couple guys fitting that description.

"Yes," we both nodded.

"You are flying to Changsha?"

Another yes.

"You are in a band?"

I thought you'd never ask.

"We are."

"You have American friends waiting there for your arrival, yes?"

"Yes."

"One woman and three men?"

Unless our bass player had suffered an identity crisis on the two-hour flight, that would also be accurate.

"Yes."

"Good. You come with us *now*." It was not a suggestion.

I glanced at Gavin. We'd both known going into this that a scenario exactly like the one that was suddenly playing out was a very real possibility. I just hadn't thought it would happen so quickly. We'd only been in the country for two hours.

But the situation did make sense. There were six of us traveling to China, headed for the city of Changsha. We hadn't all made it onto the connecting flight because Gavin—God bless him—had managed to lose his boarding pass while traversing the massive Beijing terminal.

The rest of the group had gone ahead with the planned itinerary, leaving the two of us to stay behind on a two-hour layover to catch the next available flight. The crew going ahead of us would've had to clear Customs when they landed. They would've handed over their passports—the Chinese Customs agents quickly surmising they were the wrong people with the wrong names—and then the proverbial excrement would've hit the fan. They'd have been arrested, the Changsha airport would've notified the Beijing airport to be on the lookout for a conspicuous pair of foreign stragglers, they'd have spotted us, confirmed our traveling companions . . . and *that,* my dear Watson, was why we were now being arrested before we'd even had a chance to step outside and breathe in some of that thick, beautiful Chinese smog.

I patted myself on the back for the Sherlockian deduction, thought better of it, then wiped it off for getting into a situation that would require deductions of that order in the first place. What was that old "Quotable Quote" from *Reader's Digest* I'd proudly memorized as a kid?

Wisdom is the trait that keeps you out of situations where you need it?

Yep, that was the one.

Man, I was great at memorizing wise quotes! What a pity memorizing wise stuff never has any useful life applications. Somebody should speak to someone about that.

We stood up and grabbed our backpacks. I gave Gavin a solemn nod that said *it was nice knowing you.* He returned one that said the same, plus an impressive number of expletives my eyebrows hadn't managed to convey. And then three heavily-armed Chinese guards encircled us and led us away.

I was worried for two reasons. The first was that they were leading us past the gate our plane would've been pulling into at any moment, through a set of double doors marked SECURITY: NO ENTRY, and down a narrow hallway that stopped dead at an imposing steel door with who knows what on the other side.

The second was that the *woman* who'd been apprehended with the group ahead of us just so happened to be my mother—she was the sole reason any of us were here in the first place.

This was all her fault.

The steel door swung open from the inside, and we were unceremoniously ushered into the dark.

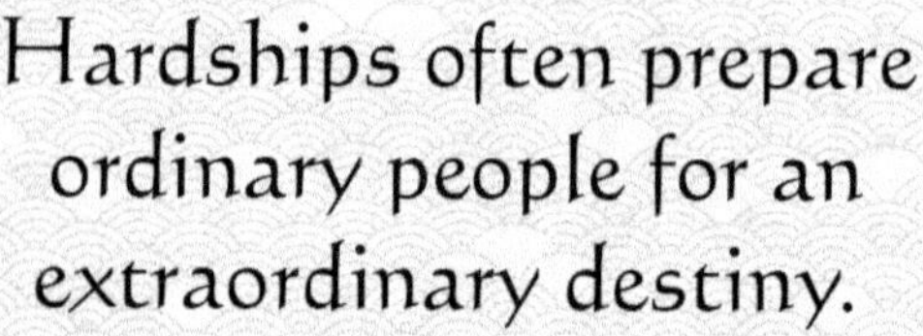

Hardships often prepare
ordinary people for an
extraordinary destiny.
– C.S. Lewis

二

Almgrens Vs China

CHANGSHA, CHINA, 1988-89

The People's Republic of China was officially established in October 1949 by the Communist Party of China and its leader, Mao Zedong.

Under Communist ideology, religion was heavily discouraged by the State. Vast numbers of missionaries began being expelled, and local churches that were short on doctrine and theology were more or less left to fend for themselves.

From 1966 until Mao's death in 1976 ended the Cultural Revolution, most expressions of religious life in China were effectively banned. Under new leader Deng Xiaoping, persecution of Christians in China became sporadic, possibly even arbitrary. It kinda just depended on the weather, Deng's mood, or how late breakfast had been served that day.

The Communists "wink-winked" at the Three-Self Church, a Protestant organization that was willing to submit to the direction of the Chinese State. But believers were also arrested, imprisoned, and sometimes tortured for their faith. Bibles were destroyed, churches and homes were looted, and Christians were subjected to a variety of humiliations. Several thousand Christians were known to have been imprisoned between 1983 and 1993.

In the winter of 1988, my family decided to roll the dice and throw our hat in the ring. Jail? Torture? *Public humiliation?* Sign us up!

My parents uprooted us from the quiet, boring town of Wichita Falls, Texas, and moved us halfway around the globe, smack dab into the middle of this political upheaval and religious oppression. Though both of my parents had been in the Air Force, this move wasn't military-related. Mom and Dad had felt the call of God upon their lives and were moving us there as missionaries.

This was problematic for any number of reasons, the primary one being the aforementioned point about it being pretty much illegal. (As you'll learn soon enough, a couple of us in the family never concerned ourselves much with such trivialities.)

Since the Commies weren't terribly keen on allowing missionaries into China, those hellbent on going in anyway were forced to enter the country under semi-false pretenses. An organization called University Language Services (ULS) at Oral Roberts University in Tulsa, Oklahoma, provided the necessary cover by placing Christian missionaries as English teachers in schools throughout China. These folks were expected to act like professional academics by day and to do their mission work on the hush-hush by night. And once over there, everyone was on their own.

The schools paid a salary, and many of the missionaries had modest supplemental support from home churches back in the States. From what I'm told, it was a bit like enlisting in the military in that you had no say in what city or school you ended up at. You went wherever China and ULS told you to go.

Our family was sent to the city of Changsha in China's south-central Hunan province. We were stationed at the National University of Defense Technology (NUDT), a military academy under the direct leadership of China's Central Military Commission.

Since its inception in 1953, NUDT has been regarded as the number one military academy in the entire country and is still one of the most difficult universities to enter. It is the Communist Party's preeminent school and research facility for developing national defense science, strategy, and technology. It's also a leading institute for the

Chinese space program, as well as China's supercomputer development.

The sprawling 922-acre campus was surrounded on all sides by a 10-foot-high concrete wall with razor-sharp glass embedded in the top. There were four entrances to the campus, each patrolled by armed guards 24/7. The compound for the foreign English teachers consisted of a four-story apartment building with eight units—two on each floor—a small dining hall, a recreation room, and a few administrative offices. The complex was additionally surrounded by more of the same concrete-and-glass walls, cordoning off the foreigners from the rest of the campus—a "compound-within-a-compound"—giving the whole place the delightful, homey air of a minimum-security prison. It was widely assumed all the units were bugged.

We had our own private guardhouse and gate, and nobody came in or went out without signing in with the guards. To grossly understate it, if someone were looking to do some covert missions work in China, *this* particular university was the very last place on earth anyone in their right mind would ever pick for a staging ground.

A week after arriving, my parents started their new positions as English teachers—Dad at the university, Mom at the on-campus high school. My sister, Kyle, and I were enrolled in the on-campus elementary school.

Sorry, that sounded funny when I read it back to myself.

"Enrolled" sort of gives the impression we'd been granted admittance to some exclusive institution we had aspirations of attending. On the contrary, Mom and Dad had simply flung us into the deep end of a Chinese school because there was nowhere else to put us.

None of us had bothered to learn any Mandarin before we left the States, an inconvenience that didn't strike Mom as a particularly valid reason for not dumping us into a school that didn't speak anything but that. She just patted us on the head and offered, "You'll figure it out."

Figure it out.

That was a mantra in our family.

I did manage to learn *hello, goodbye, thank you,* and how to count to ten in Mandarin before the first day of school, effectively equipping myself to confidently navigate the entering or exiting of various rooms, and dazzle my new classmates with my bilingual prowess should any of the teachers have a pop quiz of *How Many Fingers Am I Holding Up?* planned (they did not).

Apart from the whole "not speaking any English" thing, Chinese schools also differed from their Western counterparts in that the school day started at 8 a.m., and then let out at noon for an afternoon siesta of sorts. Everyone would go home for lunch, take a nap, and then return to school at 2:30 for a couple more hours of class time. Also, the school week was six days (I blame the Communist Party's notorious lack of an appreciable sense of humor on a lifetime of missing out on Saturday morning cartoons). Saturday school was definitely an eye-opening culture shock, and one was tempted to remind themselves: *When in Rome* . . .

Fortunately for us, we were not in Rome; we were in China, and they had no such saying. So, we skipped school on Saturdays.

There were no churches in the city to attend, but every Sunday morning dozens of students would gather at "English Corner," a pavilion in nearby Martyr's Park where students from all over the city would come to practice their English and inquire about the Western culture with whatever foreigners happened to show up (there were, at most, a few dozen Americans in the entire city of six million people). It became the weekly target of the missionaries in the area.

The locals' English proficiency ranged anywhere from barely conversational to nearly fluent. Most of them dutifully showed up every Sunday hoping to practice their vocabulary and phrasing over discussions of American culture, philosophy, or Michael Jackson, but the missionaries always seized the opportunity to evangelize. There was no such thing as a conversation too mundane or arbitrary that it couldn't immediately be redirected into a discussion about God.

"You are from America, yes?"

"Yes, we are."

"Michael Jackson! I love the moonwalk!"

"He's very talented, but have you heard about the man who can walk on *water?*"

"What? *Who is this man?* Tell us more!"

And so it would go.

Whether you're a believer or not, it's amazing how often the details of the Bible are taken for granted in the Western world. Whether you're a Muslim, Buddhist, agnostic, or militant atheist, there is still a passing familiarity with the stories of the Bible. *Everyone* knows who Jesus is.

Right?

The fact of the matter was that the vast majority of the Chinese population did not. They were utterly intrigued. Never mind all the magical and supernatural stories, the mere concept of a *personal* deity who loved them and cared for them, was watching over them, and might even intervene on their behalf was captivating. They were easy pickings, and they converted in droves.

(Of course, it's also possible that, since every TV show in the country featured kung fu masters who could fly through the air and knock people over with invisible energy balls from 50 feet away, New Testament miracles weren't as tough a sell as they were at the MIT robotics department.)

But those Gospel conversations weren't just saved for the people who showed up at the park on Sundays; students would stay after class to discuss assignments, and my parents would seize the opportunity to introduce them to the faith.

As the months passed and the new converts became interested in learning more, it became no longer feasible to relegate teaching moments to a few passing encounters between classes. My parents and the other missionaries in our apartment building began organizing weekday evening meetings in our homes. Our floor would be entirely blanketed wall-to-wall with students participating in our makeshift home church services.

Naturally, all these gatherings had to be done under the auspices of game nights, movie marathons, or cooking parties. That two or three dozen students from campus were on record signing in at our guardhouse on any given night was unavoidable, so the best we could hope for was to make it as innocuous-looking as possible. And so, they'd slowly trickle through the gate bearing board games, traditional Chinese instruments, a wok, or any variety of dead (and occasionally alive) animals. It was a grand and convincing show.

For a while.

A little over a year into our stay, an incident in our building attracted some unwanted scrutiny. During one particular weekly meeting, one of the American women in the apartment above us had left her camera out, and one of the visiting students that evening had walked off with it. The school launched an investigation to determine the culprit, and that ended up uncovering a whole lot more than the missing Kodak.

Dad returned home from work one afternoon and informed us that a number of his students hadn't shown up for class. A few of the other missionaries in the building said the same thing. It wasn't a random sampling of students who weren't accounted for either—it was the ones who had become regular fixtures at our weekly evening gatherings, whose names had popped up enough times on the sign-in forms at the guard station to pique the interest of the authorities investigating the stolen camera. A second investigation was started to determine why the same names kept showing up on such a regular schedule.

When the students failed to materialize after a few days, curiosity turned to concern. We started asking around, and that's when the news broke from their fellow classmates and friends about what had happened: the missing students had been rounded up—snatched straight from their dorm rooms in the dead of night—and "dealt with."

Dealt with *how* was left to the imagination.

And it wasn't just the students. Many of their family members had vanished as well—unsuspecting people whose only "crime" was being related to someone who'd found themselves in hot water with the State. Dozens upon dozens of people simply disappeared with absolutely no forthcoming explanation from anyone.

Apparently, we had not been nearly as inconspicuous as we'd all imagined. Or maybe we had been, and the units actually were bugged. Either way, our family was immediately booted out of NUDT.

The students and family members who'd gone missing were never seen or heard from again. Nobody knew if they'd been imprisoned, executed, or conscripted into some involuntary medical experimentation.

They simply *vanished*.

In the process of evicting us, the Communist Party officials at NUDT sent out letters to all the other schools and universities in Changsha explaining what we'd been up to and warning them not to hire us. All the schools received the memo except one: Hunan University, about five miles across town.

With no other options, my parents quickly applied to work there and were accepted. Compared to our previous post, Hunan University was idyllic. It was a regular university campus: no armed guard stations, no Communist Party officials dotting the walkways, no bugged apartments. Instead of psychotically booby-trapped border walls, it was surrounded on three sides by scenic forests and parks.

Mom and Dad unassumingly resumed their mission work. Kyle and I *enrolled* in a brand-new Chinese school, made new friends, and mostly stayed out of trouble. Life was copacetic. Until I accidentally ended up in a counter-communist protest that got out of hand and turned into a revolution where 10,000 people got massacred, and they kicked us out of the entire country instead of just the school.

Okay, maybe not *exactly* the way I just described. Allow me to clarify:

Our new school was a couple miles from our new home, and since school buses weren't a thing there yet, Kyle and I made the daily trek on foot. About six months into our stay at Hunan U, our elementary school started buzzing because kids up at the high school had suddenly begun walking out of class on a daily basis. Student walk-outs aren't a thing that ever happens there.

Not even for seniors.

There were whispers and rumors among the missionaries that the students weren't happy about . . . *something*, but no one knew for sure what was going on, and it didn't seem like a big enough deal to any of the adults to get any details.

A week into the inexplicable walkouts, Kyle woke up sick one morning, leaving me to hoof it to school alone that day. Normally, when the morning session let out at noon, instead of going home for lunch and a nap like all the other kids, Kyle and I would walk a couple blocks over to the music building for our mandatory daily piano practice. On this particular day, the main gate to the building was chained shut. There would be no piano practice that day, a travesty I regarded somewhere between Second Christmas and the Second Coming.

Since I was by myself, I decided to head back home in a manner I absolutely loved doing whenever I could find an opportunity: hitchhiking.[2]

I began waving my hand at anything that drove past, and within minutes, a dump truck came to a stop in the middle of the road. A dump truck whose "dump" was standing-room-only filled with college-aged kids, packed in like sardines. I asked if I could climb in, and a cluster of hands immediately reached over the side and hauled me up. Once aboard, they asked where I was headed. I told them—*home*. The sardines began tittering excitedly, insisting I should come with them instead. Naturally, I wanted to know where they were going.

At this point in time, we'd been in China for a year and a half—completely immersed in a Chinese school—and my Mandarin was, well, good enough to be getting an education a couple grade levels above my American counterparts.

But it wasn't *fluent*.

What I *thought* they said they were headed to was a "parade," which seemed exponentially more fun and exciting than heading "home," where I'd have to do "chores" and "homework" and "get yelled at" and such.

Parade it is.

When we arrived at our destination 20 minutes later, the driver got out and opened the back gate, and we all spilled out into a throng of people. Thousands of people packed the streets in every direction. This was gonna be some parade!

Several of the students I'd been crammed in with were holding long bamboo poles, connected by cloth banners wrapped around the ends. One of them asked me if I wanted to carry one of the poles holding up one side of a banner.

Are you kidding me?

Instead of *watching* a parade, I actually get to *be in it?*

Yes, please!

---

[2] Changsha was relatively crime-free, so even at the age of 12 I had a lot of freedom to roam around the city as I pleased. Usually, I'd ride my bike or hop on the bus. But since tiny, blue-eyed, blond-haired humans were basically one step up from a zoo attraction, I'd occasionally amuse myself by flagging down a moped or rickshaw and asking for a ride, which the locals—once they got over the shock—were all too happy to oblige.

A person with a bullhorn pulled himself up onto a traffic light stanchion and started barking orders. The congregating masses began forming into orderly clusters, apparently dividing themselves up by schools. Or something. I still had no real idea what was going on.

I was handed my end of the banner, and my pole partner on the other end slowly moved apart as we unfurled it. We were motioned out to the front of our cluster of students, maybe 100 people in all. Then the person on the bullhorn gave a command, the entire crowd let out a cheer, and as one, we set out on our parade.

As we walked, I couldn't help but notice there were no bystanders or onlookers out on the streets watching the parade. As far as I could tell, every living person in this sector of the city was *in* the parade, which was curious. And more than a little irritating. I'd never been in a parade before, and now here I was in my very first one, and there was no audience to bask in my contribution to it.

It was also a bit of a bummer that there weren't any marching bands or BMX riders or acrobats or giant helium floats—anything at all, for that matter—to provide some much-needed entertainment.

Maybe that's why there's no audience, I thought, *we're the least entertaining parade in parade history.*

Out of curiosity, or possibly boredom, I leaned forward and swiveled my head up to see what the banner I was carrying one half of said. Perhaps it was announcing where all the free ice cream at the end was being passed out? I read it once, a second time to make sure I hadn't made a mistake, and then a third time in the hopes it had morphed into something other than what it definitely said the first and second time:

DEATH TO COMMUNISM OR DEATH TO US!

Uh-oh.

At twelve, I wasn't well-versed in geopolitical affairs, but I did have the sense to understand that marching down the middle of a major road in Communist China sporting a 10-foot-wide sign calling for "death to communism . . . or else" probably wasn't ideal. Certainly not one of my better ideas.

But I was in it now, what was I gonna do—drop my pole and hitch a ride home? I'd rather face the entire Communist Party than my mother after she found out I'd skipped piano to help spark a political revolution. She was obsessive/compulsive about my piano practice. And also about me not inciting revolutions. Moms, amiright?

The word I'd mistranslated as *parade* was actually *march*—or more specifically, *demonstration*. Students city-wide had begun demonstrating the week prior, following the April 15 death of Hu Yaobang, the former General Secretary of the Communist Party and a popular politician among college students for his pro-reform stances. (Think the Bernie Sanders of China.) But the economic and political reforms that endeared him to the younger generations made him the enemy of Party elders, and he was eventually forced to resign.

Born in Liuyang, just 40 miles from Changsha, he was already viewed as something of a local hero, and his death transformed him into a martyr. It sparked vigils and protests both in Beijing, where they remained peaceful, and in our city, where they turned uncharacteristically violent.

The day after my . . . uh . . . *parade*, we found out that a few hours after I'd left and hitched a ride home, full-scale rioting had broken out in the spot I'd just been marching. Arsonists and looters ransacked nearly 40 stores, and more than 300 people were arrested.

Over the next two months, the protests grew in scale and scope as students throughout the country staged continuous demonstrations, went on hunger strikes,[3] and occasionally lit themselves on fire, eventually culminating in the infamous events of June 4, 1989: the Tiananmen Square Massacre.

Fed up with the protests and unable to squelch them, the Communist Party declared martial law and ordered the military to converge on Tiananmen Square, where more than 100,000 students were gathered. The tanks rolled into town (providing one of the most iconic images of the 20th century when a lone, unidentified man armed

---

[3] At one point, an estimated 3,100 students were on hunger strikes, garnering media attention from around the world. Incidentally, the first hunger strike began in Tiananmen Square on May 13, with students picking that date because the General Secretary of the Communist Party of the Soviet Union, Mikhail Gorbachev, was scheduled for a Grand Welcoming at that location in two days. Remember him for later.

only with a briefcase and sack of groceries stepped out into the middle of the road and blocked their path), the troops opened fire on the protesters, and thousands of students were killed.[4]

While the Western media instantly labeled the event a "massacre," the Chinese government rounded up thousands of suspected dissidents, threw them in prison or executed them, then denied to the outside world that anything had ever occurred there.

In the ensuing weeks, Westerners throughout China were kicked out of the country en masse. Rumors and whispers were flying everywhere about what had actually taken place, and Beijing didn't want those whispers reaching the ears of foreigners who might leak it out of the country. Party officials strenuously "suggested" that those of us who were ordered out refrain from discussing any of the things we'd just read, heard, or seen.

And above all, we were instructed never to come back.

---

[4] Initial estimates put the death toll around 1,000, with another 7,000 wounded. In 2017, the BBC reported that newly released documents from the then-British ambassador to China, Sir Alan Donald, revealed the death toll to be closer to 10,000.

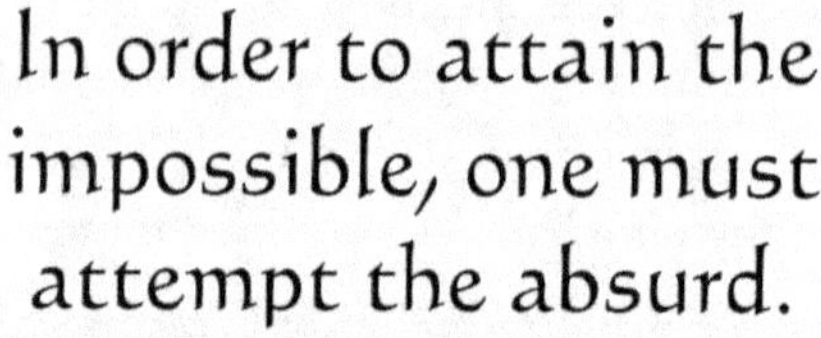

In order to attain the impossible, one must attempt the absurd.

– Miguel Cervantes

Why, sometimes I've believed as many as six impossible things before breakfast.

– Lewis Carroll

Mission: Impossible

We left China and camped out with some missionary friends in Hong Kong for a month while my parents contemplated our next move. They finally decided on Thail— sorry, *God* told them to move to Thailand, which became our home for the next year (with a six-week interlude in Malaysia thrown in for good measure). Mom had mercy on us that year and opted to homeschool us rather than toss us into another foreign school.

After two and a half years flitting about Asia, we finally returned to the States in the spring of 1990, to our old home of Wichita Falls. With nowhere to live, we camped out as a family on the floor of our best friends' house while we figured out our next move.

Two weeks in, my granddad passed away in Maryland, so we flew up there for the memorial service with all the suitcases we'd brought back from Thailand, which was everything we owned. There was no reason to return to Texas, and nowhere else obvious for us to go, so some of my parents' old friends from Christ for the Nations drove over from Pittsburgh and picked us up in a church van. Neither of my parents had any real idea what we were doing there, but flying by the seat of our pants was par for the course.

We were invited to stay in the home of a guy from our new church who opened up his house to missionaries, itinerants, or anyone in need of some temporary lodging. Dad looked for work while Mom finished up our homeschooling. A few months later, we found a permanent house to rent and finally unpacked our suitcases.

It was one of the first evenings in our new home, sitting around the dinner table, when my mom dropped the bombshell. "I've been given a mission by God," she announced dramatically over tuna casserole.

This was not an earth-shattering revelation. Mom was perpetually under the assumption that absolutely any idea that popped into her head without her actively and intentionally calling it up was a Divine Directive. Move to China? That was God. Make a tuna casserole? Also God. Order me to do the dishes—even though it was Kyle's night—because I had failed to compliment her casserole in a timely manner? You guessed it—*God*.

Kyle and I rolled our eyes at each other.

Without waiting for anyone to ask a follow-up question, she continued, "I know this is going to sound crazy," (that went without saying) "but I've been carrying this mission for almost two years now. And it's *big*."

She then proceeded to explain that when we'd been at NUDT in Changsha attending some track-and-field meet her students were in at the city's giant soccer stadium, God had told her it was her mission to bring a Christian concert to China, something that had never been done before in history.

And not *told her* as in she suddenly felt strongly compelled to go put on a concert of epic proportions for reasons she couldn't explain; *told her* as in, God Almighty *audibly* said to her ear holes, "SUSIE, I NEED YOU TO THROW A CONCERT FOR ME!"

She recounted the details of sitting in the stands during the 400-meter dash (or maybe it was the long jump?), looking out across the sea of communistically dour faces in the crowd, and coming to the full realization that everyone there was in desperate, dire need of a

Christian rock experience, as one typically does after watching Chinese collegiate pole vaulting and discus events for six hours straight.

I was skeptical about the audible nature of this alleged Divine Directive. "Are you sure you didn't imagine it?"

"Son, I know what I heard."

"Okay, but did anybody else around you hear it?" I wanted to know, very validly and non-communistically.

"What difference does it make?" she answered. "God can speak audibly to one person in the midst of a sea of people so only that one person can hear Him if He so chooses."

"I'm not trying to limit God or anything and say it definitely wasn't that," I quipped back, "but isn't this the textbook definition of an auditory hallucination?"

"No, it was *not* a hallucination; I know what I heard!"

Yes, that's exactly what people having a hallucination say.

But that was the end of that.

Finishing up her summary with an enthusiasm and satisfaction that wasn't really warranted without the *Mission: Impossible* theme song playing in the background, she sat back in her chair and awaited our collective gasps of awe and wonder.

I wasn't sold. Mom and Dad had an illustrious history of hearing grandiose messages from God that later turned out to not be God, often with cringe-worthy results.

When I was in second grade, God told my parents He was sending us to India. Specifically, to Bombay. They were so convinced of this Divine Directive that Mom came down to my school and made arrangements to get the rest of the year's lesson plans and assignments to take with us so I wouldn't miss out on any schooling when we left the country.

As any 7-year-old naturally would, I spent a couple weeks bragging to anyone at school who would listen that we were moving to India, which pretty much cemented my status as Coolest Kid at Saint Paul Lutheran Elementary (no small feat when one of the fifth graders was in an arm cast from football and two of the sixth graders were rumored to have made out in the barrels at recess).

But those arrangements ultimately fell through, and the move was scrapped. So, I had to trudge back to school with my tail between my legs and explain to everyone that we were no longer moving to India, which pretty much cemented my status as Lamest Kid at Saint Paul Lutheran Elementary—the pathetic kid who tried to impress everyone by making up a tall tale about moving to an exotic foreign land.

When we were in Thailand, God told my parents we were going to adopt a little Thai girl named Bee, who was currently living as a foster child with another missionary family that had a ton of kids of their own. Kyle and I were thrilled to be getting a new sibling and spent hours regaling Bee with epic descriptions of Wichita Falls, Texas, where we were all going to live happily ever after together.

Mom and Dad even made it a point of taking her along with us on outings, spending as much quality time with her as they could to make sure she felt welcomed into her new family. That went on until something way over my pay grade threw a monkey wrench into the process, and the adoption plans fell through. We were all disappointed and very sorry for getting her hopes up, but God had made a mistake, and Bee was unfortunately going to have to find herself a different family to adopt her.

About six months into our Thailand stay, God told my parents that our missions work was done and it was time for us to go back to America. The only problem was that we were so dirt poor at the time that we could barely scrape together enough money to get ourselves and all our luggage from our home in Si Racha to Bangkok by taxi, two hours away. Purchasing four trans-Pacific plane tickets was as far out of reach for us as leasing a wing in Buckingham Palace for the summer.

But God told my parents to take a leap of faith and go to the airport nonetheless—the God of the Universe is not concerned with mortal bank accounts. He was about to unleash a miracle of Biblical proportions on our behalf.

So, we packed up all our belongings—about 11 suitcases—and headed off for the Bangkok airport to await God's airport-themed manna from heaven.

What form might it take? None of us knew, but we all had our guesses. Dad thought some businessman traveling with his own family might overhear us discussing our situation and charitably inject himself into the conversation to offer us his tickets (Dad was pretty sure they would be in First Class). Kyle and I were of the opinion that we were going to happen upon four plane tickets that just magically appeared out of thin air and landed in the seats beside us. Mom was convinced a bona fide angel in human form—like Clarence from *It's A Wonderful Life*—was just gonna stroll right up to us and whip out his celestial Amex card.

The correct answer, it turned out, was *none of the above.*

After waiting around at the airport for 13 hours for the last flight to leave and no miracle taking place, Dad had to call a missionary couple back in Si Racha to ask if they would mind driving up in their van to pick us up and bring us back. We would remain in Thailand for another six months.

So, my skepticism about this latest God-directed Don Quixote quest of hers felt well-earned.

Naturally, I had a few questions.

First and foremost: *Are you out of your mind?*

Secondly: *Are you* sure *you're not out of your mind?!?*

And finally: *Are you just messing with us? Because I'm quite certain that you are literally* OUT. OF. YOUR. MIND!!!

All of that was internal. There was a barrage of more reasoned, coherent questions that actually made it past my lips:

"Who's going to play the concert?"

(I don't know yet.)

"Are you talking about enlisting a church worship band to go over there?"

(No, it has to be a big-name act.)

"Do you know any big-name acts?"

(No.)

"Do you have any connections to any big-name acts?"

(Not exactly.)

"Do you have any idea how to get a hold of any big-name act?"

(Not yet, but I'll figure it out.)

"Do you know *anything* about the music business or concert promotion?"

(No, but how hard can it be?)

I'm told it can be difficult.

"How on earth are you going to get China to agree to this?"

(That's a tomorrow problem. We'll cross that bridge when we come to it.)

"Do you even know who to contact in China to float this idea to?"

(China has a vibrant entertainment industry. I'm sure someone in that realm knows how to make it happen.)

"Do you *know* anyone in China's 'vibrant entertainment realm?'"

(Not at the moment, no.)

"What if you actually get an artist or band to go over there and they get arrested…or worse?"

(If this is God's plan, He'll protect whoever He sends.)

"Okay, Mum. Sounds like you've got a real winner on your hands."

I figured she had a better shot of resurrecting Elvis and staging a concert on the moon.

"Crazy" is a term of art;
"Insane" is a term of law.
Remember that, and you
will save yourself a lot of
trouble.

– Hunter S. Thompson

The question isn't who is
going to let me; it's who is
going to stop me.

– Ayn Rand

四

Mother Dearest

For anything that follows in this book to retain any semblance of plausibility, you're going to need to understand my mother. If I tried telling this story without including this necessary side trek, you'd immediately accuse me of making the whole thing up because regular sentient beings who haven't crash-landed on this planet don't behave this way.

Much like Dickens needing to set the table for his *Christmas Carol* with a thorough testament to just how incontrovertibly dead-as-a-doornail Marley was, I'm going to need you to be fully convinced of the state of the woman at the center of our story.

Ready?

Let's go.

My mother is an enigmatic creature. She's a mercurial, tempestuous, hypercreative, hyperactive, hyper-clueless, stubborn-as-a-mule, Energizer bunny/mad scientist spitfire little five-foot Jew of a woman who perpetually resides in her own alternate reality and has the same aptitude for self-awareness as she does for starting at center for the Boston Celtics—a description she'll no doubt find wildly inaccurate, severely misguided, and horribly offensive because she fancies herself five-foot-two.

She is a woman of *extremes*. She has boundless energy. She has incomparable creativity. She has unprecedented resourcefulness. She has limitless drive. She has unparalleled tenacity. She has unbridled optimism. She has an unmatched sense of adventure. She has unrivaled convictions. She has unwavering faith in her God. And she hasn't stopped talking since I met her.

Many of her traits are mutually contradictory. She is fun-loving and gregarious and stubborn and spiteful, and welcoming and inclusive and judgmental and vindictive, and thoughtful and caring and petty and immature, and self-sacrificing and self-effacing and irrational and irascible and maddening and endearing, and she could fit all of those in before breakfast was over. Also, it's possible she has rabies. (To be fair, I wrote this chapter a long time ago. She appears to have mellowed out somewhat since then.)

Her only settings are *one* and *eleventy*, and she does not care what you or anyone else thinks about what she's doing.

If, for example, what you thought she was doing was trying to single-handedly orchestrate an unprecedented international spectacle that is seven kinds of impossible and four kinds of illegal because she insists God told her to—and that perhaps she ought not be doing that thing—she does not care one iota that you think so.

The Jew part up there wasn't pejorative—her dad's side of the family is Jewish. If they didn't think she was a little off-kilter before (they did), she did herself no favors when she ran off at the age of 18 to join the Air Force, where she also found Jesus. Thankfully, she also found my dad there, which meant I got to make an appearance.

If Mom was a raging hurricane, Dad was the calm eye in the middle of the storm. Dad's side of the family is of Swedish descent, and he fit the Nordic stereotype of rarely showing any emotion whatsoever. He was always cool, calm, and collected. Maybe *too* calm. It was often impossible to decipher whether he was furious, elated, or had just gotten struck in the back of the neck with a bear tranquilizer dart. All three came with the same expression.

You'd probably think that the melding of Scandinavian and Jewish philosophies would yield some kind of belief in a supernatural deity who wielded a cosmic hammer—just not on Saturdays—but no, they both went full-on Jesus-freak.

They married a mere six weeks after meeting each other, had me a year later at Sheppard Air Force Base in Wichita Falls, Texas, and then went straight from the Air Force to Christ for the Nations Bible Institute in Dallas, where they learned how to speak in tongues and dance in the aisles with their eyes closed and hands raised. They probably also learned a lot about the Bible, but the only passage I was certain they had covered in class was "spare the rod, spoil the child." Over the next 16 years or so, I would remain as unspoiled as the virgin, Arctic snow.

When their two years of Bible training were up, we moved back to Wichita Falls, where Dad worked full time as a roofer, and Mom worked full time at making sure I didn't accidentally burn down our apartment complex (which she assures me was a much tougher job than roofing in Texas in July).

But if I was a handful, half the blame for that rests squarely on her shoulders. As I mentioned, she was hyper-creative and never stopped moving. She was constantly doing, making, inventing, creating *something*. We didn't have a lot of money—certainly none to spare on room decorations—so mom went down to Sears, got a dozen refrigerator boxes, and cut out giant silhouettes of the more noteworthy animals on Noah's Ark: lions, giraffes, elephants, zebras, rhinos, penguins, walruses, and anything else you might spot on safari that she could find wall space for. She hand-painted each one meticulously, and by the time she was done, I had a menagerie of exotic animals following each other two-by-two around the room up to the Ark.

When Jams (those crazy-patterned shorts) became a popular fashion trend in the early '80s, Mom didn't let the fact that we couldn't afford them keep me from having a drawer full. She'd take Dad and me down to the fabric store, tell us to pick out whatever prints we wanted, drag out her sewing machine and set to work, making us a collection of shorts that were indistinguishable from the real thing.

If she wasn't painting or sewing, then she was teaching herself to play the guitar, or writing plays for the Sunday School kids at church— which she'd also direct—or acting at the community theater, or wallpapering bedrooms, or going to night school to earn her teaching certification, or patching the holes in the ceiling I'd created trying to parachute off the dining room table.

About that . . .

When I was around five, we'd all gone to an air show that featured a bunch of paratroopers dropping into the crowd, and I decided right then and there that if parachuting wasn't the very next activity I attempted in life, life no longer had any meaning. Again, I was five.

The next day I waited until mom was outside sunbathing, stacked a chair on top of the dining room table, nailed my bed sheet corners to the ceiling with masonry nails, tied string around the corners of the sheet and my wrists, and jumped off the chair, anticipating a leisurely Marry Poppins-esque glide down to the floor. It will not surprise you to learn that this method doesn't actually work. I mean, *at all*. I crashed to the floor, sprained an ankle, busted my lip, and ripped several chunks of plaster out of the ceiling.

Mom heard the crash and came running inside to find me in a bleeding heap, a bedsheet tied to my limbs, and the ceiling on the floor, which was not where we normally kept our ceiling.

Once she was done screaming and delivering the obligatory spanking that accompanied just about every activity I engaged in, she congratulated me on the creativity of the attempt and asked what I thought went wrong with the experiment.

I found this incredibly patronizing, as it was patently *obvious* what went wrong: the nails were an impedance, and I hadn't jumped from high enough up. Both issues could be easily remedied by making a second attempt . . . off our second-floor balcony. For some reason, she nixed that idea.

During the summer, our family took frequent Saturday trips to a nearby lake. After several weeks of watching speedboats whip around the lake with skiers in tow, I lost all interest in my snorkel and meager blowup raft. I wanted to water ski.

Unfortunately, families who decorate with refrigerator box hippos do not, as a general rule, possess high-end watercraft. Or even low-end watercraft, for that matter. What I *did* possess were two plastic baseball bats—a big fat red one and a little skinny yellow one. If I lashed them to my feet with bungee cord and got someone to sprint through the shallow water fast enough lugging a rope, there was no good reason why I couldn't become a prolific skier in maybe two or three tries.

Mom thought this was a fantastic idea and volunteered to be the "boat."

Now, I'm not sure that Usain Bolt, sprinting on solid dry land, could pick up enough speed to raise a skier out of the water, but I do know that my diminutive mom, trying to run through knee-deep water for a skiing novice with bats strapped to his feet, could not. After a dozen attempts to no avail, I begrudgingly accepted that God simply made Mom too slow to bring my idea to fruition. That meant this particular failure was on her. The concept itself was flawless.

I told her so. And she agreed. But she complimented the effort, commended the ingenuity, and vowed to start training in case I ever decided to try again.

That was her M.O.

Express your creativity. Don't be afraid to fail. You never know unless you try.

We'd eventually come to have more than our fair share of disagreements later in life, but that's one thing she did that deserves a ton of credit. A lot of parents listen to their kid's hair-brained ideas and then shoot them down with adult-y explanations about how and why it's a dumb idea that would never work. My mother may have *known* that the vast majority of my childish schemes didn't have a snowflake's chance in hell at succeeding, but that didn't stop her from encouraging the attempt.

The worst that can happen is that it doesn't work. Now try something else.

Around the age of six, I became obsessed with the Lone Ranger and demanded that my parents immediately acquire four items of *absolute necessity* for me: a cowboy hat, a mask, a gun, and a horse. My parents and grandma chipped in for my birthday and bought me the cowboy hat and mask, along with a matching set of fringed leather chaps and a vest. They scrimped on the Colt .45 six-shooter I had my heart set on, gifting me a cap gun instead, much to my chagrin. Even at that young age, I was acutely aware of how ineffective cap guns were at stopping *bad guys*. But then they redeemed themselves with the final gift: a lasso. It came with a note:

If you catch a horse, you can keep it.
Love Mom & Dad

I was amenable to this arrangement, much to their chagrin. I took that lasso with me *everywhere:* school, church, the grocery store, the pool, the mall (it was Texas—you never knew when a wild mustang might find its way into the JCPenney's shoe department). Everywhere. For two years straight. My parents never told me to stop or that "enough is enough." They just encouraged me to go right on horse-hunting until I caught my horse. I never did manage to snare one (though I did lasso a goose one time at a public park and nearly lost an ear for it).

Around that time, we realized a mouse had taken up residence in our kitchen. Numerous attempts at baiting a mousetrap with cheese or peanut butter had failed to capture the beast, so I decided to take matters into my own hands. I would wait up all night on the dining room floor for the monster to make his appearance and then *kill it* . . . somehow.

Mom assured me this was a brave and noble quest, and that all the villagers in all the lands would probably sing songs and tell tales of my heroic vanquishing of the mighty creature terrorizing the bag of dog food to the right of the stove. I didn't want to let the villagers down. This was going to require careful planning.

The first order of business was *personal protection.* My Aunt Joy, a nurse, had terrified me with descriptions of how they treated people who'd contracted rabies—14 hypodermic needle shots right to the stomach, she said. (In retrospect, I have no idea if this was actually true, but it was terrifying.) So, I'd need to cover every square inch of my body. That meant a long-sleeve shirt and overalls, rubber rain boots, my winter gloves, earmuffs, a bandana to cover my face, my dad's roofing helmet, and a snorkel mask. It was virtually impenetrable, and I was pretty sure it could withstand a bear attack. All I needed now was a weapon.

I had one of those bow-and-arrow sets with the suction cup tips, which would not do. Anyone who knows anything about the Wild Wild West knows you never bring a suction cup to a rodent fight. That's Cowboy 101. What *would* do is the same bow firing a Phillips head screwdriver. Dad dutifully fetched his from his toolbox, and I was all set.

Perhaps due to his military background, Dad also informed me that one shouldn't have to man their post alone—they should always have a buddy—and he was going to stand guard with me all night. Mom bid us good luck and good night and took herself off to bed. Dad turned off the dining room light, switched on a flashlight, and settled in beside me. I lay prone on my stomach, bow and screwdriver at the ready. That mouse didn't stand a chance. Five minutes later, I was sound asleep.

Now, Dad could've carried me to my room, tucked me in, and slept comfortably in his own bed. Instead, he spent the night right there next to me on the linoleum floor. When I woke up the next morning, Mom simply said, "Way to stick it out . . . you'll get 'em next time!"

There were few things she disdained more than a person giving up when the going got rough, tough, or uncomfortable. The way she saw it, failure was acceptable. Quitting was not.

Dad reinforced this idea whenever he could. When I was six, he read me a book that had impacted his life when he was a kid, and was about to do the same for me: *Never Quit*—the autobiography of Glenn Cunnigham, who, at the age of eight, survived a schoolhouse fire that left his legs so badly burned doctors recommended amputating both to save his life. He refused and was told that if the infection didn't kill him, he'd never walk again. He vowed to prove them wrong, and eventually did so in epic fashion by making the US Olympic track team.[5] I probably reread that book on my own another two dozen times.

Perhaps the greatest lesson I ever learned in my entire life came in third grade. Mom had used her GI Bill benefits from the Air Force to put herself through night school, earning a teaching degree. Before she went into the workforce full time, she wanted to take one year to homeschool my sister and me.

Mom ran our homeschool routine with military precision—up at 6:30 as if we were going to regular school, get dressed, and come to the table where breakfast would be waiting along with a sheet of paper listing out all the assignments we had for the day. The school day

---

[5] He actually made it twice—in 1932 and 1936—winning a silver medal in the 1500m at the Berlin Games and becoming the world-record holder in the mile race from 1934-1937.

ended when the assignments were completed, not when the clock said 3:30.

Towards the end of the year, I came to the breakfast table one morning, poured my cereal, and glanced over at the sheet mom had prepared. There was just a single item written on it: *Get the tire over the fence.*

I didn't know what that meant, but I knew it was the only thing on the list . . . which meant I was gonna be done early today!

When I was finished eating, Mom took me outside to show me the assignment. She'd found a spare tire from God-knows-where and had placed it in our next-door neighbor's backyard. A six-foot privacy fence separated our yards, and the assignment was as self-explanatory as the sheet had spelled it out: I had to somehow get the tire over the fence into our own yard.

"How am I supposed to do that?" I wanted to know.

"That's entirely up to you," she said.

I tried to pick it up, testing its weight. I managed to flip it upright, but couldn't lift it higher than my waist.

"It's too heavy," I informed her, "there's no way I can lift this over the fence."

"Then you'll have to figure out some way other than lifting it," Mom replied.

"But I don't *know* any other way to get it over!" I whined, slowly beginning to understand the difficulty of the challenge.

"Yes, I'm aware of that, son. It wouldn't be much of an assignment if you already knew how to do it. Your job is to figure it out."

Figure it out.

"I don't care how you do it," she continued. "Build a catapult, dig a tunnel, whatever you can come up with—"

Matches?

"—without burning the fence down."

Drats!

"But the school day isn't over until that tire is in our yard. Now, I'll leave you to it. Happy scheming!"

Then she went back inside.

I tried lifting the tire one more time, but it was exactly as heavy as I remembered it being from one minute ago. There was simply no way my pint-sized, eight-year-old self was getting this stupid tire over the fence. So, I knocked it back over and plunked myself down into the middle of it like an innertube. At least I didn't have to do any actual *schoolwork*—I was just going to sit out here until I reckoned I'd been out there long enough for Mom to agree with me that the task was impossible, and then she'd let me off the hook to go play.

It didn't take long for the sun to start beating down, which was my cue to head back in and announce that I'd given it my best, and my best simply wasn't enough. Mom had done a whole section on Greek epics that year, so I even knew what term I was going to spring on her to impress her with the impossibility of the task she'd given me: *Sisyphean.* I walked back into the house to state my case.

"Done already?" she asked. "That was fast!"

"No, I tried, but I can't do it. I don't think anyone could do it except maybe Dad or Arnold Schwarzenegger. You gave me a Sisyphean task!" I readied myself for her approval of the vocabulary word and the sure-fire dismissal of my case that would accompany it.

"Well then, you turn around and march your little *bee*-hind right back out there and try some more. You are not coming back inside this house until the job is done. Do you understand me?"

"But what if I have to go to the bathroom?" I demanded.

"You can come inside to use the bathroom, and I will call you inside for lunch if you're still out there then. But you're not stepping another foot inside this house for any other reason until that tire is over the fence, got it? Now scram!"

I turned around and stormed back out, muttering hateful eight-year-old epithets under my breath.

Stupid mom and her stupid assignments and her stupid tire and stupid fence and her stupid rules and stupid homeschool and stupid lunch and stupid house and everything is STUPID!

For the next couple hours, I made up games to play with the stupid tire, collecting rocks and trying to toss them into its center from various distances. It passed the time. Didn't do much to inch towards a solution, but at least I wasn't bored. At one point, Mom came back out to check on my progress, of which there'd been none. She was not pleased to find that no progress had been made, other than a bunch of new rocks scattered about.

"Can I come in now?" I pleaded. "It's roasting out here. What if I die of heat stroke? I bet you'd be sorry *then.*"

"You're not going to die out here. If you get too hot or thirsty, go turn on the hose. You're welcome to as much hose water as you want."

I started to cry. Stupid Mom didn't get it. This was *impossible.*

She came over and put her arm around my shoulder, looked me in the eye, and said, "Son, you are allowed to cry as long as you need to. You can pout all you want. You can sit out here all day long, feeling sorry for yourself. But with God as my witness, you are not coming back inside until that tire is over the fence." Then she left.

So that's what I did. I cried. I pouted. And I sat there in the hot Texas sun, feeling sorry for myself.

But then a funny thing happened. After a while, the self-pity started giving way to anger. Not at Mom, at the tire itself. It was just a stupid, worthless, beat-up little insignificant tire.

It wasn't better than me.

Nope, I wasn't gonna get beat by a tire, especially not a *stupid* tire. I'd show it who's boss! It was time to stop pouting and figure this out.

Around the time I'd normally be getting done with my schoolwork, I walked in the back door and announced we were the proud new owners of a tire in our backyard. It had taken a dozen or so tries, each one failing for one reason or another, but incrementally getting closer than the previous attempt. The final solution was a half ramp/half pulley contraption using a couple of 2x4's I found on the side of the neighbor's house, and a length of rope I found in our garage. Using the neighbor's busted basketball goal as a fulcrum, I tied one end of the rope to the tire, and the other end I passed through a cinder block. Pulling the rope as hard as I could, and with the cinder block for added weight, I managed to guide the tire up the ramp and over the fence.

"What an ingenious contraption!" Mom exclaimed when she saw it. "Great job. Now you can go play."

And that was it. No lectures or lengthy spiels about what we'd learned that day or how it might be applied to life. I'd eventually come to those realizations on my own, though it would be many years later before I looked back and saw the lesson in it.

Nothing is impossible. There's always a solution.

Figure it out.

That was Mom—always insisting on figuring it out. Even if it was something patently absurd and ill-advised to be figuring out.

I don't want to leave you with the mistaken impression that Mom's solutions were always neat, or practical, or effective, or well-thought-out, or rational, or safe, or sane, or legal—more often than not they weren't—just that they were solutions. But, once she'd gotten her mind set on something, trying to talk her out of it only made her do it harder.

The year she homeschooled us, she decided that for P.E. class one day, we needed to learn how to row a boat. For some reason. We didn't have a boat—row or otherwise—so Mom went to Target and bought one of those two-person inflatable rafts with the detachable oars. Although there were several boat-friendly lakes nearby that would've been perfectly accommodating and ideal for amateur rowing lessons, mom decided we were going to Sikes Lake for our crew practice.

Now, let's be very clear on this point: Sikes Lake was a misnomer. Sikes Lake was to lakes what Wichita Falls was to falls—a three-story, man-made hunk of fiberglass built along the side of the highway in the 1980s because the actual falls our humble town was named for had gotten washed away in a flood in the 1800s. Our "falls" was basically a glorified lawn fountain—the kind of tacky water feature you might find at a family putt-putt golf center.

Sikes Lake was more or less the same deal. It was a minuscule body of water that nobody was allowed in. Technically a reservoir, it was little more than a well-manicured duck pond behind the library, with a walking path around it that made a one-mile loop.[6] It was a popular fishing spot, and Mom and Dad loved to take us over to walk (or skateboard) the loop in the evenings. So, it was impossible not to be aware of all the signs everywhere saying *No Swimming. No Wading. No Boating.* Mom was definitely aware. But the day's lesson plan required reinterpreting them into polite suggestions rather than hard, fast rules.

Signs can't tell our family what to do.

Mom drove us down to the duck pond and then sat in the parking lot for an hour blowing up the raft because she hadn't bothered to get an air pump. ("Why would I buy a pump when my lungs work perfectly

---

6 For the purposes of this book, I Googled Sikes Lake to see if it was still there and how big the loop was. Not only is it still there 40 years later, it's actually called Sikes Lake Duck Park now.

fine?") She got the raft about 90% full before discovering there was a hole in it, but by then she'd just spent so much time blowing it up that she decided it shouldn't matter. In her mind, the laws of physics could be matters of opinion and up for debate, dependent on how much time and energy she'd already invested.

So, we walked our not-quite-inflated raft down to the *No Boating* duck pond, where all three of us climbed in. Once we were all aboard, Mom pushed us off from the rocky bank with one of the oars and immediately lost her grip, dropping it into the water as our raft sailed off without it.

Predictably, the pressure of three bodies in the raft just made the air leak out faster, and within minutes, the raft was sagging in the middle, slowly bending in half as the center crept down towards the waterline.

"Hey lady, your boat is sinking!" came a shout from the shore, as three boys my age rounded into view toting fishing poles.

"I know my boat is sinking, what do you want me to do about it?" she yelled back at them irritably.

"You should row back to shore!" came the response.

Row back to shore. That was a great idea. Wonder how many oars that might require? We currently had *one*.

"Hey lady, one of your oars is over there!" one of the boys shouted helpfully, pointing with his rod at something about 40 feet to our left.

"Don't worry about what we're doing!" Mom screamed back. "We're having P.E. class!"

Great call, Mom. I bet that was exactly the missing piece of information they were looking for.

"Hey lady, you know this lake is full of water moccasins, right?" one kid hollered.

That tidbit jolted her back to reality.

Mom grabbed the remaining oar and began paddling furiously, on one side of the sinking raft and then the other, making it about ten yards from the shore before the center finally dipped below the surface, water flooded in, and the whole thing capsized. The pond was only about waist-deep at that point, but Mom grabbed both of us—and the submerged raft somehow—and sprinted to the shore before the cottonmouths devoured us.

Stellar P.E. class there, Mum!

That was not at all an atypical day at Susie Almgren Elementary Homeschool: she'd decide we needed to learn proper rowing technique (because she'd learned it at summer camp when she was 13 and thought it was a practical life skill), and then we'd just stand around and watch her blow up a raft for an hour, watch her ignore all the signs telling people to stay out of the water, watch her casually disregard everything she'd ever taught us about air pressure, and then sit in a sinking boat for about 15 minutes doing absolutely nothing while she freaked out and frantically raced around with her one paddle trying to outrun snakes.

We didn't learn anything about rowing that day, but at least we got to go home soaking wet and smelling like fish. Later that evening, Dad wanted to know what in the world she'd been thinking. "There are signs posted everywhere that say *No Boating*. What were you thinking?"

Mom's response? "Oh, for Pete's sake, it wasn't a boat! It was a *raft.*"

(Years later, when I was getting into similar scrapes on a fairly regular basis, Mom would swear up and down she had no idea where I got it from.)

Even the authoritarian Communists who policed China with an iron fist and had zero tolerance for the kind of "creative interpretation" of the rules mom was so fond of couldn't do much to dissuade her from something she'd made her mind up about. Especially not when it came to Christmas.

The only living human who is in the running for possibly having more Christmas cheer than Mom is Will Ferrell's Buddy from *Elf.*

Growing up, Mom lived and breathed Christmas. Our tree always went up the day after Thanksgiving, and it usually didn't come down until it was so brittle and dead that accidentally bumping it with the vacuum cleaner rained down more needles onto the floor than it left clinging to the branches. Usually right around Easter. (I was pretty sure we were the only kids on the block who got their Easter baskets under a dead Easter pine tree.)

Before we had a house with a fireplace—and since Santa couldn't come without one—she made one out of cardboard boxes. It was about five feet tall, sturdy enough that you could set stuff on the mantle, and she hand-painted the whole thing to look like real brick.

Every night for the duration of December, we had a "special family tradition" event of some sort—making homemade ornaments, stringing popcorn to go decorate trees in the park for the birds, acting out the Nativity story, or mom's *coup de grace:* the gingerbread houses.

She insisted on making those herself, from scratch, cutting out all the sides and facets with poster-board templates she'd also made, and then gluing it all together with sugar she melted down on the stove until it was a scorching hot, sticky brown mess that she invariably scalded herself with. Some families marked the passage of time with penciled height marks on their kitchen doorjambs. At our house, much like cutting down a tree and counting its rings to see how old it is, you could tell how many Christmases Mom had seen by simply counting all the burn scars on her hands and arms from all the stupid melted sugar for the gingerbread houses.

Oh, and you know those travesties normal people call "ugly Christmas sweaters" and invented parties for solely to wear ironically? Mom just called them "sweaters." Half of her closet was hideous Christmas sweaters that she wore to school year-round.

Like I said, Buddy the Elf had serious competition.

When Christmas finally rolled around our first year in China and we found out it wasn't celebrated—barely even recognized—Mom handled the news like she was the ninth person to reach the ark.

"Living in a God-forsaken Communist country that doesn't celebrate Christmas or sell Christmas trees because they don't have any idea what those are is *not* a good excuse for us not to have one!" Mom was explaining to us logically and loudly one day.

We were just going to have to find one, that's all. How hard could that possibly be?

Turns out it could be pretty freaking hard.

The first thing Mom did was enlist one of our closest Chinese friends, Wendy Lee, a spunky 20-something-year-old we were all quite fond of for her "atypical" Chinese attitude. She was up for some mischief, even if she didn't quite understand what it was about.

"You want a *what*—a tree? Why do you want a tree? Are you going to plant it?"

"No, I don't want to plant it," Mom told her, "I want to put it in the living room."

"Why would you want to put a tree in your living room? It's too big. You should get a plant instead," Wendy replied. "I will take you to a nice flower shop tomorrow."

"I don't want a flower shop, I need a Christmas tree," Mom insisted.

"I don't know that kind of tree. What does it look like?"

Mom drew her a picture.

"Oh! Okay, yes! I have seen this kind of tree before—I know exactly where they are! I will take you there on Saturday."

What were the odds of that? A Changsha nursery that sells Christmas trees without even knowing they're Christmas trees!

At NUDT, the foreigners' compound we lived in had a van on the premises and a driver on staff to take us wherever we wanted to go as long as we gave him some advanced notice. So, Mom reserved the van for Saturday.

When Saturday morning arrived, Wendy Lee showed up at our door wearing her trademark black high heels and debutante silk gloves. And she was carrying a hacksaw. "I will explain on the way," she announced cheerfully.

The forthcoming explanation was that there was, in fact, no such place in Changsha that "sold" Christmas trees. Nothing of the sort. But Wendy knew of a place where they grew in the wild, and that's where she was taking us.

She barked orders to the driver, sending him through a maze of turns until even he admitted he had no idea where we were. This was a part of Changsha he'd never seen before. We wound our way up a small mountain until we were near the top. Then Wendy directed him up another ridge, through an ornate gate that looked like the entrance to a temple of some sort, and eventually ordered him to pull over and stop on the side of the road. A few hundred yards up ahead, we could see the tip-top of a nine-story pagoda just over the crest of the hill.

"Right over there," Wendy pointed.

She was pointing out into a field. If you squinted, it was possible to make out some shapes in the distance that may or may not have been evergreens. "Let's go!" she ordered.

We climbed out of the van, climbed over the fence that lined the road we were parked on, and set off through the field. As we got closer, we could see that, sure enough, those were definitely the kind of evergreens Mom was in the market for. She looked over the handful of options, gave her stamp of approval to one, and Dad set to work sawing it down.

As soon as it hit the ground, Wendy began yelling, "Okay, everyone, grab on, and let's go! Go, go, go, go, *go, GO! We have to go NOW!*"

"What's the rush all of a sudden?" Mom wanted to know.

"We cannot be here!" Wendy screeched. "It is private property—very off-limits! If we are caught, it will be very, very bad for all of us, especially me. Now *run!*"

So, everybody reached in and grabbed whatever we could find to hold onto and high-tailed it back to the road with our poached Christmas tree. When we were within earshot of the driver, Wendy began frantically waving and screaming, "Start the car! Start the car! Turn around and open the back!"

The driver stared at us dumbfounded.

"Do it, do it, do it, do it NOW!" Wendy screamed again.

Finally, our driver sprang into action. He fired up the van, whipped it around, and threw open the back door just as we made it to the fence. We heaved the tree up and over the fence (*Get the Christmas tree over the fence?*), then Dad and the driver shoved it unceremoniously through the back door and over the seats, the point of it jammed up against the windshield. We all piled in—half of us relegated to the floor since the tree was taking up so much room—pulling the side door shut as the driver gunned the engine and floored it.

"Yes! We made it!" Wendy was laughing hysterically.

Turning to the driver, she commanded, "Don't slow down until you get to the bottom, unless you want to end up in prison!" This only made him speed up, careening down the mountain like a terrified skier trying to outrun an avalanche.

We made it to the bottom of the mountain and fishtailed to a halt, the driver and Wendy turning to make sure nobody was following. Then, as if nothing out of the ordinary had just happened, the driver hung a left and merged back in with the regular traffic.

"What was all that about?" Mom wanted to know.

"It is a very famous monastery," Wendy explained. "Nobody is allowed in. Trespassing there is a very serious offense. If you get caught, it's maybe . . ." she trailed off, making a slicing gesture across her throat.

"Well, thank you, Jesus, for keeping us all safe!" Mom declared to the heavens on behalf of all the van's occupants.

Then to Wendy, "But you really should have told us in advance where you were planning to take us."

I had to know.

"Mum, just out of curiosity, would it have made a difference if Wendy told you where she was taking us?"

Mom thought about it for a moment and then answered, "Eh, probably not."

She *really* had to have that stupid tree.

Getting the tree into our apartment proved even more difficult than pilfering it from the sacred forest. It hadn't looked all that big when we'd been out in the field, but now that we had it propped up next to the entrance of our building, it was huge. Try as they might, Dad and one of the other missionary guys were unable to find an angle to turn the corners up the stairs with it. All that work, and it was just going to end up being displayed in the lobby, or outside somewhere.

"Over my dead body!" Mom declared when Dad informed her that the tree's new home was going to be on the ground floor. "Go find me some rope!"

Knowing better than to argue, Dad set off on a campus-wide scavenger hunt. A few hours later, he was back with a 50-foot length of rope.

My first thought was that Mom was planning to use the rope to wrap up the boughs like those bailing machines at the tree lots. Cinched up tightly, a couple adult males might be able to maneuver it up the stairs.

But no, Mom had a different idea. She was going to go upstairs to our third-floor balcony, throw one end down, tie it around the trunk at the lowest branches, and then haul it three stories up. Or, rather, have all four men in the building haul it up for her.

It turned out to be an entire-building affair. Because the tree was getting pulled up upside-down, someone had to stand post on the ground and second-floor balcony to push it free from the overhang above them it kept getting hung up on. The guys pulling it up got it as far as the second floor a couple times before losing their grip and dropping it.

The third time was the charm. After much grunting and grimacing and heaving and straining, seven missionaries finally managed to wrangle the tree up and over the third-story railing. To say it had seen better days was a comical understatement. The thing was a mangled mess. Between dragging it a couple hundred yards through the field, stuffing it into the van, and then dropping it on its head from two stories up a couple times, it looked like something we'd found on the outskirts of Chernobyl.

But she had her stupid Christmas tree—probably the only one in the whole city of Changsha—and that's all that mattered. If Charlie Brown and the Peanuts gang could still find the true meaning of Christmas with their pitiful little shrub, we'd be just fine with our giant, mangled Chernobyl tree.

She pulled a similar Christmas tree stunt in Thailand. After our brief fieldtrip to the Bangkok airport for the miracle plane tickets that never materialized, a missionary family who was leaving for the States indefinitely let us stay at their place. Their place had 16-foot ceilings, and you are out of your ever-loving head if you think Mom had any intention of allowing any empty space between the top of the tree and the ceiling. If God hadn't meant for us to have a 16-foot tree, He wouldn't have installed the ceiling so high off the ground. Or so she explained it to us.

The problem with Thailand was twofold: like China, Christmas wasn't really observed, what with them being a Buddhist nation and all. So, nobody was selling Christmas trees. Unlike China, we were now less than 900 miles north of the equator—a section of the globe best known for its palm trees, not its Douglas firs. There were simply no evergreens to be had for several degrees of latitude, legally or otherwise. But if you think that mild ecosystem inconvenience was going to keep Mom from having her 16-foot Christmas tree, you haven't been paying attention.

On one of our little tuk-tuk rides into town one day, Mom had spotted some pointy-looing tree-type thingy out in a field off the side of the highway that wasn't fenced in or off limits or anything. So, that was going to be our tree.

The problem was that we didn't have any vehicle, let alone one large enough to transport the size of tree Mom had her eyes on. Down in Si Racha, it was pretty much nothing but mopeds and tuk-tuks.

The tree was about two miles away, so we hailed a tuk-tuk to take us there. Or as close to *there* as we could get. Where it was growing was not a "destination" you could drive to. Mom just told the driver to pull over on the side of the road as soon as she spotted her tree, which he did, but then he seemed a little confused as to why we were all thanking him and sending him on his way. It wasn't like he was letting us out at the market—we were on the side of the highway in the middle of nowhere.

Naturally, the tree was on the opposite side of the highway we'd been dropped off on, so the four of us had to play human *Frogger*, trying to make it to the side we needed to be on without getting squashed by the endless stream of kamikaze tuk-tuks and mopeds.

Once across, we made our way out into the field to Mom's tree, and upon arriving at it, I had to laugh. There was no way this thing was coming home with us. Mom's "Christmas tree" was only that in the sense that it was tapered from top to bottom. Beginning and end of similarities. To this day, I have no idea what species of flora was in front of us, but it looked prehistoric. Like something right out of the Jurassic Age. Also, it was about 25 feet tall. Unless Mom had secret plans to contract God to install a retractable roof in our friends' living room, this prehistoric monstrosity wasn't going anywhere.

"Cut it down," Mom said to Dad.

"What do you mean *'cut it down'?"* Dad wanted to know. "We can't take this thing home with us—it's twice the size of the house!"

"Yes, I can see that," Mom shot back. "Obviously, we're not going to take the *whole* thing."

We all looked at her, waiting for the missing piece of the puzzle.

"Oh, for Pete's sake! Just climb up there and cut off the top half!" she commanded, as if it were the most obvious course of action in the world.

So, Dad and I took turns sawing and climbing, climbing and sawing, until we'd cleared out enough of the lower branches to climb, relatively unimpeded, about eight feet off the ground. Then Dad went up, sawed through the trunk, and shoved the top portion of the tree to the ground.

Once it was on the ground, Dad determined that it still needed a few more feet cut off the lower end if it was going to stand up in the living room. Once that excess was removed, Dad determined that another couple feet needed to come off to get this down to a manageable weight. Because the four of us were going to have to carry it home.

Two miles away.

The good news was that the branches on this thing were so sparse and spread out that it wasn't hard to wiggle your head and shoulders in towards the trunk once we'd lifted it up into the air. So, with the four of us lined up according to height—Dad in the front, Kyle in the back—we set the trunk on our shoulders and began the long walk home.

For the next couple hours, we walked down the shoulder of the highway with Mom's stupid *Land Before Time* Christmas tree, stopping and dropping it to rest whenever it got to be too much, and then hoisting it back up to soldier on. To anyone driving past, it must've been quite a sight. At one point, a tour bus slowly rolled up alongside us at a slow crawl, all the tourists on board snapping pictures of . . . whatever the hell they were witnessing—a giant Megasaurus Rex tree on its side, eight legs poking out the bottom, slowly making its way down the road. Who could blame them? I'd probably pull over and snap a few shots myself if I witnessed the same thing.

We eventually got it home, where the front double doors made it fairly uneventful to get it inside and stood up against the wall. That's where we discovered Dad had hacked off a little too much at the bottom. Our wimpy little Jurassic Christmas tree ended up being a measly 12-feet tall.

It wasn't a 16-footer, but Mom decided those extra four feet weren't worth quibbling over. This was a tropical zone. It was about 105 degrees out. It was a Buddhist nation that didn't do Christmas. We didn't have a car. Thailand didn't have any Christmas trees. And yet, here we were with a 12-foot Christmas tree next to the couch.

If mom wanted something done, she got it done.

That's   all   there   was   to   it.

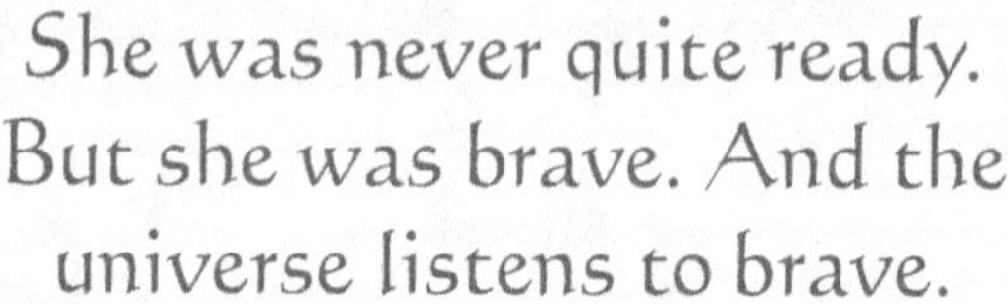

She was never quite ready.
But she was brave. And the
universe listens to brave.
– Rebecca Ray

It's kind of fun to
do the impossible.
—Walt Disney

Just keep swimming.
– Dory, *Finding Nemo*

五

Woman On Fire

f Mom was going to throw a concert, the first thing she needed to do was find an act—a *big-name* act—that was willing to go to China and sing a bunch of songs in public about God that were absolutely illegal to be singing in public in China. So, she did what any grade school teacher from Texas with zero knowledge of the music industry would do: she went and got herself a teaching position and carried on with normal life, waiting for God to drop something international-concert-related into her lap. Which is basically what happened.

She landed a job teaching seventh grade at Pittsburgh East Christian School, which was attached to Pittsburgh East Church, one of the bigger congregations in the Pittsburgh area. She stayed there for three years before changing jobs for a new school district and better pay. Three years and not a stitch of forward progress on that Moon Mission of hers.

Driving home from her new school one day, Mom heard an ad on the radio for some event Pittsburg East was putting on next month. Since their facility was so large, they were always hosting national conferences, or flashy Christian entertainment events like John Jacobs and the Power Team, or monthly concert series featuring big-name artists—events that were big enough to warrant advertising on the radio.

Concerts.

Concerts featuring *Christian artists.*

Concerts featuring *big-name* Christian artists.

Concerts featuring big-name Christian artists *at the church attached to her old school.*

These concerts had been going on the entire time she'd worked there, but Mom's strong suit was piecing together gingerbread houses, not obvious dots, so it took her a few years to finally draw that connection. But once she'd finally assembled that hyper-complicated 4-piece puzzle (always start with the edges!), she reached out to someone at her old school, who told her to contact someone at the church, who put her in touch with someone else at the church, who allegedly knew a guy who knew a gal whose cousin's barber's babysitter's aunt knew someone back at the church where this whole game of duck-duck-goose had started in the first place. You know the organizations I'm talking about—a few dozen staff, nobody knows what anyone else is doing.

Anyway, my mom was eventually put in contact with whoever was in charge of booking the events at the church and laid it out for them, "I'm trying to make arrangements to take a Christian band to China. I don't have any idea how to get in touch with any of the Christian bands. Can you give me any clues or any help on how to make those kinds of arrangements?"

The person on the other end said they'd see what they could do and would get back to her.

A week later, they called back with the name of an agent, Scott Huie. They weren't going to make any warm introductions to facilitate the process, but they did give Mom his number, saying, "Give him a call. That's where I'd start."

Huie was the agent for the Newsboys, a pop-rock group from Queensland, Australia, widely regarded as the biggest Christian band in the world at the time. Formed in 1985, by 1996, the Newsboys had already released a half-dozen critically acclaimed albums, racking up four Grammy nominations along with 10 Dove Award nominations (winning 3) in the process. They'd just completed their fourth world tour, easily selling out arenas, often packing out stadiums.

In a 1998 interview with *Pollstar*, Newsboys founder Peter Furler recounted the surrealness of playing the Astrodome in Houston for the first time, knowing they were sharing the same stage as their hero acts like U2. In the echelon of Christian music, they were at the pinnacle. If you were looking for a "big-name" Christian act, you'd be hard-pressed to find one any bigger.

Go big or go home.

So, Mom called the booking agent for the biggest Christian band in the world, introduced herself, and briefly explained what she wanted to do: take a Christian band to China.

It was brief because that was literally the full extent of her idea. No dates, no venues, no relevant information, no nothing. Just a vague concept.

Again, for the #1 touring act in the Christian market.

It would be like calling up Tesla, asking for Elon Musk, and telling him, "I've got an idea for an EV passenger van for folks in Papua New Guinea who don't have paved roads or electricity yet. Wanna help?"

To her credit, Mom didn't beat around the bush. "This is the preliminary, just-getting-started phase. I don't have any details, and I don't have any specifics. I'm just wondering if you guys would have any interest in going?"

When she was finished making her … um … *pitch*, she sat back and waited for the inevitable response. Laughter? Derision? Or would he simply hang up on her like some punk kid making a prank call.[7]

To her surprise, Huie did none of the above.

"Here's the deal," he told her. "We usually play for a flat fee, or a portion of ticket sales. But for this once-in-a-lifetime opportunity to

---

[7] Kids, a "prank call" was something your parents used to do for fun back before everyone had cell phones with caller ID and screened everything and demanded that you text first to ask permission to *call*, and people actually looked forward to the phone ringing. It was a delightful way to cure boredom on a slow Saturday by irritating strangers at random numbers in the phone book.***

*** Kids, a "phone book" was a huge, cinder-block-sized piece of literature they mailed out every year to every single resident in town. It contained an alphabetical listing of everyone who lived in that city, along with their address and phone number. You may have Google today, but you can't kill spiders with a search engine.

play in China, if you agree to cover all the expenses—roundtrip airfare, hotels, transportation, meals, et cetera—we would be willing to do it for no extra charge. That's it. Just take care of all the costs to get us there, take care of us *while* we're there, and then get us home. If you can do that, we won't ask for any additional fee."

That's it.

Mom didn't have a clue how much it cost to fly, feed, house, and transport an international touring band and their crew, but it sounded exorbitant. However much it was going to be, she didn't have it. Not even remotely. Talk about a major bummer. For a normal person, this would've been a gut punch, or at least a healthy reality check.

"Perfect, that sounds fabulous!" Mom replied. "I'm cool with all of that, so let's just move from there."

That ended the phone call.

Under ordinary circumstances—or at least for ordinary human beings—having no way to contact a famous band and having a famous band say they'll go anywhere you want them to as long as you pay for the entire thing are roughly the same. I wanted a Lamborghini at the time but didn't know where they sold them in Pittsburgh. If you drove me over to the dealership, showed me the fleet, and told me I could have any car on the show floor as long as I came up with the quarter million dollars it took to drive it off the lot, I'd be in the exact same boat as not knowing where the dealership was in the first place.

But Mom was not an ordinary person, and she hung up the phone with the same enthusiasm as if Huie had told her the Newsboys were 15 minutes from soundcheck on the Great Wall. She'd already received her mission from God, and now she had her marching orders. The *How* of it was someone else's problem.

Let me rephrase. The *monetary situation* was someone else's problem. Mom was not without her own conundrums—she'd only gotten one side of the concert equation to agree to participate. It took two to tango. It didn't matter a hill of beans if she walked out the door and tripped and planted face-first onto a winning Power Ball ticket, she still needed the people on the other end to agree to it. China was almost certainly going to insist on having a say in the matter.

While our family was quite close with two missionaries who still frequently went into China, neither of them knew anyone over there who might be of service. They didn't even know anyone who knew someone who knew someone who might be able to help. Their sphere of influence was pretty much limited to the underground churches they smuggled in Bibles to and ministered with. They did their best to *avoid* officials and anyone in power, not network with them. Nope, the only connections we had to anyone in China would not be of any service.

So, not knowing who to contact in China, not knowing how to contact anyone in China, not knowing which departments in China needed to be contacted, not knowing where to even begin the search in China, and not speaking a word of anything that remotely passed for Chinese, Mom decided to go to China.

Alone.

For all her amazing attributes and admirable qualities, two essential human traits that eluded my mother wholly and unconditionally were basic land navigation and languages that weren't English.[8]

She could convincingly sell the phrase, *Le chat est dans la cuisine en train de boire du lait*, but that was about the extent of her bilingualism and was only sparingly useful. Not a lot of situations call for anyone present to inform anyone else in French that *the cat is in the kitchen drinking milk.* Come to think of it, I don't think an appropriate context has ever come up as long as I've known her.

You know what—screw it. Let's roast this remarkable woman for a couple pages, shall we? Trust me, it'll be fun!

Back when we lived in China, Kyle and I were incessantly tasked with serving as the designated interpreters for all social interactions for our family because Mom and Dad simply could not wrap their heads around the Chinese language.

Like many Asian languages, Mandarin is tonal, which means you can say the exact same word with four different inflections, and they all mean four completely different things.

For example, the word "ma" can mean *mother, numb, to scold,* or *horse,* depending on if you raise, lower, lower-then-raise, or keep your pitch level. (You can also add *ma* to the end of a sentence to indicate a question.) The difficulty of Mandarin is not in the pronunciation of

---

8 She'd always insisted Pig Latin was a language—one she spoke fluently—but that only worked on me until I was seven.

words—the pronunciations are actually quite simple—it's getting the tones right that's the deal-breaker. Dad was certifiably tone-deaf, so he had an excuse. Mom, on the other hand, disagreed with the entire premise. The way she saw it, it didn't matter that a billion people had thousand-year-old grammar rules. If she didn't agree with them, she could just veto their whole language.

Since she's generally incapable of determining when a subject is a matter of opinion and when it's a matter of fact, Mom unilaterally decided that tones were the equivalent of accentuating syllables in English. Americans pronounce *laboratory* LAB-ra-tory, while Brits say la-BOR-a-tory. Regardless of how it's pronounced, English speakers on both sides of the pond can understand what word is being said.

Mom was of the opinion that the same principle ought to apply to Chinese tones, and the painful fact that it most definitely did *not* was irrelevant to her. She had Declared It So, which meant she was right, the billion or so Chinese inhabitants were wrong.

But at least the pronunciations were still easy. Somehow, our esteemed parent people figured out a way to butcher those as well.

Case in point: every street vendor in China sold a bottled soda[9] we all loved called *qi shui* (pronounced "CHEE-shway"), with the "CHEE" descending down to the leveled-off "shway."

Now, we already know that you can say "chee" in four different ways to get four different meanings. But that's only *if* you say "chee" to begin with, which my parents steadfastly refused to do. They insisted on pronouncing it "SHISH," which isn't a word at all. In fact, the sound *ish* doesn't even exist in Mandarin. (And if you're wondering, the answer is no, they never got the tone right either. Instead of a down-tone, they'd both inflect *up* on the non-existent word.)

So armed with their nonsense phrase, Mom and Dad would stroll up to a vendor and proclaim, "SHISH-WAY!" with all the misplaced confidence of a 10-year-old demanding the car keys. They wouldn't even bother with any other words that would form a complete

---

[9] Northerners, I don't want to hear any of your crap about how it's called "pop." This is a book about cross-cultural affairs. Assimilate! Southerners, God love you, but I'm not calling Mt. Dew "Coke," no matter how much profanity you can call up trying to explain it to me. It's not a Coke. Learn different words for different things already. This is why your education system is the way it is.

sentence, such as "Do you have...", "I would like...", "Can I get...", etc., that might provide some much-needed context to indicate to the confused vendor what the hell they were attempting to accomplish. Nope, just a bold, two-syllable declaration of absolute gibberish.

Kyle and I thought it was hilarious, which just made Mom and Dad mad, which made them try even harder to get it right without our help, but for whom "trying harder" simply meant "yelling it louder" rather than "attempting a different freaking pronunciation."

It was awesome.

Bolstering the daily comedy sideshow was that, while "SHISH-WAY" didn't mean anything at all, the similar-sounding *xie xie* (pronounced "SHAY-SHAY") means "thank you." So, a lot of times, thanks to my parents' supreme ineptitude at pronunciation consistency, they'd stroll up to the vendor and say something he vaguely recognized—*thank you*—at which point he'd return the phrase with a raised inflection as if to say, *Thank you? Why are you thanking me?*

Naturally, Mom and Dad would hear him say "SHAY-SHAY?" back at them and think he was confirming they wanted the drink they didn't know the word for and hadn't actually ordered. Then a hysterical, incomprehensible battle of sheer nonsense would unfold.

"Shish-way!"

"*Xie xie?*"

"Shish-shay?"

"*Xie xie!*"

"No, not *xie xie*, SHISH-way!"

"Ah! *Xie xie!*"

"Yes! Shay-shway!"

"*XIE XIE?*"

"Oh, for Pete's sake, *SHISH-WAY!!!*"[10]

---

[10] If you remember *Arrested Development*, one of the show's long-running gags involved Lucille Bluth adopting a Korean kid who greeted her with "An-yang," which meant *hello*, but she thought he was telling her his name was *An-yang*. They'd stand there yelling "an-yang" back and forth at each other, though for entirely different reasons. The show won six Emmys for Outstanding Comedy Writing. I got to live it in real life.

This would go on for several more rounds until the poor vendor would raise his hands in hopeless bewilderment, at which point Kyle or I would step in and remedy the situation. We'd order our drinks, pay the man, and then walk off with Mom invariably steaming, "I *know* he knows what I was saying! I don't understand why everyone in the country always has to be so *difficult!*"

When we eventually left China after a year and a half of complete cultural immersion, the only four phrases my mother was able to speak that anyone in their country was capable of understanding were: *hello, goodbye, thank you,* and *I want that in hot pink.*

So, yeah, that was the eloquent polyglot—who couldn't order an orange soda from a cart that sold nothing but orange soda—about to head off to the Far East all on her lonesome to broker terms for an international Christian concert with the Communists.

Good luck with that.

Then there were the aforementioned navigational shortcomings. Calling my mom "directionally challenged" would be like calling Stephen Hawking "figure-skating impaired." I promise I'm not exaggerating when I tell you that, clinically speaking, she's whatever the polar opposite of a homing pigeon is. The woman has been perpetually lost for as long as I can remember. I can't count how many times dinner was two or three hours late when I was in high school because Mom got lost coming home from work, or the mall, or the mailbox. We'd been in Pittsburgh for almost six years when I left for college, and even up to that point, she was frequently calling home to have someone talk her through locating the freeway onramp so she could leave downtown. And that's in a city where all the signs were written in English.

But at least she could fall back on the excuse that Pittsburgh is laid out like a bunch of drunk raccoons threw a pile of sticks on the ground, city planners traced where they landed, and then built their roads to match.

West Palm Beach, where I was now living, was laid out in a perfect grid. The summer after I graduated college, Mom came down to visit for a week. Since I still had to work, she'd go to the beach every day until I got off. And every day, for five days straight, we'd have the same conversation every morning.

"Son, tell me again how to get to the beach."

"It's real simple, Mum. Your car is parked outside on the curb, already facing the direction you need to go. Get in your car, turn it on, and then drive straight as an arrow until it dead-ends at Southern Blvd. You with me?"

"Southern Blvd. Got it."

"Great. Turn left, then Southern Blvd. will basically dead-end at the ocean in about a mile. You can turn either left or right, and you'll eventually come to a clearly marked public beach whichever way you turn."

"Okay, that sounds easy enough. Have a great day at work, and I'll see you at dinner!"

Around dinnertime, I'd get a call. It would be Mom, and she couldn't figure out how to get back. And every day, for five days straight, we'd have the same conversation every evening.

"Son, how do I get back to your house?"

"I don't know, Mum. Where are you?"

"I'm still at the beach."

"What beach are you at?"

"The sign says Municipal Beach."

"Okay, super simple. Head south until you get back to Southern Blvd., then turn right. Follow the—"

"Hold on!" she'd snap, "I don't have any idea which way *south* is. Tell me in terms of *right* or *left*."

"Are you serious?" I'd ask, incredulous.

"There's no need to get sarcastic with me," she'd fire back. "I don't live here. How would I have any idea which way is north and which way is south?"

"Mum," I would say gently, "do you see any distinguishing landmarks or topographical features around you that might offer some clues?"

"I see a few condos, but I don't know what direction that is."

"Do you see, I dunno, a large body of water nearby?"

"Yes, obviously, that's where I've been all day!"

"Okay, Mum, that incredibly large body of water you've been splashing around in all day is the *Atlantic Ocean*. Florida is on America's Eastern Seaboard, not the great Pacific Northwest. If you're facing the ocean, you're facing *east*. Are you able to extrapolate the other three directions from that admittedly limited data point?"

"Well, I know *west* is behind me, so left would be *north,* which would make right *south."*

"Correct. That's the direction you want to go—*right,*" I'd say encouragingly. "Now here's a convenient little life hack for you: whenever you're visiting me in Florida, if you can see the ocean, put the ocean on your right. Now you're facing north. Every time. You'll never get lost in West Palm Beach again. Got it?"

"Aye, captain. By Jove, I think I've got it! I'll see you in 10 minutes."

Then she'd call back 45 minutes later, going, "Am I supposed to be at The Breakers Hotel?"

"What? No!" *How the*— "Mum, you went the wrong way."

"You told me to go *right*! I was facing the ocean, then I turned around and went right. Just like you said."

"I told you to go *SOUTH!* I told you to go *right* if you're facing the ocean, not *in general.* ("Hey Mom, if you ever find yourself lost on our planet, just turn right?") If your back was to the ocean—which is *EAST*—then your right would've been *north."*

"Son, I don't need a geography lesson right now. I just need to know how to get back. How do I get to your house from Breakers Hotel?"

"Go out the main entrance and head south until you get to Southern Blvd."

"Okay, which way is south again?"

"GAHHHHH!"

To repeat, all this was in a city laid out in a grid, with the second largest body of water on earth denoting *east* and every sign written in her native language. And she still couldn't figure it out.

To put it delicately, Mom couldn't navigate her way out of a two-car garage if both bay doors were missing. If there were more than two turns involved, she'd be worse off than if you threw a pillowcase over her head and dropped her in the middle of a corn maze. She was like if Mr. Magoo and Helen Keller had a love child, raised it on Twizzlers and Holy Ghosting, and then tossed their little Anti-Magellan out into the world with nothing but a fanny pack and some florescent Dollar Tree sunglasses to figure things out.

Yep, that was Mom.

Up until now, someone in the family was usually on hand to extricate her from whatever loony-tunes predicament she'd managed to find her way into. The way I figured, if she went over to China unsupervised and simply managed to not get stranded in the middle of a koi pond, or locked in a train station bathroom for a week, or end up wandering around Bolivia shoeless, the trip could viably be considered a roaring success. Anything above and beyond those entirely plausible scenarios would be a divine miracle. Finagling an international concert? Not a snowflake's chance in hell.

But Mom wasn't interested in listening to anyone explain why this was an objectively terrible idea.

I don't want to hear why it won't work.

Anyway, she'd already formulated a plan. A cleverly sophisticated two-step plan:

Step 1: Go to China.
Step 2: Start doing *something* and see what happens.

It wasn't the most formidable plan I'd ever heard. Then again, this wasn't my mission.

So, Mom bought a ticket to our old city of residence, Changsha, and, on a leap of faith, just . . . *went*.

Now that we've just spent six pages throwing Mom under the bus, allow me to pull her back out, dust her off, squeegee off the tread marks, and give her some kudos for a brief moment before we continue our story.

While it's absolutely true that Mom couldn't communicate with anyone in their native tongue to save her life, she possessed a hidden talent for usually getting whatever she wanted anyway through the ancient art of pantomime. Sure, it wasn't always the most complicated thing to communicate—you walk into a shoe store, pull off your shoe, point to it, and the shopkeeper deduces you're looking for a pair of shoes. Not that impressive.

But raise your hand if *you* know the pantomime for "I want four tickets to the Beijing acrobats show" because I've witnessed her pull that one off.

The four of us had been traipsing around Beijing all afternoon trying to find a ticket office because Mom was adamant about seeing the famed Beijing acrobats. We finally came across one, but it wasn't a box office at the theater where the acrobats were performing—which only sold tickets to that particular show—it was a generic box office that sold tickets to literally everything Beijing had to offer: movies, sporting events, Forbidden City tours, panda-spotting expeditions, skydiving, you name it.

By the time we found it, Mom was fed up with Kyle and me making fun of her lack of communication prowess. She told us all to wait outside on the sidewalk while she went in and secured the tickets herself—to prove she didn't need our help. Through the window, I could see there were six or eight ticket windows, with at least a half-dozen people in each line. Mom got up to the front of her line and spent about five minutes gesturing and waving her hands around nonsensically while the ticket lady stared back at her blankly. She wasn't getting it.

Exasperated, Mom looked around the lobby, saw a wooden chair sitting against the side wall, walked over, and picked it up. Then, in the middle of the ticket office, with about 40 onlookers watching stupefied, she laid down on the floor on her back, feet straight up in the air, held the chair up towards her feet, and started slowly rotating the chair while pedaling like she was on a bike.

Chinese acrobats, duh!

She exited the building a few minutes later with four tickets to the show that night.

I defy any of you to even come up with that, let alone pull it off.

So, she wasn't completely without her methods.

om arrived in Changsha and made the executive decision to go stay at the Lotus Hotel, a fancy establishment we poor missionaries used to go eat at maybe twice a year when we were homesick enough for real American food that we were willing to tolerate whatever offerings their "authentic Western buffet" almost approximated.

She stepped out to the taxi stand and began attempting to communicate in the way only she could. "*Wo yao* (I want) Lotus Hotel," she began repeating. She tried it by raising her head up, then tried again lowering her head down, and tried yet again keeping it level, obviously under the impression that as long as something was moving in an obvious direction, it wouldn't matter if it was her voice or her noggin. (It matters.) They understood that she wanted *something*, but *Lotus Hotel* was still English.

This went on for several minutes, going absolutely nowhere, when a college-aged man approached the scene and, in perfect English, asked, "May I help you?"

Mom quickly explained that we used to live here nearly a decade ago and that she was trying to get to a hotel that was around then—if it still existed.

The man got the name of the hotel from her, then launched into a conversation with the cab driver, who nodded and said he knew where it was. The young man then introduced himself. His name was David, he'd been studying abroad in Australia for a couple years, and was now home visiting his parents.

Mom introduced herself in return and explained she was in town to try to organize a concert. David jotted something down on a piece of paper and handed it to her. "If there's any way I can be of assistance," he told her, "here's my number."

Mom thanked him and got in the taxi. As luck would have it, the Lotus Hotel was right where we'd left it, and Mom got herself checked in.

The following day, she managed to find enough people working the hotel's front desk who spoke enough broken English to combine their broken pieces into communicating where she wanted to go: the stadium where she'd originally heard her voice from the heavens bestowing her mission. There weren't a lot of stadiums in the middle of the city—just the one, in fact—so finding it was easy enough for the cab driver.

Mom got out and set off in search of a way in. She circled the entire facility to no avail—every door was locked, with chains and bars across the gates. Was it deserted? She wasn't sure if the place was even still in use.

Finding nobody to speak to, Mom returned to the hotel and took another wild shot in the dark—she called up the newspaper, found someone there who actually spoke English, and asked how much it would cost to take out an ad in the paper advertising a concert.

You know, like back home.

In America.

Where we have a non-state-run free press and that's a thing you can do.

"No, no, you cannot do that. It is not possible," said the person on the other end of the line. "You would have to contact the head prefecture official and request permission. You cannot put an ad in the newspaper without getting it approved. I'm very sorry."

State approval to take out an ad in the local paper?

This wasn't Kansas anymore.

As Mom hung up the phone in the hotel lobby, another college-aged guy materialized out of nowhere and asked if he could be of any assistance. If you're keeping score, that's two random English-speakers in two days approaching her out of the blue and asking if they could help. This was all the proof Mom needed that God was pulling the strings

Thrilled that someone else spoke conversational English, Mom once again explained that she was trying to bring over a band, but she didn't know who to talk to about it. (Mom doesn't remember this guy's name, so we'll call him Andrew.)

Andrew wasn't positive, but he thought she was probably being directed to the Department of Cultural Affairs. He also informed her that the Lotus Hotel was drastically overcharging her. He knew of much more affordable accommodations and offered to help her transport her things if she wanted to move. Mom agreed. Andrew made the arrangements, called a cab, and off they went.

The new digs Andrew had in mind were indeed significantly cheaper, but only because they were the opposite of an upgrade. Mom wasn't entirely sure if Andrew had brought her to a hostel or a dorm, only that—as she put it—the $5.00 a night they were charging for the room was about $3.50 overpriced. But she didn't want to insult her new friend by asking him for some nicer options, so she sucked it up and settled in.

Andrew ended up getting roped into Mom's merry band of misfits after she informed him that—unrelated to her concert scheming—she was planning to look up one of our old piano teachers.

Anna was the mother of our first piano teacher, So Mei. When we changed schools to the other side of town, So Mei referred us to her mom, who was right down the road from our new place and more convenient for us to get to. Mom still had So Mei's old number from back when we lived there and gave her a call. To her surprise, So Mei answered and passed along Anna's contact information.

Whenever we used to get care packages from the States, we'd always made a point of sharing our favorite snacks and goodies from home with people who'd never even heard of, let alone tried, America's finest food [adjacent] products. Anna had gone ga-ga over peanut butter and Pringles potato chips, so Mom had brought both on the off chance she was able to find her. For reasons I can't begin to fathom or explain, she chose to pack a glass jar of peanut butter for her international travels rather than a plastic one.

As this visit would require a series of bus rides with multiple transfers, Andrew offered to accompany her. On the bus ride there, Mom dropped the jar of peanut butter on the bus, shattering it. Andrew attempted to pick up some of the pieces, gashing his finger in the process and requiring Mom to play medic to stop the bleeding. And you know how the old saying goes: "Once you've spilled blood and peanut butter together, you're bonded for life."

After parting ways, Mom decided to give David a call. Andrew had been helpful, but David was a few years older and had more of a professional comportment. Plus, he spoke impeccable English.

David answered the phone, and Mom quickly brought him up to speed regarding her chat with the newspaper and their direction that some vaguely-named government officials needed to be involved. David confirmed that it was indeed the Department of Cultural Affairs she needed to meet with, and he agreed to take her there himself.

Arriving at the office, David instructed Mom to have a seat and wait while he went off in search of someone to speak with. So, she sat and waited.

And waited.

And then waited some more.

After a short eternity, David returned with an older gentleman who introduced himself as Mr. Wu, Changsha's Director of Cultural Affairs. He led the three of them back to a private office, closed the door, and told Mom to have a seat.

Since David understood the basic gist of what Mom was trying to do—bring an American band over for a concert (though wholly unaware it was to be a Christian band)—he began conversing with Mr. Wu while she sat back and watched. The two men prattled back and forth for an uncomfortable amount of time, never breaking their dialogue even once to ask Mom to explain some details or clarify some points. She just sat there in silence, wondering how long this was going to go on before she was finally asked to contribute to the discussion.

As the conversation wore on, Mom began to suspect Mr. Wu wasn't stopping to ask her any questions because he had no intention of indulging her on this outlandish quest she was on and zero inclination to humor her in the process. Or maybe he and David were simply making fun of this crazy, presumptuous foreigner who didn't speak the language but still expected some government favors or assistance nonetheless? Whatever they were discussing, her input wasn't needed, which definitely wasn't a good sign.

Silently, Mom began brainstorming which departments to go plead her case to next as soon as this one ushered her out the door and had a good laugh behind her back.

After 20 minutes of politely ignoring her existence, David finally turned to her and said, "Okay, it is agreed that it would be a very good thing for you to bring an American band here for a concert."

What was that?

That was not at all what Mom had been expecting. There had to be a *"but . . ." "It would be very good, BUT . . ."*

Yep, that was probably it—throw her a morsel, then let her down gently. Mom held her breath and waited for the inevitable diplomatic spin as to why this "very good thing" wasn't going to fly.

"The only thing they are able to offer," Daniel continued—*here comes the letdown*—"is to cover the cost of all their hotel accommodations, all their meals, and all transportation between the airport and hotel."

Mom's jaw hit the floor.

But Daniel wasn't done. "They will also provide the venue, all the sound and lighting production, and will take care of all of the advertising for the concert. Unfortunately, they are not able to provide the airfare for the band to travel. The band will have to cover their own expense to get here, and Changsha will take care of everything else."

Mom was ready to fall out of her chair.

All of this had just been negotiated without any input from her? By a guy she'd known for all of two minutes at the airport while he helped her get a taxi?!?

Mr. Wu stood, smiled, shook her hand, and then gave her all of his contact information. From that point on, he would be the liaison between the band and China. But being that it was still 1996, nobody had cell phones or email yet; all communications would have to be in the form of faxes.

There was just one tiny hiccup with that: Mr. Wu didn't speak, read, or write any English, and Mom's Chinese hadn't improved in the slightest. So, David the Airport Taxi Angel volunteered to serve as translator for whatever communications were to come. That covered Changsha's end. Now, Mom just had to get fluent in Chinese real quick . . . or find someone who was.

Having made a successful trip beyond even her wildest dreams—one that involved not even a little bit of falling down a well or ending up for sale in South America—Mom hopped on a plane to return home. She'd signed up for a courier service for the return flight since they covered the airfare, and was scheduled for a brief layover in Japan. However, her flight out of China was running behind, and she got into Japan too late to make a connection. With no more flights out scheduled until the next morning, the airline put her up in a snazzy hotel for the night.

Mom's new flight the following day had some interesting passengers aboard: five Chinese baby girls, not more than 10 months old, were being transported by a team of caretakers to be united with their adoptive parents in America. Since watching five sets of hopeful parents meet their new babies for the first time had all the promise of one of those god-awful Hallmark Special tearjerkers Mom couldn't ever get enough of, she decided to stick around at the gate to bask in the joyful introductions before heading off to find her connecting flight.

Arriving at O'Hare in Chicago, once all the laughter and crying and hugging and *ooh-ing* and *ahh-ing* had subsided amongst all the elated new families, Mom found herself in a conversation with one of the newly minted fathers, who happened to be Chinese-American. She mentioned what she'd just been up to in China, and the man handed her his business card and insisted she reach out if she ever needed help with anything.

(To make an apt SAT analogy: Mom is to airports as New Age hippies are to Taos—that ill-fated, ticketless trip to Bangkok notwithstanding. I swear, if she ever decided to trade in her travel New Testament for a sack of activated crystals and then flew into the Taos airport, she'd run smack into God in the flesh at Alley Cantina's nacho bar.)

She arrived back in Pittsburgh under the adorable impression that all the heavy lifting was now complete. The Newsboys had agreed to go as long as all their costs were covered, and China had agreed to cover all the costs other than the airfare. That meant the only thing left to do was come up with a half-dozen plane tickets. That was the final piece of the puzzle, and then all this concert-ing could get to a-happenin'. Why, this concert was going to happen in a matter of months, if not weeks! Right?

Right?

Hahahahahahahahahha, no! Oh my goodness, no.

No, no, no, no, no, *no.*

Silly reader.

As Mom was about to find out, all the *easy* parts of the puzzle had been solved.

Now, the real fun was about to begin.

Not long after Mom got back to the States, a fax came in from China requesting information about the band she was planning to take. She'd gotten approval to bring *a* band over, but there'd been no discussion about a *particular* band. Mr. Wu needed to confirm that whoever she had in mind was going to conform to China's rigid standards and practices: no heavy metal, no punk rock, nothing lewd or indecent, nothing provocative or overly political, etc. There was a laundry list of stuff the act couldn't be, do, say, or sing about. [11] (Failing to make the list: *overtly religious*.) To stay in the good graces of the Communist censors, Mr. Wu needed to review a copy of the band's lyrics.

Mom called Scott Huie and requested whatever lyrics he could send her. The Newsboys' latest album, *Take Me to Your Leader*, had been a smash hit on the Christian charts, with 10 of its 11 tracks cracking the Top 10 and 5 different singles hitting #1 at some point. The lyrics ranged from innocuous and abstract—where it was unclear what the song was even about—to the kind of casual *God* references that frequently popped up in secular music without being ostentatiously religious, to the beat-you-over-the-head-with-its-overt-proselytizing lines such as *God is not a secret to be kept*.

So, Mom combed through several albums' worth of lyrics, cherry-picking the most harmless and "non-God-y" in their catalog to send over for approval. I'm not sure if she was simply playing dumb because the request had been worded in such a way that it could be "conveniently misunderstood " or if she genuinely didn't understand the assignment—neither option would've surprised me—but she was not the least bit interested nor concerned that the songs she was submitting for review were *not* the songs the Newsboys would actually be performing.[12]

A couple dozen sheets were faxed to Mr. Wu's office, which required David to translate them into Chinese before being dispersed around to whatever governmental officials got to have a say in the

---

[11] The Communist censors don't mess around. When The Rolling Stones played their first show in China in 2006, they had to submit their setlist in advance to Shanghai's Ministry of Culture. The censors forbade them from playing five of their biggest hits: "Beast of Burden," "Brown Sugar," "Honky Tonk Women," "Let's Spend the Night Together," and "Rough Justice."

[12] When Harry Connick Jr. played China in 2008, he accidentally submitted an old song list for approval. The Chinese authorities forced him to perform the submitted list rather than his actual setlist since they hadn't reviewed the planned set. Since his band didn't have the music for the old list, they mostly sat on the stage doing nothing all show while Connick played piano by himself.

matter and sign off on such things. Six weeks later, a fax came back saying the band's lyrics were approved.

Six weeks.

Mom was about to learn that six weeks would be about the average length of time any correspondence in either direction took to get a response. This was going to be slow going.

(I should probably also mention that, while Mom had immediately contacted Huie to let him know the Newsboys' lyrics had been approved, she neglected to inform him that she'd filtered out all the lyrics the Chinese officials might find objectionable for religious reasons. So, not only was China blissfully unaware that the Newsboys were a Christian band who'd be singing a whole bunch of Christian songs that hadn't been pre-approved, but the Newsboys didn't know that *China didn't know* they were a Christian band. They had no idea what Mom was setting them up to walk into. She was definitely pulling some strings, but she was weaving a tangled web with them indeed.)

The next thing China wanted were statistics on the band's shows: the number of stops on their tours, average venue size, average number of tickets sold, average ticket prices—stuff like that.

Oh, and she needed to throw in whatever marketing materials they used. While the band's lyrics had been deemed acceptable, they still wanted to make sure this was a legitimate, respectable band. If they were going to throw open their doors to a Western band for the first time since 1985, it wasn't going to be for some middling act. They wanted to be sure they were getting the goods. (To be fair, they were.)

What China was requesting was all data that Scott Huie could come up with (in a few weeks, hopefully), but he didn't have it in the format they were requesting it in this time: *Chinese.*

Since David didn't actually work for the Department of Cultural Affairs, his ability to translate what needed translating was wholly dependent on his personal availability, which was unpredictable at best. So, in a comical effort to keep the trains running on schedule—or whatever passed for "on schedule" given their 6-week lag time—Mr. Wu concluded that having Mom send everything back to him in Mandarin was the most reasonable course of action.

Of course, Mr. Wu. Would you like that in hot pink?

A month later, Mom had the tour data she needed from Huie in hand. Now she just needed to somehow convert it into Mandarin.

Thinking for a bit, it suddenly came to her: the guy in the Chicago airport—that one who was there to adopt one of the babies from her flight! He'd given her his business card and told her to call if she ever needed anything. Well, she ever needed something. She ever needed something very badly.

It will probably not surprise you in the least to learn that Father O'Hare answered Mom's call, readily agreeing to do whatever translations she needed. So, she faxed him the stack of forms and then waited for them to come back to her in Chinese.

Hurry up and wait.

It was a maddening game.

Weeks went by before the forms returned. When they finally did, Mom observed that they were definitely written in Chinese, as promised.

Were the translations accurate?

Who knows!

That would be a question for someone who could actually read the language, which she still couldn't do. Father O'Hare could've sent back a translation of last year's tax returns—or the stats from the back of Topps' complete set of 1981 baseball cards—and Mom wouldn't know the difference. She just had to trust that whatever she was flinging off into the fax ether was what she needed it to be. The Chinese weren't into baseball.

Unfortunately for Mom, the translation turned out to be perfect. It was exactly the information Mr. Wu needed to confirm the Newsboys had the kind of stardom and notoriety their city officials were stipulating. Unfortunate because Mom had now shown herself capable of fulfilling any requests he sent her in native-perfect Mandarin. And he was already armed with more requests.

The next thing he needed was a list of all the Newsboys band members who would be coming over, along with all their passport information.

In Chinese, of course.

Once again, Mom contacted Scott Huie for the information, then sat around waiting until he could get back to her with it. When she finally had it in hand, Father O'Hare wasn't available this time to do any translating.

Scrambling to come up with a Plan B, she reached out to the mother of one of her current first-grade students, whose parents were both professionals who'd immigrated to America from China years ago. Once again, Mom found herself explaining her situation to a stranger, and once again, a stranger stepped up to the plate to take a swing, once again knocking it out of the park. Mrs. Chang translated the requisite materials, Mom faxed them off to Mr. Wu, and he immediately replied with—

Sorry, he *eventually* replied with yet another request.

A doozy of a request.

That last round of forms Mom had sent over—the ones containing all the ticket sales and venue sizes and whatnot—had shown acceptable facts and figures. But it had also come from her personally, an Average Joe citizen, on plain ol' office paper. Bearing no authorized markings to certify their legitimacy, those figures could've come from literally anywhere. They could've been invented out of whole cloth. It could all be counterfeit!

Mr. Wu insisted she enlist an official source to vouch for the legitimacy of the Newsboys, attesting to their popularity and acumen on official letterhead.

From the American government.

That's it? Just go ask "the government" for a tiny favor?

So, Mom contacted the government.

This wasn't actually a novel concept for her. She'd always been an overly participatory citizen, frequently firing off letters to her Congressmen and Senators to request this or demand that, to proclaim her support or spell out her disapproval for whatever policies and agendas happened to be the pressing issue *du jour*. I don't know if she'd ever received any responses from her elected representatives or if her letters had ended up in a pile of unopened mail on someone's floor. I also wouldn't be surprised to learn that every single one of them had been opened and read aloud on the floor of the Senate and that the entire United States Congress was actively screening her mail.

Whatever may or may not have happened previously had no bearing on what happened this time, and before long, Mom had a certified letter from Pennsylvania's Republican senator, Rick Santorum. On official Congressional letterhead, Senator Santorum attested to the fact that the Newsboys were indeed a legitimate, popular, reputable band who played to capacity crowds around the world. Mom faxed the English letter to Mr. Wu, and David was thankfully available to translate it.

And so, with the accompanying official Congressional Seal of the United States proclaiming its authenticity, Changsha's Department of Cultural Affairs finally decreed that all the obligatory boxes had been ticked.

The Newsboys would be allowed to come to China.

That left just two remaining details to resolve: there was the matter of coming up with the band's airfare, and then there were the actual concert dates that had to be solidified. The former would materialize in yet another unexpected manna-from-the-sky fashion, while the latter would prove to be the most challenging and time-consuming ordeal of the whole project.

At the time, Mom was attending Greater Works Church of Pittsburgh and had briefly discussed this concert mission she'd been on for nearly a decade with her head pastor, Gary Mitrik. Unprompted, Pastor Gary decided to inform the entire congregation one Sunday morning what Mom was up to. Greater Works regularly funded a number of missions projects, so it was announced that, for one month, all offerings that were taken up would go towards getting the Newsboys to China. By the end of the month, the church had collected $13,000, more than enough to secure six roundtrip plane tickets.

That just left the concert dates.

It had been nearly three years since Mom first reached out to Pittsburgh East to inquire who she needed to contact to book a band. Since then, she'd managed to secure a verbal agreement from the booking agent for the biggest band in Christian music, had traveled to China blindly and returned home with a verbal agreement that China would host a concert on their own dime, had gotten lyrics approved, mountains of data translated and approved, Congress to vouch for it, and funding for the band to travel. She'd done as much as she could personally do.

Mom would still continue to act as the liaison between the two parties, but what was left now was a matter for China's concert promoters and the Newsboys' booking agent and management to hash out amongst themselves. And the Newsboys were about to get a rude awakening to the difference between Eastern and Western booking practices.

Once Changsha's Cultural Affairs had been notified that all the boxes had been ticked and all the arrangements were in place, Mr. Wu contacted Mom with a prospective concert date: *Could the Newsboys come next Wednesday?*

That was pretty much how we remembered everything operating back when we lived there. It was not at all uncommon to be sitting down to dinner and be interrupted by a knock at the front door. A handful of students, or colleagues, or officials, or barely-acquaintances would be standing there to cheerfully announce, "We are taking you to dinner now!"

Now?

No plans, no prior arrangements, no pre-approval, nada. They'd just show up unannounced and tell us what was going to happen. That we were smack dab in the middle of dinner at that precise moment was entirely beside the point, an irrelevant detail. There was no thought on their part that they might be interrupting something. Then, so as not to be insulting or appear ungrateful or rude, we'd have no choice but to stick our still-hot plates in the fridge, put on our shoes, and go hop on our bikes for a spontaneous 16-mile excursion to whatever "very famous" noodle shop our hosts for the evening had in mind. That was just the culture.

You had to hand it to them. They knew how to do the whole "living in the moment" thing like nobody's business. Still, there was something to be said for occasionally observing clocks and calendars.

Obviously, things in the West operate a wee bit differently. Plans are made in advance, prior engagements are honored, and nobody shows up at your doorstep in the middle of Meatloaf Monday to passively kidnap you for spaghetti.

So, the answer was *no*, the Newsboys would not be able to come next Wednesday. In fact, with their current tour schedule, they wouldn't be able to come any time in the next year.

Somewhat miffed, Mr. Wu told Mom he'd get back to her with other potential dates after consulting with his department. For the umpteenth time, Mom found herself waiting in limbo.

When Mr. Wu finally got back to her, it was not with a set of reasonable concert dates; it was with a bizarre request that bordered on ludicrous: When the Newsboys got to China, would they mind performing the song "The Lonesome Cowboy?"

Never mind the sheer audacity of asking a huge international act to play requests like they were some party band; more to the point: *What in the world song* was *that?* Mom had never heard of such a tune, nor had I.

This was the mid-90's. There was no iTunes or Spotify or Shazam on the market. If you wanted to find an obscure song title, the only way to do it was to head down to the local record store and hopefully find a helpful sales clerk who would tolerate your vague, off-key humming.

So, off Mom went to every record store in the Greater Pittsburgh area in search of this mysterious song. When those stops turned up nothing, she hit up every music store she could find in the phone book, spending hours sifting through thousands of pieces of sheet music. All to no avail. Nobody had ever heard of a song called "The Lonesome Cowboy."

She was stumped.

The only thing either of us could think of was that something had gotten lost in translation. When we lived in China, *Little House on the Prairie* was broadcast on TV every Sunday evening and had been hugely popular with my parents' students. We'd first found out about it when one of the students was over for dinner and informed us, "It's time for our favorite American show, 'Small Apartment on the Grass!'"

Small Apartment on the Grass?

We had no clue what show that was, but we turned on the TV and *Ohhhhhh* . . . "Small Apartment on the Grass." *Little House on the Prairie.*

ToMAYto-ToMAHto.

That had to be the explanation—something had gotten drastically, comically lost in translation.

Uncharacteristically defeated, Mom faxed Mr. Wu to let him know that nobody in our country was familiar with a song by that name.

When Mr. Wu finally responded with some additional information that supplied the missing clue, the ridiculousness of the initial request multiplied exponentially: "Cowboy" was indeed a mistranslation; the correct word was "Goatherd." The song China wanted the Newsboys to perform in the middle of their concert was "The Lonely Goatherd" from the musical *The Sound of Music.*

Yes, you read that right.

China's Foreign Affairs Bureau was submitting a formal request that an internationally acclaimed rock band perform a Rogers & Hammerstein showtune written for a puppet show about yodeling goats.

Mom made an executive decision and decided not to pass that request along to the Newsboys.

There were more pressing matters at hand to share with China. In late 1997, the Newsboys' lead singer, John James, was stepping down. This meant drummer Peter Furler was moving up to vocals, keyboardist Duncan Phillips was switching over to drums, and auditions were being held for a new keyboardist. China needed the updated roster and all the paperwork on the new member. They also wanted to know if this was unusual behavior for a very famous band. Mom assured them that it was perfectly normal for big-name bands to occasionally rotate members, a truth that would unwittingly set the stage for a series of ridiculous lies down the road . . .

Months had passed when China finally reached out with a pair of tentative dates for the following spring. By this time, Scott Huie had one of his assistants at First Company Management, a woman by the name of Velvet Russeau, acting as Mom's primary point of contact for the band.

Mom passed along the dates to Velvet, who ran them up the chain to Huie, who compared them against the Newsboys' upcoming calendar, then signaled back to Velvet that the dates in question worked, who notified Mom, who then faxed Mr. Wu that it was a go.

This was finally it.

An actual concert with dates was now officially on the books. There was nothing else to do other than count down the months. Mom began counting.

The months slowly ticked by until the concert was just around the corner when China reached out to Mom with a small problem: the circus had just announced it was coming to town, and the concert venue was being rebooked to accommodate the "very famous!"

acrobats from Beijing. They were deeply sorry for the inconvenience, but the dates that had been penciled in for the better part of eight months were no longer going to be feasible.

Annoyed but not entirely shocked (the Chinese were as inclined to scrap plans at the last second as they were to invent them out of thin air), Mom passed along the bad news to Velvet, then waited for Mr. Wu to get back to her with a new set of dates.

Again, the months passed by, and eventually another pair of dates were offered, considered, and agreed upon—another nine months out, this time in the summer of 1999.

Mom crossed her fingers.

The summer of '99 rolled around, and wouldn't you know it, a wrench that hadn't been thrown into the gears yet was promptly discovered and immediately tossed into said gears: the Newsboys were still in the studio trying to finish their upcoming album. They were under contract to have it completed by a certain date, and the recording was taking longer than anticipated. They apologized profusely to Mom, saying there was simply no way they'd be able to take a side trek to China and still meet their recording deadline. So, now it was their turn to axe the concert dates and request new ones.

This being familiar operating territory for China, they understood. *Things happen.* It was not a big deal. They immediately proposed a new set of dates for the last week of October, which the Newsboys promptly accepted. No harm, no foul.

But this third-time's-the-charm pair of dates came with a caveat: it would be the last time China would negotiate. If things fell through for any reason, regardless of which party was responsible, no more dates would be offered, and the concerts would simply be called off.

So, October was to be it.

Come then, or don't come at all.

On October 15, 1999, Mom's phone rang. It was Scott Huie. He was calling personally to deliver some unpleasant news. The Newsboys were currently in the midst of another international tour, the dates of which had been booked to accommodate the two shows in China on October 27 and 28. Currently in Florida, the band was scheduled to fly from there to China before continuing on to

South America. Unfortunately, they'd hit a snag with their visas and needed to return to Australia for the proper renewals to get into Brazil. There was simply no logistical way for the band to travel to Australia and China in the allotted window. As such, with the deepest and sincerest of regrets, they would be unable to go as planned. Huie apologized profusely a few more times and then hung up the phone.

So that was that.

The end of the line.

Ten years' worth of work . . . *gone*. Just like that, in the blink of an eye.

Done.

It was enough to send a person yo-yo-ing through all five stages of grief simultaneously.

A *normal* person, that is.

Which is not the kind of person this story is about.

Instead of shock, anger, depression, or denial, a calm peace settled over Mom.

Done?

Done happens when you're dead. Last she checked, she was still fogging a mirror.

Sure, there was a concert on the books less than two weeks off and no band to go play it—a mild inconvenience for sure—but that was a very glass-half-empty way of looking at the situation.

Another way of looking at it was that this entire operation was a complex machine with a hundred moving parts, and only *one* of those parts was missing. Granted, it was a fairly significant part, but it was still just a single part.

The other 99 pieces were still in place.

The concert was still booked, the tickets were still sold, all the accommodations and arrangements were still made, and $10,000 was still available for . . . whatever. Plus, it wasn't like the concert was scheduled for *tomorrow*. It was still 12 days off.

288 hours.

That meant she wasn't remotely done.

Not by a long shot.

It was time for her to drag me into this ridiculous story.

Know the rules well, so you can break them effectively.

– Dalai Lama XIV

Basically, what I'm trying to tell you is that it's almost impossible to drive a jet ski at nighttime unless you're in a city with lights lit up so you can navigate. Besides being pitch black, that water turn black at night. Listen, I don't recommend it.

– DJ Khaled

On Ninjas and Sharks

So, you've met Mom, but I don't think I've formally introduced myself yet. I should probably go ahead and do that before we get too far down the road, and for the same reasons. As you may have gleaned from bits and pieces of the story so far, I inherited her knack for getting into dubious situations for questionable reasons that made perfect sense in my head at the time. On a fairly regular basis.

The apple does not fall far from the trapeze. Or whatever.

None of it was my fault, obviously. Mom made us read constantly, which was something I actually enjoyed. I consumed books by the dozens—whatever I could get my hands on—getting lost in fantasy worlds and the endless adventures of Robin Hood, Zorro, Davy Crockett, Sherlock Holmes, Robinson Crusoe, Tom Sawyer and Huckleberry Finn, The Hardy Boys, Young Indiana Jones, The Knights of the Round Table, *The Chronicles of Narnia*, or anything by Louis L'Amour. I devoured these tales of epic quests and romantic adventures, imminent danger and daring escapes, narrowly-averted disasters, and harrowing survivals where the hero barely makes it out alive before riding off into the sunset to fight again another day. Those were *my people*.

Regular, everyday life was so monumentally *boring*. Nothing interesting or adventurous ever happened. Especially not when you were six. And stuck in stupid Wichita Falls, Texas.

There were never any quicksand episodes where you had to flatten out—*so as not to sink!*—and search around for a branch to extricate yourself from certain doom and pull yourself to safety. Never a reason to hide out in a mountain cave to escape the gold robbers who'd just spotted you spying on their wilderness hideout.

Then there was my ultimate fantasy scenario: trekking through some sort of dense forest or jungle that required you to hack down vines with a sword or machete. All the best heroes had to hack their way through vines at some point. With large cutlery. How else were you supposed to earn your "Hacking Through Vines" Boy Scouts badge? But that situation never came up in Texas either.

Nope, nothing but mundane school, and church, and piano lessons, and chores, and baseball or soccer practice, and brushing your teeth, and being sent off to bed at 7:30 every night (where at least I could get out my flashlight and read under the covers) on a never-ending cycle.

Wash, rinse, repeat.

The worst decision my parents ever made was to warn me about the kidnapper van that was all the fear-mongering rage for parents in the '80s. (This was right around the time society was also collectively freaking about people hiding razor blades in apples for trick-or-treaters—an urban legend there were no actual documented cases of. It was a very stupid time.)

"Now listen, son," my parents would sit me down and explain, "there are bad people out there who steal kids. They drive around in windowless vans and try to lure kids in with candy."

This piqued my interest.

Tell me more about these vans.

From then on, I was constantly on the lookout for a windowless van with a mustachioed Willy Wonka hanging out the side door ('80s child predators always had a mustache). Not so I could heed my parents' warning and sprint in the other direction—precisely the opposite—because I desperately wanted to get kidnapped. Getting kidnapped was *adventurous*. Then I'd get to use all my wiles to find a way out. There was never a doubt in my mind that I'd escape from even the biggest *gang* of kidnappers. No matter how much candy they offered me!

(That I never did manage to spot such a van and get my kid-self napped was, according to Mom, either a blessing or a curse, depending on what she'd caught me doing earlier that day.)

My top three movies at the time were *Swiss Family Robinson*, *The Goonies*, and *Red Dawn*, and I was utterly convinced I was destined to stumble upon a buried treasure map, or have to fight off pirates with an elaborate array of homemade booby traps, or hightail it out into the wilderness to wage guerilla warfare with my pocketknife and suction-cup bow-and-arrows against the Russian invaders that were definitely coming any day now (until Rocky finally vanquished them for good with punching). It was inevitable.

When Steven Spielberg's *Empire of the Sun* came out the year before we left for China, Christian Bale became my new hero. He was just a couple years older than me. Wandering around a war-torn China with no parental supervision and then getting tossed into a Japanese internment camp? Sign me up!

So, that's where my head was—anything that could take me out of monotonous real life and present some actual adventure and/or danger was what I was all about.

It would not be a passing phase.

When we announced we were moving off to China, Mom's entire family thought we were certifiably nuts. "What about the poor kids? They're going to be so *deprived!*" was the general consensus.

Deprived?

Moving to China was the closest thing to an actual adventure I'd ever had the chance to participate in so far in my 11 years. I felt the polar opposite of *deprived.*

It was finally happening!

China was where Shanghai was located, which is where the expression *shanghaied* came from. If there was a chance I could somehow find a way to get myself kidnapped *in Asia*, then I could probably just die right then and there and go straight to heaven. The rapture was all well and good, but it was a distant second to getting *shanghaied.* Mortal life on Earth couldn't possibly offer anything grander after that.

That is, until I learned about Bible-smuggling.

When I first found out that a group of missionaries regularly smuggled Bibles over the Hong Kong border into mainland China, I thought they were pulling my leg. Someone must've found my diary and thought they'd have a little laugh at my expense by regaling my gullible, impressionable little mind with made-up stories about covert operations involving very real threats of arrest.

But, no, it turned out to be an actual thing they actually did, and a team of four men—including my dad—was about to embark on such a weekend expedition. Dad was wondering if I happened to have any interest in joining them.

Are you kidding me?

They had me at "smuggle." I didn't need to hear the rest of the sentence. Smugglers were always the coolest characters in the movies. Han Solo was a smuggler! We could've been smuggling diamonds, knock-off Gucci bags, or live ferrets—I couldn't have cared less. That it happened to be Bibles, meaning we'd be putting ourselves in danger on a righteous mission for *God*, was just icing on the cake.

On the morning we were slated to take the train north to the end of the line at the Shenzhen border, I woke up early without an alarm clock, like it was Christmas morning. I donned my parachute pants, stuffed the myriad of pockets to the seams with New Testaments, and then pulled a pair of sweatpants over the top to hide the subterfuge.

I checked my reflection in the mirror.

Just another ordinary, nondescript, scrawny 11-year-old kid in a baggy t-shirt with Michelin Man legs.

Perfect.

The Commies would never suspect a thing.

This was apparently a regular run the Hong Kong Christians did— each person transporting two full-sized duffle bags loaded with Bibles—with something like 60-70% of them usually making it over the border without getting confiscated. Since the Hong Kong-Shenzhen border was a regular business-crossing hub, they didn't bottleneck the constant flow of foot traffic by funneling each person through an individual bag check. Guards loosely patrolled the crowded walkways, stopping people randomly to search their bags.

That there was only a small chance of being arbitrarily singled out of the crowd for a search didn't matter in the least. As far as I was concerned, that 50-yard walk through No Man's Land carried the exact same thrill of adventure as Indy getting chased out of the cave by the boulder.

I was living the dream.

Asia was constantly presenting opportunities for exactly the kind of exciting, "non-ordinary" life that made American life so banal and predictable to me. As I saw it, life in the States was a lot like bumper bowling—there were always railings, fences, traffic lights, crosswalks, building codes, or FDA guidelines to keep you on track while you navigated life on autopilot. It didn't matter how you threw the ball, there were guardrails to bounce off and keep you enough on track to ensure you'd knock down a few pins at the end of the lane. It was all too easy. I needed the threat of the gutter to make the experience worthwhile.

If you bought a ticket to travel in the States, everyone had assigned seating. That was *boring*. If the train from Guangzhou to Changsha was overcrowded because assigned seating was a hilarious, imaginary fiction, you simply went out to the end of the train car and laid down in a pile of cabbage with the half-dozen goats that were along for the ride.

In the States, if you wanted a Thanksgiving turkey, you simply hopped in the minivan, drove 10 minutes to the grocery store, and picked a frozen Butterball out of the freezer.

BORING.

In China, you had to ride your bike an hour to the live market that more closely resembled a petting zoo than a grocery store, strap a live chicken to the back of it, possibly run your bike into a pond to avoid being trampled by a heard of water buffalo making their way down the middle of the street, kill the chicken in your own kitchen, then dump your dead bird in a bucket and walk it a quarter mile to the school cafeteria and ask them to cook it for you because the ovens we were outfitted with weren't large enough to accommodate a bird larger than a parrot.

It was glorious.

When we got booted out of NUDT and all those people disappeared, it started to dawn on me that my little adventurous fantasy world was a bit more real than I'd given it credit for. The great thing about the stories was that, no matter how harrowing things got for the protagonists, you always knew it was going to turn out okay in the end.

Out here, in the *really* real world, not everything had a neat, happy ending.

This inconvenient fact of life was hammered home for good when one of my dad's students, Philip, at Hunan University took me on a Saturday outing one day. It wasn't at all uncommon for Mom and Dad to turn me loose with one of their students playing tour guide for trips to the zoo, the movies, or the park—wherever.

On this particular day, Mom was wrapped up in some art project that probably involved a hot glue gun, and Dad was playing in an all-day basketball tournament at the school. That left me freed up to go off on another adventure.

Philip and I hopped on a bus and rode it downtown, planning to just stroll around and hopefully score some ice cream. We ended up in the vicinity of the very soccer stadium where Mom had heard her mission from God—and would eventually go looking for years later—and saw people making their way in. A soccer game? Maybe a Shaolin kung fu demonstration? We decided to go check it out.

The ticket windows were closed, which was weird, so anyone who wanted to wander into the stadium was free to do so. We bought a panda-shaped ice cream from a street vendor outside and went in, making our way about halfway up the stands at midfield. For the size of the stadium, it was sparsely packed—no more than 10,000 people spread out in the stands wherever they felt like sitting. There was nothing happening on the field. Very odd.

After about a half hour, there was some motion down near one of the tunnels on the far corner of the field. There was no public address announcer telling us what was about to happen, so we just had to watch and figure it out. A dozen men in police officer uniforms walked out to midfield in two lines of six, with four men in drab blue peasant clothes walking between them.

Philip leaned over to me and whispered, "Public execution."

When they reached midfield, the four men were made to kneel and then blindfolded. Then, without so much as an acknowledgment to the crowd, one of the police officers drew his pistol, stepped up to the back of each man in turn, and casually fired a bullet into the back of his head. Each man fell face-first into the grass and lay still. Four shots, all in the span of about 30 seconds.

As soon as it was over, another group of officers jogged out of the tunnel carrying stretchers. They loaded the dead men onto the stretchers and carted them off—back to the tunnel. And that was it.

All the spectators in the crowd stood up and made their way to the exits. I was in mild shock, still trying to process what I'd just witnessed.[13] It didn't look or sound anything like the shootings I'd seen in movies. No Hollywood sound effects, no dramatic fall. Just *pop!* Done. The sound of the pistol reaching us a split second after each man lurched forward—the way the sound of fireworks at a Fourth of July show always lags a bit behind the explosion. The whole scene seemed weirdly sterile and *impersonal.*

Philip explained to me on our way back, "I overheard someone say on our way out of the stadium that all the men were thieves. The authorities like to hold these public demonstrations from time to time to remind the citizens to stay in line. This is why we have very little crime."

Understood.

Stay in line.

The visual of those four men falling face-first into the ground stuck in my head for the rest of my life.

God help me if I ever land on the wrong side of the authorities in this country.

When we finally left China for good, it wasn't *quite* for good. There was one last little foray to be made.

A brand-new team of missionaries had just arrived in Hong Kong, and they were planning on smuggling Bibles into the mainland via night boat up to Guangzhou rather than over the Shenzhen border. Dad had agreed to go along as a guide, but nobody on the team spoke Chinese. Did I want to come along as the interpreter?

Does a panda eat sushi in the woods?

Yeah, I was in.

---

13 This is probably the first my parents are hearing about this as well. Sorry about that, Mom and Dad. What was I supposed to do—come home and tell you Philip had taken me out for ice cream and a firing squad?

Going into China by boat meant we were virtually guaranteed not to get stopped by anyone, which meant nothing about the trip was dangerous. But I was 12, and the boat sailed out of Kowloon Harbor at 9 p.m., which meant I would get to stand up at the bow in the middle of the night staring out into the blackness, conjuring up whatever imaginary dangers I felt like imagining. Smuggling, boat rides, and middle-of-the-night anything were all the ingredients anyone needed to have one last final adventure.

When we got to Thailand, I was able to cross another item off my fantasy swashbuckling bucket list: *hacking through vines with a machete.*

Our family had taken a trip up to Chiang Mai, in the northern, mountainous region of Thailand. Once there, Mom insisted on booking a three-day jungle trek, which I didn't need to hear anything further about. *Jungles* were the official adventure epicenter. Everyone knew that. Tarzan lived in the jungle. Indiana Jones was always off in the jungle. Batman may or may not have had a timeshare in the jungle—I wasn't sure. I didn't really read comic books.

The best thing about this trek was that there were absolutely no vestiges of the modern world to rip you out of whatever storyline you wanted to make up along the journey. It was just the four of us in our family and a single guide traipsing through unvarnished nature.

Day 1 was an all-day hike through the jungle, which unfortunately had well-worn trails to lead the way. This was unacceptable. Adventurers did *not* use walking trails.

Our guide had a machete strapped to his backpack, so I asked if I could use it. He shrugged and handed it to me. I took it and walked off the trail to the left until I was maybe 30 yards away from everyone else. Then I just walked parallel to them for the rest of the day, hacking through whatever vines and branches had the misfortune of trying to block my path. If the jungle tried to play nice and clear itself out for me to make the going a little easier at any point, I simply veered off until I found a way that was blocked and required some hacking. Hacking through vines was a scene straight out of the official movie of missionaries, youth groups, and Christian schools everywhere: *The*

Princess Bride. The only thing missing was a princess and some steroid rats.

I felt sorry for all those boys back in America who had to go off to school or soccer practice or the mall with no reason or hope to hack through vines with a machete.

Sucks to be them.

Day 2 of the trek was an elephant ride. Not one of those lame elephant rides like at the circus, where you climb on for a photo op and then a handler leads you around in a circle for two minutes. This was an honest-to-goodness, all-day ride where they cinched a bench up on the elephant's back, and then two people climbed on from a tree branch and held on for dear life for the next six hours as we made our way up and down mountains. Mom and Dad shared an elephant in the back, Kyle and I got the elephant up front.

I've been asked in the past, "Shane, what's it like riding an elephant down the side of a mountain?" and the answer is very simple: take a Sprinter van up to the top of a very steep incline, get out and sit on the roof, and then have a buddy coast down the slope while you attempt not to fall off. That's it. Oh, and pray the animal doesn't trip.[14]

Up there, I couldn't believe I'd ever been impressed with horses before. A horse was basically a chihuahua compared to an elephant. Seven-year-old me was such a *child.* The only thing spoiling the experience was that I was perched on a bench. Next to my stupid sister. Tarzan would never be caught dead riding around the jungle like that. I slid off the bench and straddled the elephant's neck, resting my elbows on its massive head. Now *that* is how you ride an elephant!

The elephant ride ended at a large, open-aired bamboo pavilion at the edge of a river, where a few other tour groups were also wrapping up their day's activities. Everyone slept outside on the ground, just the way God intended. In the morning, our guide gave us instructions for Day 3's leg of the trek: grab a machete and go chop down a bunch of bamboo. We were going to lash it together into a raft and float back down the river to where we'd started.

---

[14] After spending the entire afternoon anxiously waiting for one of our animals to stumble and send us flying off the side of a cliff, we later learned that elephants have a type of padding on the bottoms of their feet that conforms to whatever they step on, making them one of the most sure-footed animals on earth.

This wasn't wanton, superfluous machete-wielding—it was bona fide "grab a blade and get to chopping or you don't go home" machete-wielding. It was *necessary*. So, we scavenged and chopped for half an hour, until we'd collected enough shoots to make a raft about five feet wide. Our guide deftly lashed it all together, and off we sailed from whence we came.

Exactly like Tom Sawyer and Huck Finn.

To this day, that Chiang Mai jungle trek remains one of the fondest experiences of my entire life.

Coming back to the States after all that was a culture shock. I'd gotten used to running around barefoot with a sword, digging up clams on the beach for dinner because we were too poor to afford anything fancier than rice. Now, I had to contend with stuff like getting jumped by the neighborhood bullies for wearing a New Kids On The Block t-shirt on the first day of school.

I should probably explain that.

When we got back home to America, I had maybe four shirts to my name. On the first day of eighth grade, all four of them were dirty. Someone from the church had given my sister a gift basket for her birthday a couple weeks earlier, and in it was an oversized NKOTB t-shirt. I'd missed all those fifth-through-seventh-grade years that are some of the most formative, so I had no idea they were a boy band. I'd never heard of them. I didn't have anything else to wear, and I thought it would be a clever way to introduce myself to all my new American junior-high classmates. I just thought, "This shirt says *New Kids On The Block*, and *I'm* a 'new kid on the block;' everyone will think I'm awesome and hip and welcome me with open arms!"

Yeah, not so much. All they opened was a can of whoop-ass at the bus stop.

The most excruciating part of the reverse culture shock was discovering that America was still exactly the way I'd left it—in its natural habitat, there was almost no adventure to be found anywhere. Which meant I was gonna have to create my own. Which meant I was about to learn that artificially manufacturing adventures where they do not organically grow is not a recipe for staying in the good graces of the law.

It all started when I met my best friend, Pete Moretti, who was always up for whatever hair-brained nonsense I had cooked up for that day's activities. Sometime around ninth grade, I'd spent the night at his house, and we'd stayed up all night watching an *American Ninja* marathon. Naturally, we both agreed that we needed to become professional ninjas.

That summer, on a vacation to St. Louis—where grandpa was guaranteed to take me shopping at least once for whatever I wanted—I revealed that I was getting too old for Toys 'R' Us, convincing him to take me to a martial arts store and buy me a ninja suit instead. To complete the ensemble, I also threw in a pair of nunchuks, a *sai* (Raphael's weapon from *Ninja Turtles*), and a handful of throwing stars.

Grandpa couldn't make hide nor hair of why I needed any of it or what I was planning to do with it. "Aw, babe," he'd say, "wouldn't you rather have a new baseball mitt or a transistor radio to catch the ballgame?" (Even though it was 1992, Grandpa was a WW2 veteran who insisted on listening to Cardinals games on the radio every night—despite the fact that he had a perfectly good working TV set—and couldn't fathom why any teenager would ever want to do anything other than have a catch in the backyard.)

The first thing I needed to do with my new weapons was injure myself very badly, which is exactly what I did since not knowing how to use them didn't seem like a compelling reason not to do so anyway.

The neighbors across the street from my aunt's house had a boy about my age, and he invited me to spend the night the same day Grandpa hooked me up with the new ninja gear.

Now, one of the well-kept secrets in the vibrant ninja community that the average layperson will never understand about ninja-ing is that whenever you show off your ninja gear to somebody—especially someone you just met—you can't reveal that you just got it. You have to act like it's been in the family lineage for hundreds of years, that you're a secret ninja master for whom it's hardly a novelty, and that you happen to have it on you at all times and are genuinely surprised anyone would have questions about the large, pitchfork-shaped object clearly concealed under your shirt that wasn't there yesterday. ("What, *this* old thing? I'm so used to always having this *sai* shoved down the front of my pants that sometimes I forget it's even there!")

Then you whip the *sai* out of your pants and attempt to demonstrate your ancient mastery by spinning it around on your finger like Raphael always does effortlessly in the cartoon—only this is the first time you've ever attempted it, so the *sai* barely completes two full revolutions before it flies off your hand and impales your foot in the webbing between the two smallest toes, pinning it to the hardwood floor.

So, yeah, ninja-ing was going to take some practice.

Once I brought it all back to Pittsburgh, the way Pete and I decided to practice was to take every weapon we could get our hands on out into the woods behind our house and wage full-on battles with imaginary enemies ducking out from behind trees. Or we'd use them on each other. We were fine either way. Unfortunately for Pete, he didn't have a cool ninja suit like mine. So anytime we headed out to the woods for ninja practice, he would have to dress up like Rambo instead: camo pants, black tank top, a healthy heaping of warpaint on his face and arms—you know the drill.

We also discovered that the woods we were honing our ninja skills in bordered the Green Oaks Country Club, and that one of the many paths crisscrossing the woods opened out into the far end of their driving range. If we concealed ourselves in the tall grass that separated the woods from the manicured range, we could sprint out when no one was looking, nab whatever golf balls had made their way out this far, then take them back into the woods and see how far we could whack them with nunchucks or the broad side of a samurai sword.

On one such golf-ball-thievery mission one Friday afternoon, someone back at the clubhouse must've spotted a black-clad figure 400 yards downrange materialize out of the bushes and snake a handful of balls off the ground before darting back into the head-high grass because a golf cart was soon speeding across the driving range in our direction.

"Quick, hide!" I yelled at Pete. I crouched deeper into the grass while he ran off towards the woods.

The golf cart came to a stop where the range ended and the grass that I was hiding in began. A kid who couldn't have been more than 16 or 17 stepped out of the cart and started scanning the area.

What was he, a caddy?

They sent a freaking caddy *out here on a recon assignment involving ninjas? Do they not know who we are?*

Unless it's Bill Murray, never send a caddy to address your ninja infestations.

It crossed my mind that the kid probably had no idea who we were or that he had ninjas on his hands, but since he wasn't a grownup, it probably wouldn't hurt to reveal myself and give him a good scare. I pulled out my samurai sword and casually walked out of the grass behind him, clearing my throat to get him to turn around and notice me.

I'm not sure what I was expecting to happen. I think maybe I thought he'd be like, "Oh, my bad, I didn't realize you were out here on official ninja business. I'll let you get back to it and be on my way. Peace out!" and then hop in his cart and go back to the clubhouse.

But I suppose life doesn't prepare teenage, country club golf caddies to be unexpectedly confronted with ninjas materializing out of nowhere and brandishing a fully-functioning samurai sword since samurai swords are obviously intended to be wielded by samurais, and I was clearly a ninja. We're supposed to have *katanas*. Duh.

Instead of quickly piecing all that together and introducing himself, he screamed bloody murder and took off running *into* the grass I had just stepped out of—in the direction of the woods. Where Pete was hiding.

My best guess as to what happened next is that Pete heard a scream, followed by someone tearing through the grass in his direction, and naturally assumed it was me. So, he stepped out from behind his tree to greet "me" with a Rambo knife in one hand and a second knife clenched firmly between his teeth—like a pirate swinging aboard a wandering vessel for a good pillaging session—directly into the path of the terrified caddy, who screamed again, veered off his current trajectory, and went noisily crashing into the woods.

If you asked me, the whole thing seemed like a giant overreaction. The very last thing either of us was interested in was harming anyone (other than each other)—we were just out here for some practical ninja field training and to enjoy our Friday. That caddy could've easily been a new friend if he hadn't been so keen on screaming and running off into the forest like a lunatic. We were *friendly* neighborhood ninjas.

We shrugged, had a laugh, and decided to climb a tree and throw rocks at stuff.

We'd been sitting up in our tree—with a clear view of the driving range and clubhouse—a good while when Pete pointed over at the country club parking lot and asked, "What do you think's going on over there?"

I turned and looked where he was pointing. A small convoy of police cruisers with flashing lights a-flashin' was pulling up to the main entrance. Bringing up the rear of their convoy was a large vehicle that was either an oversized navy blue ice cream truck or a SWAT van. It was hard to tell from this far away.

What *was* going on over there? Bomb threat, maybe? Why would anyone want to bomb a country club? They were generally a peaceful, kindly folk.

"You don't think there's any chance that might have anything to do with *us*, do you?" Pete asked.

I didn't see why it would. We were just a couple of harmless 15-year-olds goofing off in ninja suits and warpaint and feudal weaponry, stealing golf balls off their driving range in the middle of the day.

On second thought, I could see how it possibly *might* be about us.

"Do you think maybe we should leave," I wondered, "just in case it *is* about us?"

"Couldn't hurt," Pete said.

So, we climbed down out of our tree and slowly made our way back through the woods, in the direction of home. We'd gotten about halfway through the woods when we heard what sounded like dirt bikes or four-wheeler engines revving in the distance.

Were they sending the SWAT team on wheels into the woods looking for us? Uh-oh.

If SWAT was indeed out here combing the trails on motorized vehicles, we'd never be able to outrun them to the edge of the woods where the first row of houses began. We were going to have to hide out here in the woods. Exactly like Rambo in *First Blood.* Or *Red Dawn.* Take your pick.

This Friday was slowly turning *awesome.*

To our left, the woods sloped down sharply to a creek that cut through it and emptied into the Allegheny River a half mile away. If we could make it down to the creek before being spotted, we could jump in, cover ourselves with a hollowed-out tree trunk, and casually float down to the river without being noticed. The Allegheny eventually ran into the Mississippi River, which emptied into the Gulf of Mexico, which was vaguely where the Caribbean was located, which is where all the pirates lived, and they'd probably welcome us right into their fold when they saw how much cutlery we came bearing.

The only problem with this foolproof plan was that there were no hollowed-out tree trunks conveniently lying around for us to grab. Also, the creek was only knee-deep.

What we did have working in our favor was that the edge of the creek on the side we'd just come down had a lip that overhung the water by at least a foot, maybe more. We could lay down on our backs in the water and wedge up against the creekbank, the overhang shielding us from view. It wasn't *exactly* like Robin Hood hiding in the castle moat with a reed breathing tube, but it was close enough.

So, we laid down in the creek for about an hour, listening to engines race up and down the trails until they eventually concluded there was nobody out here and called off the search. We came out from our hiding spot, pruned to the point of aching, and decided to trek back to the neighborhood through the middle of the creek to hide our scent. Just in case they decided to return with the K-9 unit.

The next morning, Mom came into the dining room where we were eating breakfast, the Saturday paper opened in front of her. "This wouldn't, by chance, happen to have anything to do with you two idiots, would it?" she asked, folding the paper back and thrusting it out so we could read the incredible headline on page 4:

Ninjas Terrorize Local Country Club

That was obviously fake news. We hadn't "terrorized" anyone. We had just dressed up in assassin costumes and stolen their golf balls and then jumped out of the bushes with a small armory of functional weapons when they came looking, scaring the bejeezus out of them enough to call in the SWAT team and—okay, yeah, we terrorized them.

Fair was fair.

The problem with teenagers in general is that they think they're invincible. The problem with teenagers who regularly find themselves in situations that would typically result in a trip to the local hospital or county jail—but never quite seem to end up there—is that after surviving enough idiotic stunts, their invincibility becomes a certainty. And when those teenagers inevitably leave home still living in the fictional movie la-la land in their head, that's how you nearly get kicked out of college for almost killing one of your classmates with a shark.

I'd initially gone off to Palm Beach Atlantic University intending to major in marine biology. I'd seen enough movies to know this was a noble profession involving lots of high-speed boat chases, an abundance of scantily-clad damsels in distress, copious amounts of explosions, and the occasional sea-monster battle. I was baffled as to why anyone would ever major in anything other than marine biology. (I would've picked archaeology because of how much Nazi-punching it entailed, but it was 1995, and I was still under the youthful impression the Nazis had gone extinct.) Above all, I *really* needed to ride a shark.

When I got to school and discovered none of that stuff was actually on the syllabus, I changed my major to communications and just signed up for SCUBA as an elective instead.

Spring semester, I got certified and completed the requisite four dives to get an A. Sophomore year, I signed up for SCUBA II, which required 12 dives that got progressively deeper. Nearing the end of the course, we were out for a pretty deep dive—about 90 feet down—when I spotted a huge 9-foot nurse shark resting in the sand.

I decided this was my big opportunity. [15]

Since the shark was facing away from me, I swam up behind it and attempted to grab its dorsal fin. As soon as I made contact with the animal, it bolted like a bat out of hell, leaving me in its dust.

Unfortunately, the direction it shot off in was on a direct collision course with my buddy Chris, 30 yards away, who was busy examining seashells on the ocean floor. He happened to glance up at the shark, which was about 20 feet away and barreling straight at his face. I telepathically tried to communicate to him that nurse sharks are non-

---

[15] Nurse sharks are one of the few shark species that don't have to keep moving to breathe, so it's not uncommon for them to just be lounging in the sand. It *is* rather uncommon to just happen across one undetected. Also, nurse sharks are almost completely non-aggressive to humans—there are no recorded fatalities of nurse shark attacks ever. They're basically like giant ocean catfish.

aggressive—they're basically giant catfish—and that this particular one had just gotten spooked by me trying to ride it and didn't mean him any harm.

But it turns out saltwater is a poor conductor of telepathic vibes, and Chris didn't get my message. He just thought a shark was coming to eat him, so he let out a scream. (I assume it was a scream, anyway. I couldn't hear anything, but a stream of bubbles exited his mouth while his breathing regulator floated away. Most likely a scream.). The shark veered off at the last possible instant, leaving Chris panicked, out of breath, and flailing to locate his regulator.

Fortunately, the dive master was about 20 feet above us and saw the whole thing. He quickly swam down and jammed his spare regulator into Chris' mouth before he could drown, narrowly averting disaster, and then gave us all the thumbs-up sign to surface.

A few days later, I received my weekly summons to the school disciplinary office, where I spent almost as much time as I did in the classroom, though never for anything truly "bad." The *bad* kids got sent there for smoking weed, or sneaking girls into their dorm room after curfew, or plagiarizing term papers. I was usually in for stuff like snorkeling in the fountain in front of the Admittance Office, or nailing a piece of AstroTurf I'd found in the maintenance dumpster to the roof of our off-campus house and then charging $2 to anyone who wanted to participate in my rooftop long-ball driving contest, or accidentally setting off all the car alarms in the Flagler Towers parking lot with an impromptu electronic symphony that brought in the Palm Beach Metro cops (more on that one in a minute).

The dean motioned for me to have a seat, opened the file in front of him, and said, "Okay, let's see what you're in here for *this* week." He quickly scanned the top sheet of paper and then looked up at me in disbelief.

"It says you nearly killed a fellow student with a shank?"

"Not a *shank*," I replied indignantly.

What kind of deranged lunatic would try to shank someone at a Christian school?

"That's a typo. It was a *shark*."

The dean looked at me incredulously. "How in God's name do you 'almost kill someone with a shark?'" he demanded.

That seemed like a fair question. I told him the story.

When I was done, he leaned forward with his elbows on his desk, dropped his head into his hands, and let out a deep sigh. After thinking in silence for a moment, he raised his head and said, "Okay, you haven't actually violated anything in the rulebook, so I'm not sure what we'd discipline you for. So, can you please just give me your word that this won't ever happen again? No more shark-riding."

I gave him my word. No more sharks. *During school.* I could live with that.

Oh, you're probably still wondering about that cop-related car alarm event. Very well. Here's what had happened:

I'd asked one of my neighbors if I could borrow his truck to run to the grocery store. He agreed to let me use it if I promised to wash it when I got back. I agreed.

Flagler Towers was the guys' dorm on the south edge of campus. It was a 4-story, 72-unit condo building that the school had purchased from the city. Each "dorm" was actually a 2-bedroom, bath-and-a-half apartment with a kitchen, living room, and a sliding glass door that led out to a full-length balcony that overlooked the front parking lot and swimming pool.

There was a hose inside the pool area, and students were always pulling up next to the pool fence to wash their vehicles. That's exactly what I was doing this Saturday afternoon after making my store run. I had the windows down and the doors open while I soaped the truck, blaring music for the people at the pool.

Within minutes, two campus security guards pedaled up on their bikes and told me they'd received a noise complaint and that I needed to turn down the music. These particular two guards didn't like me one bit (possibly because they were often the ones to catch me doing whatever it was that I was doing that "technically" wasn't against the rules, and possibly because I always referred to them as *rent-a-cops*).

"Turn it down, Shane," they ordered. "You know you're not allowed to have your music up that loud on campus. We're gonna circle back around in 10 minutes and check on you. If you turn the music back up after we leave, you're getting written up. This is your only warning."

I was pretty sure nobody had called in a noise complaint. It was a Saturday afternoon, and we were out by the pool. They were just on a petty power trip with their stupid badges, handcuffs, and pepper spray—the only weapon they were permitted to carry. I turned down the music . . . and waited for them as they pedaled off. I had no intention of humoring them.

As soon as they were gone, I drove the truck around to the other side of the pool and parked it on the narrow, one-way through street, close enough for the hose to still reach. Where I was now parked wasn't more than 15 yards from where I'd been parked a moment ago, but technically, it was no longer on campus. I was on city property now. I turned the music up until the speakers threatened to blow.

As if on cue, the rent-a-cops circled back around and stopped their bikes at the truck. They looked pissed.

"I thought we told you to turn down the music," one of them said. "What's your effing problem?"

"No," I responded slowly, making sure they understood I was taking pains to speak to them like children, "you told me I wasn't allowed to have my music up that loud *on campus*. I'm not on campus anymore. This is city property. You're both out of your jurisdiction."

For some reason, they didn't like this response one bit and conferred amongst themselves for a brief moment. After discussing it, one of them spoke up: "Well, you're not allowed to take school property off of school grounds. You're welcome to stay over there blasting your music like a jackass, but you have to put the hose back on campus or we're going to write you up for theft."

Well-played, rent-a-cops. Well-played.

They had me pretty good, but it wasn't quite checkmate. Suddenly, I'd gotten a diabolical idea.

"Listen guys, I'm not trying to cause any problems," I began amicably, 100% intent on causing problems. "The thing with volume is that it's subjective. Why don't you tell me, in quantifiable terms, how high I'm allowed to have my music without getting in trouble?"

They conferred again, and then one of them said, "Seven. You can turn the music up to seven."

"This radio has a dial, it's not digital. It doesn't have a *seven*," I said. "So, now what?

"If it's a rotating knob, you can turn it up three-quarters of the dial," came the reply.

"Okay, just to make sure I'm understanding you crystal clear, you guys are telling me that as long as a stereo doesn't go any higher than 'seven,' or three-quarters of a turn, we're not gonna have any problems?"

They both agreed.

"I can live with that," I told them. "Sorry for being a pain."

As soon as they were gone, I drove the truck back around to the parking lot, parked it, and ran up to our dorm to let my roommates in on our new mission. The plan was pretty simple: the three of us were going to go door-to-door through the whole building and ask anyone who was home to set their stereo out on the balcony—turned up to *seven*—and tuned to The Buzz 99.7. Within the hour, we had about 40 participants on board. When everyone was in place, I walked out to the front of the building, snapped a twig off a bush to serve as a conductor's wand, gave the signal, and in perfect symphony, 40 stereos flipped on.

The wall of sound that emanated forth from the building that day set off every car alarm in our parking lot, most of the car alarms in the next condo over—a block south of us—and apparently even made it past the hearing aids of all the semi-deaf seniors in the assisted-living retirement home three blocks away because they're the ones who called the cops.

We were only able to tolerate the sonic assault for about 30 seconds before everyone either powered their stereos off or dialed them down to *two*. Even at *two*, 20 stereos in unison were still loud enough to sound like a block party was going on, which is where we were when the police showed up. And the *rent-a-cops* returned.

West Palm Beach's finest simply asked us to turn it down and keep it down. The rent-a-cops were furious and itching to write someone up. But there wasn't a whole lot they could do. They couldn't write a citation to the *building*, and no individual who'd contributed to the anarchy had turned up past the officially sanctioned *seven*. In the end, they wrote me up for "antagonizing authority," which isn't in the rulebook, and for which the trumped-up charges were dismissed.

Students 1, rent-a-cops 0.

There was *always* a way.

Sometimes it just meant selling everything you owned for a dollar.

My sophomore year at college, I got accused of doing something I didn't do (which may or may not have been karma, given that I'd done plenty of stuff they never found out about). Once again, I found myself hauled into the disciplinary committee, this time on some bogus, trumped-up charge of stealing a meal card from the school cafeteria.

The cafeteria manager had had it out for me for quite some time because I had a thing for testing the limits of the cafeteria's "all-you-can-eat" policy. They were of the opinion that "all-you-can-eat" meant all you could eat in one sitting at one mealtime, and I was of the mind that if we were indeed permitted to go back up through the line as many times as we wanted for unlimited food, then that was basically the same concept as bringing in a backpack full of Tupperware containers and filling them up with cereal for the road.

They repeatedly explained to me that this was against the rules, and I repeatedly explained back that nobody in the cafeteria had ever produced a rulebook that spelled out any such nonsense. So, they just kept repeating themselves, and I just kept filling microwavable bowls with Captain Crunch. We were at an impasse.

Apparently fed up with this ongoing power play, the manager simply confiscated the new meal punch card I'd purchased the previous day when I presented it at the cash register one afternoon. She delivered it to the disciplinary board and told them I'd stolen it.

The disciplinary hearing was a 15-minute he-said-she-said where we both presented our cases. The six-member panel deliberated for about 10 minutes and then acknowledged that I had a good argument with good supporting facts and that her side of the story didn't quite add up.

However, this being a Christian school, they were also compelled to *pray* about all their decisions before rendering a final verdict. And they'd all reached the unanimous decision that, even though my story checked out, the Holy Spirit had vetoed their "human logic and reasoning" and "revealed to them" that I *had* done the thing I absolutely had not done (further solidifying my skepticism at people claiming to be "hearing from God").

Seeing as the whole bogus proceedings were over a $30 meal card, the punishment their divine miscarriage of justice compelled them to level was pretty severe: I had to vacate my off-campus housing and find somewhere else to live.

At PBA, freshmen were required to live in the dorms. Upperclassmen could put themselves on a waitlist to get into one of the couple-dozen off-campus houses or apartments the school owned. They were difficult to get into, but I'd lucked out by having two upperclassmen who were already in invite me to be their third roommate; a full room all to myself. Now, thanks to those hearing-impaired God-whisperers on the judicial board, I'd have to move out.

Moving back into the dorms wasn't an option that semester, as there weren't any rooms available (and I'd acquired enough stuff to fill a small storage unit). Renting a regular apartment was also out of the question, as I didn't have any roommate prospects or make enough money to afford one on my own.

Figure it out.

After mulling over my predicament for an afternoon, it dawned on me that the judicial board hadn't told me I could no longer *occupy* my current residence, they'd just said I couldn't *live* there. Big difference. (Dear PBA, get yourself some better attorneys.)

As previously mentioned, the Flagler Towers dorms were former condos, which meant there was a living room with a couch in each of the units. I asked some buddies if I could crash on their couch at night—which they happily agreed to—and then I'd just walk the half-block to my old apartment where all my stuff was every morning to shower and change clothes.

If you don't sleep there, you don't live *there.*

Problem solved.

Or rather, problem solved for about two weeks until the school caught wind of my little loophole and issued yet another summons to the disciplinary board, which was timely. I hadn't seen them in two whole weeks and was starting to miss them terribly. This time, they came armed with a clever rewording of the injunction: I was not to have *any personal belongings* at the address on Mango Promenade. And they meant it.

It was currently Friday afternoon. The housing dean was going to meet me at the address with a few campus security guards the following Monday at 5 p.m. sharp; if any of my belongings were still on the premises at that point, I was going to be expelled from school. That meant I had the weekend to figure out where to live. And since my aforementioned financial situation hadn't changed in the slightest, that meant in three days I was either going to be homeless . . . or have to leave school and move back to Pittsburgh with Mom or Dad. Neither of those options were viable options.

Figure it out.

By noon on Monday, I'd formulated a plan, though I was a bit skeptical if it would actually work. But it was the only play I could come up with, which meant we were going to give it the ol' college try. I asked my roommate Joe Dellinger to come with me downtown. We went to the bank and requested a notary. I quickly scrawled a few sentences on a blank sheet of paper, got it notarized, and then headed back to Mango Promenade to wait.

When five o'clock rolled around, the housing dean showed up with three security guards, walked into the apartment straight back to my room, then reappeared a moment later to drop the hammer.

"Okay, Shane, you were warned," he said. "These three gentlemen here are going to escort you off the premises, and you can swing into my office tomorrow morning so we can get your academic-termination paperwork started."

"Oh, that won't be necessary," I told him. "I'm not planning on leaving school just yet."

The dean raised his eyebrows at me while one of the trigger-happy rent-a-cops reached for his pepper spray.

"Let's not make this into a bigger problem than it already is, okay?" he tried reasoning.

"There's no problem at all," I assured him. "It's just that I think you guys are a little confused."

"No, there's no confusion here," he replied. "You were told to have all your possessions off the premises by five o'clock, and you've still got an entire room full of stuff back there."

"Back there in the back room? Nothing back there is mine. It's all Joey's," I said. "I don't have so much as a toothbrush on the premises."

The dean stared at me, apparently dumbfounded that anyone would attempt such an audacious lie. "You honestly expect me to believe that all that stuff in your old room belongs to . . . *Joe* here? Looks to me like he's got his own room full of stuff right over there!"

I took out my Hail Mary sheet of paper and handed it to the dean. "Yes, it *used* to all be my stuff. But I sold it all to Joey earlier today."

The dean read it over, incredulous. "For . . . a *dollar?*"

"He gave me a really sweet deal!" Joey interrupted unhelpfully.

"Here, you can see the sale is notarized, so it's all legal," I assured him.

The dean tried arguing over it for a few minutes, but there was nothing he could do. The letter *was* notarized, so he was looking at a potential lawsuit if he decided to press the issue. And that was the end of it.

I spent the rest of the semester crashing on my buddies' couch over at the dorms, then coming back to Mango Promenade every morning to shower and change into some of Joey's clothes. Fortunately, he had fantastic taste and was just the right size.

See? There's *always* a way.

Because he was such a solid dude, at the end of the school year, Joey sold everything back to me.

For a dollar-fifty.

But it wasn't always ninjas and sharks and trying to get one over on authority. Sometimes, it was just doing something incredibly dangerous and moronic for its own sake. Like the time my buddy Rob Sloan and I decided to have a staring contest with a Category 4 hurricane.

In September of 1999, Hurricane Floyd hit South Florida. In my four years in the Sunshine State, I hadn't experienced a full-on hurricane. Of course, it didn't help that a few nights prior, I'd rented *Twister* and decided that the only thing that mattered in life was becoming a storm chaser. Our family had survived the ~~epic~~ horrific F4 tornado that destroyed half of Wichita Falls—including our entire apartment complex—in 1979 (we had to move into a trailer park for a couple years while Sun Valley Apartments was rebuilt). But I was only two-and-a-half at the time, and nobody was giving me any credit for chasing that tornado.

Rob had been a friend throughout college, was currently my next-door neighbor, and was often right in the middle of whatever legal-adjacent, ninja-based shenanigans the day called for. It didn't hurt that he also had a propensity for stumbling into situations that probably warranted a book of their own, like the time he inadvertently ended up in a runoff election for the Florida House of Representatives.[16] That's my kind of guy.

The day before Floyd made landfall, we did the responsible thing everyone else in West Palm who wasn't evacuating was doing: covered all our windows with plywood sheets from Home Depot; stocked several Igloo coolers with ice, water, and beer should the power go out for a few days; and bought a couple chain saws should we need to cut our way through downed palm trees to go back for more beer. But that was about the extent of the similarities to West Palm's responsible citizenry.

While everyone who hadn't left town was hunkering down inside their boarded-up homes, Rob and I decided to go stake out a front-row seat for this so-called "hurricane" and see what all the fuss was about. It wasn't an overly complicated plan. We were going to walk over to the seawall at the Intracoastal Waterway and find something solid to strap ourselves to so we didn't go airborne like that *Twister* cow.

A nearby neighborhood had a few dozen houses whose fenced backyards butted up against the seawall. The seawall itself was about 20 inches wide, so you could walk atop it behind the yards—a fence on one side of you, an 8-foot drop-off into the Intracoastal on the other. We were just going to walk our way along it until we found someone with a wrought-iron fence that we could loop a leather belt around. Securely buckled to an iron fencepost, we'd greet Floyd as he made his way into our lovely city and stare him directly in his stupid eye.

Or so we imagined.

What actually happens in a hurricane—that they don't teach you at Christian college—is that if you strap yourself in place to anything outside, you basically turn yourself into a human dartboard, at which drunk Mother Nature will happily fling whatever she wishes.

Fortunately for Rob and me, by the time Floyd hit West Palm, its winds had died down from 155 mph to a mere 70, which was better

---

[16] For District 89. Democrat Irving Slosberg was running unopposed, and a Republican activist had called the non-profit Rob worked at to ask if they knew anyone willing and able to run against him. Rob threw his own name out as a joke, and they actually stuck him on the ballot. He ended up losing by the narrowest of margins: 46,885–19.

but still not great. If you've never been pelted with raindrops and palm fronds at 70 mph, might I suggest that you just continue right along that happy life journey. If it happens while you're in a bathing suit— barefoot and shirtless—you end up looking like you just reenacted the whipping scene from *Passion of the Christ* and then passed out in a wasp nest. It also makes it incredibly difficult to concentrate on unbuckling your too-tightly-cinched belt.

We lasted about 20 minutes from the first raindrop to the eventual wasp monsoon before finally unbuckling ourselves in desperation mode and sprinting for home. Floyd was no nature rent-a-cop, that was for sure. He was the real deal. PBA would not be hiring him any time soon.

Hurricane–1, Rob and Shane–0.

We made it back to our house, happy to be alive, and went off in search of all the aloe and hydrogen peroxide we owned. Hunkered down indoors like responsible citizens, I couldn't help but smile about crossing yet another item off the bucket list. Student uprisings, public executions, international Bible-smuggling, elephant jungle treks, ninjas, SWAT teams, sharks, the legal system, and now . . . *Storm Chaser.*

I was 23 and pretty sure I was close to maxing out whatever adventures life had to offer. It was probably all downhill from here.

How do you possibly top all that?

Leave it to Mom, that's how.

Humanity has advanced, when it has advanced, not because it has been sober, responsible, and cautious, but because it has been playful, rebellious, and immature.

– Tom Robbins

Go, and make interesting mistakes, make amazing mistakes, make glorious and fantastic mistakes. Break rules. Leave the world more interesting for your being here.

– Neil Gaiman

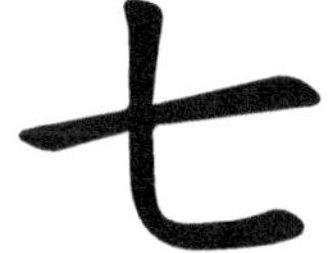

Fielder on the Roof

As a lifelong pianist and huge Billy Joel fan, it was only appropriate that the call came when it did: *It was nine o'clock on a Saturday.*

On the West Coast, that is.

On the east coast of South Florida—where I actually was at the moment—it was closer to midnight. But there's no song about that. However, it was nine o'clock somewhere, so my point is still valid. Either way, this is a story that owes its entire existence to playing a little fast and loose with things like 100% truth and technical accuracy, so it's apropos.

If Mr. Joel *had* written a song more accurately depicting my current situation, it might have gone something like this:

It's twelve o'clock on a Saturday
A lunatic's up on his roof
In a lawn chair, precariously balancing
Where he sits and sips seventy-proof

Actually, that's not too bad.

Hey guys, can we get someone in touch with Mr. Joel's people and let them know I'm writing him a sequel to his most popular and beloved song of all time?

Yes, I absolutely agree he'll be thrilled to hear about it!

As is generally acknowledged in academia, there are only a dozen or so sensible reasons for a person to ever be on the top of their roof in a lawn chair with a *Dukes of Hazard* TV tray and a tennis racket in the dead middle of the night. And as a sensible person,[17] it was for one of *those* reasons—not for, say, any of the myriad of others—that I found myself in precisely that situation on a balmy October night, barely a month removed from our tango with Hurricane Floyd.

I was up there to observe the hotly-contested game of wiffle ball home run derby in the street below between my roommate Nutter (real name Mike, though everyone called him Nutter for reasons I won't get into here), our three next-door neighbors (including Rob), and a few other friends. I would've preferred to be competing in the smack-talk-riddled derby, but Nutter had an uncanny knack for fouling balls off directly over the ridge I was now perched on, and I'd just bet him five bucks that I could sit in a lawn chair on the roof and catch more of his foul balls—without moving—than he could hit home runs.

He was indignant, and I was flat broke. The bet was on.

(It was agreed that I didn't have to technically *catch* the ball, I merely had to *intercept* it. And as a further sign of sportsmanship, I was given the choice of a single piece of sporting equipment to aid the endeavor: a hockey stick, a fishing net, or a tennis racket. I chose the tennis racket like a sensible person.)

Now, I know this raises an obvious question: *Shane, was at least some part of your roof* flat *to place all this stuff down on safely?*

No. No, it was not. Not at any part.

What a foolish question, you foolish fool.

The chair had to be balanced *just so* on the peak of the roof, straddling the ridge, lest I go tobogganing headfirst off the side of the house into the ficus hedge. The TV tray—one of those metal contraptions from the '80s with the fold-out legs—was also straddling the roof's ridge in front of me, acting as a makeshift coffee table for

---

17 Editor's note: this is *strenuously* disputed by 6 out of 5 mental healthcare practitioners and 4 out of 5 dentists.

the bevy of snacks I had also brought up: a bag of Doritos, a pack of clove cigarettes, and a six-pack of Heineken.

I settled into my chair and cracked a beer. It was going to be a great night.

Nutter stepped up to the plate—a hubcap from my rusted-out station wagon that suffered from severe ADD (Attachability Deficiency Disorder)—pointed out into the distance like Babe Ruth calling his shot . . . and promptly fouled off the first pitch three feet over my head. I could've snagged it had I not been organizing my concession stand.

I could smell my five dollars.

I was about to holler out, telling him as much, when my phone rang. I glanced at the caller ID: *Mom*. Who never called past eight in the evening. Ever.

That meant something was probably horribly wrong. My heart immediately leapt into my throat as I tried to imagine which friend or relative must've had a heart attack or car accident. My hand shook as I answered the phone, and I steeled myself for whatever calamity I was about to hear.

"He-hello?" I could barely get the words out.

"Shane, quick, do you know any guitarists who have a passport?"

I'd braced myself for any number of awful scenarios. This was absolutely not one of them.

"Um . . . *what?*"[18]

"Do. You. Know. Any. Guitarists. Who. Have. A. Passport?" she repeated slowly as if talking to a drunk (which, to be fair, she almost was).

"Uh . . . I don't think so, no. Wait, yes. Actually, I'm not sure. Maybe?"

I was suffering from mental whiplash at the moment. In the span of two seconds, I'd been jerked from trying to determine if I owned the proper dress slacks for a potential funeral to attempting to recall if anyone in my non-existent Rolodex happened to be a guitarist with a penchant for international travel. Needless to say, I was somewhat confused.

---

[18] The scientifically correct response here would have been to quote Wesley from *The Princess Bride*: "Do you always begin conversations this way?"

I collected my thoughts and tried again: "What in the *world* is going on? Why are you calling so late? What do you need a guitarist for? Why do they need a passport?"

Another wiffle ball whizzed past my ear. I could've caught that one, too, but far more intriguing subjects were demanding my immediate attention.

Thankfully, Mom backed up and started over.

She and the Newsboys were slated to leave for China in ten days for some concert thingy she'd been working on for the better part of the '90s.

"Wait, what are you doing with the Newsboys?" I wanted to know. "How in the world do you have something going on that involves them?"[19]

"Be quiet and let me talk, Shane!"

Fine. Proceed.

She continued, explaining that the Newsboys had just called her at the last minute to let her know they wouldn't be able to go do something-something China due to something-something visa, something-something reasons.

Mom had never been great at summarizing. It was typically hard enough to follow her recounting of anything when she had your undivided attention and you were securely anchored on *terra firma.* Up here on the roof, thinking about my five bucks and not falling off the roof, I was having a difficult time making heads or tails of her dilemma.

"So," Mom continued, "I've found a lead singer, bass player, and drummer here in Pittsburgh. I've got you penciled in on the keyboard, and then we just need a guitarist."

Penciled in on keyboards?

I was trying to put all the pieces together in my head, and they were refusing to fit.

---

[19] Since Mom hadn't begun working on the concert in earnest until after I'd gone off to college in 1995, I knew almost nothing of the fine details I laid out in the previous chapters. I got all of that information conducting interviews with her after I started writing this book. At the time of our rooftop conversation, all I really knew was that she'd mentioned an idea for a concert a decade earlier and that she'd gone to China around 1996 for some reason I didn't fully understand. This was the very first time I was hearing about the Newsboys.

"For *what?*" I asked, befuddled. "What are you talking about?"

"Son, I've been working on this concert for ten years, and it's happening with or without the Newsboys," she replied impatiently, as if this were the most obvious explanation in the world.

"The plane tickets and hotels are booked and paid for. The venues are set. The tickets are sold. The production is all in place. This concert is *happening.* We're going to China in ten days, and we're not going to tell anyone there that we're *not* the real Newsboys. Are you in or are you out?"

Did I just hear her correctly? She wanted to pull a fast one over on the Communist Party of China? They were going to be furious enough when they realized she'd duped them into booking a Christian band. Now she wanted to compound the situation by enlisting some random musicians to *impersonate* the offending band?!? A particularly apt maxim popped into my head. . .

If you're going to break one law, don't break two.

In my 23 years on earth up to this point, I'd been privy to dozens of my mom's more ill-conceived ideas and dubious propositions. But this one, hands down, took the cake.

Go to China in ten days, pretending to be a world-renowned band, for an actual concert in front of a real audience?

This was next-level lunacy. Even for Mom.

I was intrigued.

She was also putting me on the spot and demanding an answer. I swung my tennis racket at another errant foul ball, missing by inches and nearly losing my balance. That would be out number three for Nutter. He passed the bat off to the next man in the rotation and flashed me a one-finger salute. We were tied 0-0.

Focus, Shane. Focus.

What she was laying out for me, if I was understanding it correctly, was obviously insane. Which was not a disqualifying feature by my math—more of a selling point, actually.

Ten days to prepare for a full-length concert?

I wasn't concerned with learning whatever music I'd be required to know. *IF* I agreed to participate. I had total confidence I could handle that aspect of it, even on such short notice. I also wasn't bothered by the potential danger of the undertaking once we got to China. If anything, that was a point in favor *of*—not against—signing on.

No, the thing that concerned me was having no idea who I might be agreeing to play with, what their ability level was (my mom was not a musical talent scout), and how we were supposed to get ourselves on the same page in just ten days.

"Okay," I began, "let's save the discussion about what happens when China figures out we're not the real Newsboys, or what the *real* Newsboys might do if and when they find out we went over there impersonating them, and just discuss the logistics of pulling this off.

"Supposing I agree to this, and supposing I can actually find a guitar player—with a passport—who's willing to go along for this insane ride, how are we supposed to actually, you know, *rehearse* for this gig?"

A long pause on the other end. She hadn't considered that small detail yet. I had yet to catch one of Nutter's foul balls, but I did just score a debate point with my mom. Those were equal to 12 wiffle ball points.

"Let me think about that for a second," she finally replied. "Go make some phone calls and call me back as soon as you find something out."

Click.

I sat back in my precariously balanced lawn chair at the top of the roof and tried processing the entire exchange. Two possible ~~victims~~ guitarists immediately came to mind as potential candidates. My good buddy—and occasional beach volleyball partner—Chris Armfield was a singer-songwriter I'd played a handful of coffee shop gigs with in the past.

The other option was Gavin McLaughlin, one of my best friends at the time. Gavin had never played a single gig of any sort, to my knowledge. He was strictly a "backyard guitarist"—the guy we always insisted break out the guitar around our regular bonfires. Our good friend Dave Lashbrook lived in a little housing unit right on the Intracoastal Waterway, and at least a few nights a week, we'd gather over there at sunset, build a fire, drink a few [too many] beers, and sing classic rock tunes to Gavin's accompaniment until the sun resurfaced, no doubt surprised to find us all still sitting right there where it left us.

I called Gavin first, not entirely sure what I was going to say to him.

Fielder on the Roof

Hey dude, you wanna go to China in ten days, impersonating a world-famous band, and play a couple concerts featuring a bunch of songs you probably don't know with some bandmates you've never met?

And maybe get arrested in the process?

I hadn't even committed myself yet to signing up for this debacle that I'd only learned about three minutes prior. And God forbid he ask any follow-up questions because I certainly didn't have any answers for him. He answered on the second ring.

"Yo, yo! Whazzzup?!" Gavin's favorite salutation.

"Um, this is going to sound a little weird, but you don't happen to have a passport, do you?" I asked.

"Nope!" he proclaimed, sounding vaguely proud of that fact. It took him a few more moments to realize this was not the typical kind of phone call I was in the habit of making in the middle of the night. "Why, what's going on?"

I tried to give him the two-minute version of Mom's current predicament and bonkers solution, wrapping it all up with the phone call I'd just received from her.

"Dude, that sounds *awesome!*" he said after a long pause. "If I had a passport, I'd be all over that in a second!"

'd met Gavin—and his identical twin brother, Trevor—at the gym a few years back. Both were avid rock climbers, and Gavin had introduced me to rappelling. I'd gotten hooked immediately.

One of our favorite activities was grabbing harnesses and a rope and walking around downtown West Palm Beach in the middle of the night, looking for tall things to rappel off of.

One such foray found us on top of the five-story men's dorm right in the heart of PBA's campus. We tied our rope off to the balcony railing in the rear of the building, and I went down first.

(I should probably also mention that I had a questionable habit of wearing my ninja suit on these nightly excursions for reasons science is still puzzling over. The suit was abysmally hot, was difficult to see out of, and served absolutely no purpose whatsoever other than I thought it looked cool to dangle off the side of buildings dressed like a ninja.)

On this particular night, I stopped my descent about ten or twelve feet down to adjust my mask, which had shifted over to completely cover my left eye. Had my eye not been covered, I might have noticed the petrified look on the face of the poor freshman whose fourth-story window I'd just come to a grinding halt outside of. But apparently, one man's "cool" is another man's "Oh my god, someone, call 911! There's a freaking *ninja* outside our fourth-floor window at two in the morning!"

I finished adjusting my mask—oblivious to the abject horror currently being experienced on the other side of the window a mere three feet from me—and continued on my merry way.

I made it safely to the ground, unharnessed myself, peeled off my mask, and sat down against a dumpster, waiting for Gavin to descend. And that's exactly where I was sitting when the omnipresent West Palm Beach police department showed up a few minutes later. Six of them. None of them appeared to notice me (I'm told maskless ninjas are still at least *partially* invisible), but they did instantly spot Gavin, who was still some twenty feet off the ground. One of the cruisers trained its spotlight up on him, and he touched down a few seconds later and was immediately surrounded by a half dozen of West Palm's finest.

I could see them getting into a conversation, but I was too far away to hear anything that was being said. It didn't look heated, and none of the officers were being aggressive. They almost looked—dare I say—*amused?*

I watched for a couple more minutes, wondering what to do. They still didn't know I was there, but I was starting to feel a little guilty about leaving Gavin to deal with the cops by himself. And my curiosity was getting piqued by the fact that the entire group was now decidedly in stitches about *something*. One of the officers roared with laughter and clapped Gavin on the back good-naturedly. I couldn't take it anymore.

I quickly decided to take off the rest of the ninja suit, ditch it in the bushes, and casually saunter out as if I were out for a late-night stroll and just happened upon this amicable confrontation by chance. Then I could "pretend" to recognize Gavin and come over to say hi. It was a perfect plan. The cops would see my board shorts and tank top and never suspect I had anything to do with the reported ninja. I stepped out from behind the dumpster.

"And there's the ninja right there!" Gavin shouted instantly, pointing directly at me. I made a mental note to never invite him along on bank heists.

I sheepishly walked over to the group, preparing for a lecture, a citation, or possibly handcuffs. Instead, all of the officers shook my hand and introduced themselves. Apparently, they'd initially asked Gavin about an alleged ninja in the area, and Gavin had been more than eager to spill the beans. That's what all the laughter was about. They were collectively of the opinion that we could be out doing drugs or starting fights or vandalizing property, and so a little harmless rappelling was to be preferred over those other activities. We both nodded in agreement.

One of the officers asked us about the gear we were using, and the conversation turned to rappelling safety and techniques. We filled them in on all the various buildings around town we'd climbed and rappelled down from, which seemed to impress them quite a bit. Then one of them surprised us by issuing a standing invitation to come out to the nine-story rappelling tower the SWAT team trained on whenever we wanted.

We thanked them, shook hands again, and parted ways. As soon as they drove off, I circled back and collected my ninja suit.

That was Gavin and me in a nutshell. We'd egg each other on, get ourselves into trouble, occasionally have brushes with the law, and generally come out of it unscathed. Our friends used to joke that if it were anyone else, they'd be sitting in a jail cell. We do it and somehow end up getting an invitation to go train with SWAT.

Go figure.

Our phone call ended with mild disappointment. I knew that if Gavin was up for going to China, I was going to China as well. He was my partner in crime. It was too bad he didn't have a passport.

My next call was to Chris. I repeated the same spiel I'd just given to Gavin. Chris took it all in without saying a word until I was finished. When he finally spoke, it was pragmatic.

"First off, yes, I have a passport," he said. He paused for another moment and then asked, "How much is this trip going to cost?"

I told him that, if I understood my mother correctly, it wasn't going to cost any of us anything. The entire thing was already paid for.

"And we leave in two weeks?"

"I wish. More like a week and a half," I replied.

"Do we have a setlist yet?" he wanted to know.

"Not that I'm aware of," I admitted. "But I think my mom's working on that."

(I had no idea if Mom was working on that or not. It wouldn't have surprised me one bit if she got us all over there and then realized half an hour before the first sound check that she'd neglected to tell anyone what songs we were supposed to be playing.)

"Well, we're going to need to figure that out and then rehearse our butts off," he offered helpfully.

"Does this mean you're . . . *in?*" I was incredulous.

"Yeah, man. I'm in. This sounds like the opportunity of a lifetime!"

"Great," I said, "I'll call you tomorrow with some more details. Let me jump off and call my mom back."

Now I had a problem. I'd essentially just promised Chris an all-expenses-paid trip to China to play the biggest gigs of his life, and I still had serious doubts that any of it was even remotely possible. I already knew what logistical concerns I had to bring up to Mom, and I was pretty sure any single one of them would be a deal-breaker for this venture on their own. Then, after she listened to reason, I'd have to call Chris back the next day and apologize for speaking too soon and getting his hopes up.

Mom answered before the first ring was halfway finished. "What did you find out?"

I debated whether to start with the good news that we had a guitarist or the bad news that I didn't think any part of this plan was realistically feasible. I opted for the good news first.

"My buddy Chris has a passport, and he's in," I began. "I also spoke with Gavin, who was all about it, but he does *not* have a passport."

"Okay, no problem, I'll take care of it. We're going to need both of them since there are six members of the Newsboys."

You'll take care of it?

"Mum, I'm pretty sure the Newsboys only have five members."

"And don't most bands have two guitarists, anyway?" she continued, ignoring my incredibly relevant head count.

I affirmed that it was not uncommon for a band to have both a rhythm and a lead guitar player.

"So, here's what you're going to do," she began, improvising on the fly. "You and Gavin are going to drive down to Miami first thing Monday morning. And I mean *first thing*. You need to wake up at the crack of dawn and be there waiting outside the passport agency when they unlock their doors. Have Gavin fill out his application, and you *make sure* that they expedite it. I'll also call them the second they open and see what I can do to speed up the process."

"But . . . don't passports—even if they're expedited—take, like, a month to come in?" I protested.

"Typically, yes."

"So?"

"So . . . *what?*" she demanded. "If it doesn't get here in time, it doesn't get here in time. But the only way it has a chance is if you two are down there when they open on Monday. Then it's in God's hands."

"Terrific. Glad we got that squared away," I muttered sarcastically. Now it was time to burst her bubble with the bad news.

"Let me see if I can summarize the situation we're in, and please stop me if I'm missing something," I told her.

"You've got six guys—one of whom doesn't have a passport— who've never played music together before, and you want to take them out of the country in a week and a half to play a couple concerts with international diplomatic implications. Half of them are up there in Pennsylvania, and half are down here in Florida. Somehow, we've got to be prepared to play a two-hour concert in 12 days in Asia.

"How do you propose we get together for rehearsal? Are you flying us up there, or are you flying those guys down here? All six of us have jobs or school, and I'm pretty sure none of us can just take a month off for this."

"Nobody's flying anywhere," Mom replied. "You three rehearse down there, and my guys will be rehearsing up here."

Oh boy, this just keeps getting better and better.

"How are we supposed to rehearse *as a band* with half of the band missing?" I wanted to know. "We don't know what songs we're playing. Assuming we figure that out in the next few days, we don't know what key they need to be in. We don't know how they're going to be structured. We don't know where any of the solos are. We don't know who's going to be singing what harmonies. We don't know when or how any of the songs are supposed to start or end. These things take *months* to figure out for bands that have been playing together for years!"

I was stupefied but pressed on. "The actual Newsboys themselves rehearse for weeks, if not months, when they're gearing up for a new tour. And that's playing *their own music!*"

"Look, this isn't as big of a deal as you're making it," she replied matter-of-factly, as if addressing a child who faced the daunting task of picking up his scattered blocks before dinner. "You, Gavin, and Chris get together tomorrow and pick out ten songs that you guys want to do. They don't even have to all be Newsboys songs. The Chinese public has never heard of them, so they won't have any idea whose songs you're doing. Put your ten songs on a mix tape or burn a CD and overnight them via FedEx on Monday. The guys up here in Pittsburgh will do the same. Then all of you should have a full list of songs no later than Tuesday afternoon."

Had the A-Team been holding auditions for a new leader, Hannibal would've been out of a job (and Murdock would no longer be the insane one).

"Okay, so now we know what songs we'll be playing, but that still doesn't answer any of my other questions about the music."

"Just learn them exactly like they are on the CD," she replied with a hint of exasperation. "If you both have copies of the exact same songs and you learn them exactly like they sound on the recording, then you should all be playing the exact same thing when you get together."

Flawless logic there, Mum.

I had one last card to play. "What happens 1) if and when the Chinese authorities discover we're imposters, and 2) when they discover we're imposters performing overtly, blatantly Christian music?"

Mom answered without hesitation, "God will protect us."

I wasn't entirely sold on that premise, but I was all out of protests.

"Alright. I'll get the boys together tomorrow, and Gavin and I will be in Miami Monday morning, bright and early."

We hung up, I laid back in my lawn chair, downed the rest of my beer, and grabbed another.

Crack!

On his third up through the rotation, Nutter had finally connected on a pitch and drove a ball deep into the night. He whiffed on the next one for his last out. Nutter-1, Shane-0. Stupid phone calls. It should've been Shane 4-1.

I'd just lost five dollars. On the other hand, I was theoretically going to China in less than two weeks to play the biggest concert I'd ever been a part of in the most daring, audacious, and adventurous way imaginable.

Five bucks seemed like a fair price for that trade-off.

Luck is a very thin wire
between survival and
disaster, and not many
people can keep their
balance on it.
– Hunter S. Thompson

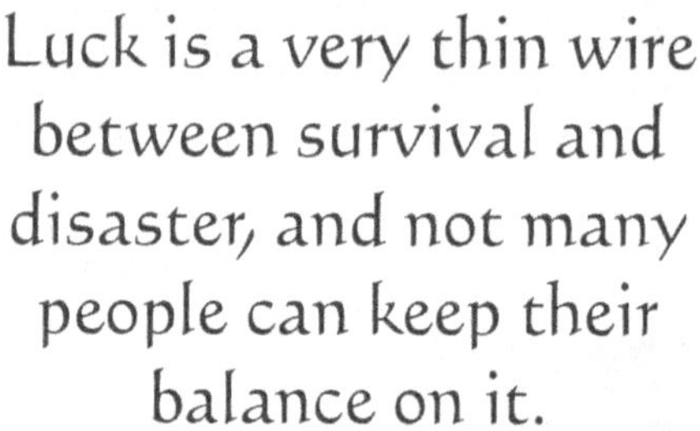

The main thing
is honesty. If
you can fake
that, you've
got it made.
– George Burns

You Got Served

Of all the dates Mom could've picked to waltz us into a high-pressure, international situation pretending to be someone and something we weren't anywhere in the ballpark of being, this one couldn't have come at a more opportune time since I'd pulled off a similar piece of chicanery earlier that summer.

Fresh out of college, I still hadn't decided what I wanted to be when (or if) I grew up,[20] so I was content to spend my first summer with a college diploma working for Nutter's painting company, St. John's Exteriors. This had its pros and cons.

The pros were that we had no "official start time" to the workday. Nutter operated under the rock-star mantra of always arriving fashionably late to everything—including job sites—so any time before 10:30 a.m. was heavily frowned upon and deemed "uncool." Also, we took two-hour lunches every day—which Nutter always paid for—and he was adamant about cleaning up and leaving the job site in time to beat the 3:45 rush-hour traffic, which he kept insisting was totally a thing.

---

[20] And here we are 24 years later with that situation largely unchanged.

The cons were that paydays at St. John's came around about as often as Halley's Comet. It didn't matter how many hours we actually worked in the course of a week, Nutter was exactly as inclined to make payroll as he was to putting in an 8-hour workday.

Essentially, it was a "job" only in the sense that paint-based activities were occasionally penciled into the calendar, and there were vague promises—and even vaguer expectations—of future compensation in exchange for services rendered.

How did Nutter manage to convince people to continue working for him week-in and week-out without paying them on Fridays?

Simple: He'd just offer you a raise.

"Nutter, are you gonna pay me any time soon? It's been, like, three *weeks* since I've seen a dime from you," someone would grouse. "If I don't get some money tomorrow, *I quit!*"

"Please don't quit," Nutter would respond. "You're the best painter I've got!" (Nutter had five full-time painters, and all five of us were the "best.") "How much am I paying you now?"

"Well, technically . . . *nothing*. That's why we're arguing right now."

"Yeah, but how much am I *supposed* to be paying you?" he'd ask.

"Twelve bucks an hour."

"And how much do I owe you right now?"

"About six hundred dollars."

"Tell you what," he'd say, "don't quit, and I'll give you a three-dollar raise. That's fifteen an hour, plus lunches. I'll get you all squared away at the end of the month. Deal?"

"Deal," we'd always agree.

That's how he kept us all around—dishing out raises that would *also* never get paid. But hey, if you're never going to get paid for an honest week's work, better to not get paid $15 an hour than to not get paid $12 an hour like a schmuck. What am I, a valet?

It was during this stretch of grueling, 20-ish-hour workweeks of what was essentially volunteer work that I bumped into an old buddy at the gym one Friday afternoon.

Jeremy Fasel had graduated a year ahead of me and had been one of the top-ranked tennis players at PBA while he was there. He was spending his summer working as a tennis pro up in the well-to-do Palm Beach Gardens area with a bunch of kids from the French Junior

National Team who came over to the States every summer specifically for high-level tennis camps.

"That sounds like a cushy gig," I remarked. "How much are they paying you for that?"

"Four hundred dollars a week," he replied. "Cash."

He might as well have said four bajillion.

'Four large? To play tennis?" I was incredulous. Not at being paid to play games—at being paid period.

"Well, there's more to it than that," Jeremy admitted. "It's also free lodging at the resort they're all staying at, three meals a day, plus we take the kids on outings every weekend—Disney World, Universal Studios, stuff like that. That's all paid for too."

I had a thousand follow-up questions, but only one that was really pertinent at the moment: "Do they need any more help?"

"Actually, yeah . . . they do," said Jeremy. "Why, do you play tennis?"

Do I play tennis?

Do. I. Play. Tennis.

So many words there, all in a row. What could they possibly mean? How best to answer this extraordinarily complex and nuanced question?

I "played tennis" in the sense that I owned a tennis racket, had taken two 30-minute tennis lessons that Mom signed me up for against my will one summer years ago, and had played casually maybe a half-dozen times over my entire four-year college career. None of those times had been with Jeremy.

"Of course, I play tennis," I scoffed indignantly.

Four hundred dollars—cash?

You bet your ass I play tennis.

"More importantly," I continued, "I speak fluent French." (Having taken four years of high school French and then another three years in college, *proficient* was the word we were looking for here. But I didn't want to come across as pretentious for using three syllables.)

"You're not kidding me?" Jeremy wanted to know.

"Not even a little bit," I replied, assuming he was referring solely to the French part.

"If you're really serious, I'll give them a call this weekend and let you know what they say."

"I'm dead serious," I told him in that fake "let's do lunch sometime" L.A.-kind-of-way that I kinda/meant but kinda/sorta didn't.

I knew Jeremy. He was flaky. He was not going to be calling anyone on my behalf.

"You got the job, man!" Jeremy called and announced a few hours later. "I told them you'd be able to start on Monday. Is that cool?"

"Oh my God, what did you tell them?" I wanted to know, mildly horrified.

"I told them I had this badass collegiate-level tennis player who speaks perfect French that, as luck would have it, just happened to be available. Everyone there is *super* stoked to have you on board!"

"What do you mean by *everyone*?" I inquired with a compounding sense of dread. "How many people are we talking about?"

"Oh, it's not a ton of people or anything like that," Jeremy explained. "There's about 30 students aged 11-18, the tour director, three or four chaperones, myself, and four professional instructors who came over with the students. About 40 of us total."

"And these kids are pretty good?"

"Oh yeah, they're amazing. This camp usually fills out a bunch of spots on France's Junior Olympics team," Jeremy informed me.

"Okay, awesome," I gulped. "Because I don't want to waste my time with a bunch of hacks."

"They're definitely not hacks, so bring your A-game. See you bright and early Monday!" Jeremy hung up.

Eff me sideways with a running helicopter.

A short sidebar about the specifics of my tennis game:

I already mentioned that I absolutely, 100% owned a tennis racket, which nobody disputes. In addition to my genuine racket ownership, I'm naturally athletic and actually had a pretty impressive serve I could uncork at a not-insignificant velocity when I felt like it. And to go along with that ferocious raw power, I had an uncanny talent for landing my serve at two very precise locations around the court with remarkable precision and stunning consistency: the back of my double partner's head and the driver's side mirror of whatever the most expensive car out in the parking lot was.

So, if you ever found yourself playing tennis with me, the bulk of your time would be spent shagging tennis balls out of the rose bushes across the street—to the smooth acoustic stylings of a Rolls Royce car alarm—while I stood over my prone partner, badgering him about how many fingers I was holding up.

These French Olympians were in for a real treat.

arrived at the facility the following Monday at 8 a.m., just as the kids were finishing up breakfast and making their way to the courts. There was no plan whatsoever, other than to hope and pray I wouldn't actually be called upon to play any tennis. I was an instructor—there to shout directions and encouragement and tennis-y sounding things like "Good eye!" and "Great return!" As long as I could stick to that, I might be okay.

The instructors and kids met out on the courts, went through 15 minutes of stretching, and then everyone, including the instructors, paired off to do some light volleying to warm up. As luck would have it, the last kid without a partner was the youngest student there— maybe 11 years old—which meant he and I got to warm up together on the furthest court, where nobody would be paying any attention to me, which was great because I was about to discover that I couldn't even warm-up volley at the level of a semi-competitive child.

As we trudged off to the far court, I took note of all the other pairs volleying back and forth. Nearly all of them were alternating forehand-backhand every other shot, placing their volleys precisely where their partner could do the same thing in return. Nobody was running—most of them were barely moving. Other than that half-pivot to hit their backhand, everyone pretty much just stood in place.

So, that's what I did when we finally got to the far court—stood stationary at the center of the baseline, where my pint-sized partner kept perfectly placing volleys I didn't have to move for. In return, I sent him sprinting sideline to sideline with every shot. Not out of spite, because I had no control over where the ball went once it left my racket. And no matter where I sent him scurrying to, he returned it to my racket each time.

"Tu le fais bien!" I hollered, hoping the encouragement gave him the impression I was doing this on purpose. *You're doing great!*

After 10 minutes of warm-ups, the head instructor called everyone to the center court and told the kids to assemble near the fence. The group slowly gathered together, as if still waking up, the youngest member panting and sweating for some reason.

"Why are you out of breath already?" the head instructor asked the kid I'd just been warming up with. "Looks like we need to work on your cardio. Hopefully, Coach Shane will stop being so nice and go a little harder on you from now on!"

Perfect, I can definitely make sure these kids run more than they're used to.

So far, so good.

The instructor announced we'd start the day with some serving drills. With all of us gathered behind the baseline on one side of the net, he walked to the opposite baseline and set a can of tennis balls on both baseline corners. Then he walked back to us and explained the drill:

"Everyone is going to line up, one at a time, and take two serves. Try to aim at one of the cans. The first person to hit a can gets *this*—" He pulled out a twenty-dollar bill, waved it in the air, and then tucked it back in his pocket. All the kids immediately began jockeying for position to be first in line.

I had been standing on the baseline, casually bouncing a tennis ball on my racket, when a sudden sensation came over me that I'd only experienced a few other times in my entire life. It is a weird and inexplicable phenomenon that anyone who's been around sports or physical activities long enough will probably recognize: Every great once in a while—when the planets are aligned and your chi is balanced and Mercury is in retrograde, or whatever—on an impulse, you'll attempt some improbable feat before your brain has time to kick in and talk you out of it. It's almost as if you're momentarily not in control of your own body, and whoever's suddenly in charge *knows with certainty* what the outcome is going to be.

I can distinctly recall three occasions when this happened to me. The first was when I was about 14. I'd had a sleepover with a bunch of friends, and we'd all watched *The Karate Kid* the night before. At the table for lunch the next day, flies were buzzing around the dining room. At my suggestion, Mom brought us all chopsticks so we could attempt to catch them Mr. Miyagi-style.

We stabbed at them for several minutes in vain before giving up and focusing on our sandwiches. As I took a bite, I noticed my buddy at the end of the table had a big, juicy mosquito sitting on his forehead. In the instant he went to swat it away, that feeling came over me, and *I knew*. Without thinking, I snatched my fork and hurled it in the general direction of his head. It cleared his skull by a matter of inches and stuck prong-first into the drywall behind him. Impaled on the second tine was the mosquito. I couldn't do it again in a billion attempts, but I *knew* the instant my hand reached for the fork that mosquito was toast.

The second time was in college. We were wrapping up an afternoon of basketball at the park and getting ready to head back to our cars. As we gathered our belongings, I was getting a particularly brutal ribbing for the abysmal shooting afternoon I'd just had. "Dude, you were like 0-for-Tuesday," someone said.

That was an exaggeration, but not by much.

"Yeah, we should've started giving you points just for hitting the backboard," someone else chirped as I picked up the ball and started walking towards the parking lot.

"Do we need to bring a 12-foot ladder out here and let you drop the ball down through the net just so you don't go home and kill yourself?" asked Nutter.

Suddenly, in that moment, *I knew*.

"Nah, I'm good," I replied. "Nothing but net." With one hand, I heaved the basketball backward over my head as hard as I could, then turned and watched it sail through the air the entire length of the court before swishing through the far net. Again, a one-in-a-million shot (unless you're a Harlem Globetrotter), but I *knew* it was going in the instant I felt the impulse to launch it.

The last time it happened, a bunch of us were driving back from a music festival and stopped at a strip mall to grab a bite to eat. There was a football in the back seat that I grabbed as I was getting out. As soon as I stood up, I saw a stop sign about 40 yards across the parking lot with an open trash can under it. *I can hit that.* I aired it out without a second thought, and we all watched in disbelief as it sailed through the air, clanged off the stop sign, and bounced into the trash can below it.

Naturally, everyone else had to try it, so we all stood there for the next half hour taking turns trying to hit the stop sign again. None of us came close.

That was the tricky thing about it—you couldn't do it if you *tried* to do it. All you could do was learn to identify that little *premonition* that struck once in a blue moon and then do whatever compulsive thing it was compelling you to do.

At that moment, bouncing the tennis ball, I *felt* it.

Without thinking, I bounced the ball high in the air—I'd been standing with my back to the court, facing the kids—spun 180 degrees, and swung as hard as I've ever swung in my life. The ball whipped down the line and drilled the near-side can, sending it flying into the fence.

The kids went ballistic.

My first instinct was to rip off my shirt and take off running around the court like I'd just scored a goal in the World Cup, complete with a headfirst dive into the net, but I immediately squashed that impulse and told myself to act like this is something I do all the time. My second thought was one of sheer panic: *What if they ask me to do it again?*

I had just used up every last ounce of tennis mojo the universe had bestowed upon me, and since I was a newly minted hero in the eyes of all my adoring new fans, the last thing I wanted to do was crush their spirits and shatter their dreams by standing on the baseline, trying in vain to land a serve in bounds for the next three hours.

I immediately grabbed my shoulder in unimaginable faux pain (also reminiscent of World Cup performances) and exclaimed, "Oh, *mon dieu!* I think I tore something! Definitely should've warmed up longer! *C'est terrible!* I'd better get some ice on this *tout de suite.*" One of the instructors ran off to fetch me an ice pack.

And that was the last time I swung a racket in two weeks of tennis camp.

After a day or two, when it was pretty obvious that there was no swelling or serious mobility issues, I decided the only option I had to avoid embarrassing myself in front of all these little French prodigies was to keep faking more injuries.

The first one I tried actually worked pretty well; the room I was staying in was on the second floor, and the stairway down to the parking lot was a double-back, with about 12 steps down to the landing and then 12 more the other way to the pavement. With a dozen kids watching, I got four steps from the bottom and then did my best stuntman trip-and-fall-and-roll-and-hope-for-the-best. I sold it, landed without hurting myself, but somehow came up with a "sprained ankle" that obviously required another icepack and a pair of crutches "just to be safe."

Perfect.

That lasted nearly a week until I bumped into one of the instructors at an off-site convenience store where I wasn't fake-limping around.

"So glad to see you are feeling better!" they said. "The kids are very disappointed that you can't play with them. They think you are like a young . . . Andre Agassi."

This was an apt comparison in the sense that Andre and I both had our ears pierced, both owned a racket, and Brooke Shields was probably secretly in love with me. I desperately needed another "injury" before I could get roped into an international friendly.

And that's how I nearly lost my right eye.

We all got a two-hour break every afternoon, and just about everyone hit the swimming pool. The younger kids loved to wrestle and roughhouse, and we'd inevitably end up having chicken fights. My plan was to get one of the kids on my shoulders and then wait for an opportunity for . . . *something* . . . to go wrong. With all the jostling and splashing and commotion, there'd be ample time to jam a toe or knock heads and develop "concussion-like symptoms" or whatever. After 15 minutes without any good windows, I pretended to slip mid-match, fall backward, and see what happened.

What happened was that the 12-year-old perched on top of me thought we were about to lose (as long as you don't fall off, the match isn't over) and grabbed whatever he could clamp onto. Unfortunately, "whatever he could" happened to be my chin and right eyeball.

If you've ever been poked straight in the eye, you kind of know the feeling. Now imagine that instead of merely jabbing you in the eye, they're using your cornea like a door handle. There was absolutely no need to fake excruciating pain. This was as real as it got.

I frantically pried his claws off my face, grabbed my eye, and found a small fountain of blood. One of his fingernails had sliced my eyelid open.

The good news was that, other than the brief pain, that was the extent of the damage. Just a superficial cut. The better news was that even superficial facial lacerations tend to bleed heavily, and once a lifeguard evacuates an Olympic-sized pool because someone's bleeding profusely from their eye socket, nobody asks that person to play doubles.

And that's how I finished out tennis camp—gauze taped over one eye, the entire international group convinced I was one functioning eye away from the Wimbledon semifinals, and having swung my racket precisely *once*.

With that prolific stunt barely three months old and still fresh in my mind, there was no reason under the sun to give a second thought to trying something else that was more or less the same thing.

Besides, if—on a scant three days' notice—I could have the entire Junior National Tennis Association of France convinced I was an international legend at a sport I could barely play, a week and a half was more than enough prep time to convince The People's Republic of China I was a member of an internationally acclaimed rock band they'd never heard of.

I actually *played* the keys.

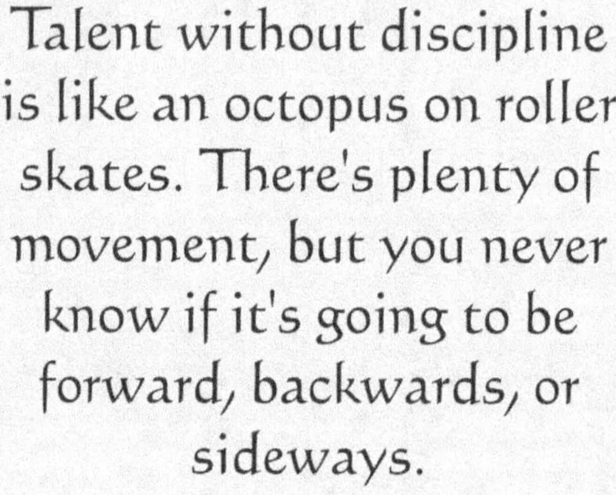
Talent without discipline
is like an octopus on roller
skates. There's plenty of
movement, but you never
know if it's going to be
forward, backwards, or
sideways.
– H. Jackson Brown, Jr.

九

Piano Man

Mom signed Kyle and me up for piano lessons when we were each four years old. She was militant about it. She'd conversed with too many adults in life who'd taken piano lessons for a few years as a kid and later expressed regret as adults that they didn't stick with it. She had no intention of letting that happen to us. Come hell or high water, we were going to stick with it.

Her first rule when it came to the piano was that both of us were going to keep taking lessons until we graduated high school. Whether or not we actually *enjoyed* it was beside the point.

Her second rule was that we had to practice every day. Every. Single. Day. Thirty minutes was the entry-level minimum, which also happened to be precisely eight times longer than the average four-year-old's attention span. At four, thirty minutes a day might as well have been however long it was between that particular day's calendar date and Christmas morning.

It was torturous.

But no amount of whining, begging, crying, pleading, stalling, bargaining, or hiding in the closet was going to affect daily practice time as far as Mom was concerned. She would've chained us to the bench if there were any spare chains lying around (there weren't because they were all being used on her other projects).

Although practice was the most dreaded part of my day, I did look forward to the weekly lessons. We were enrolled in the Yamaha Music Education System, a program created in Japan in the 1950s that was designed to cultivate a love of music by encouraging personal exploration and creativity.

It was a group learning environment structured like a school classroom. There were a dozen or so kids in the class, each one with their own electric piano instead of a desk. At the front of the class, the teacher would play musical phrases, and we'd try to replicate them. They'd start off simple—usually not more than three or four notes at a time—and progressively build, like that old Simon game where you had to mash colored buttons in increasingly complex patterns.

We were taught the basics of reading music with flash cards: how to count notes and rests, read time and key signatures, tempos, and dynamics. We learned rhythm by playing the triangle or wood block to vinyl records of kid songs we all knew. A portion of each class was dedicated to "free play" time—just improvising and making up whatever we wanted.

(This segment was done with headphones on all the kids for the sanity of the teacher and whatever parents were observing, as nobody in their right mind would voluntarily subject themselves to fifteen minutes of a dozen novice toddlers banging out twelve different made-up tunes simultaneously.)

Each lesson would end with all of us grabbing a guitar or recorder, or jumping on the xylophone, and reviewing the day's material on a different instrument. In this way, we weren't just learning how to navigate the piano keyboard using rote memorization of finger placements. We were learning how to follow *music,* which became an integral part of picking things up by ear.

It was relatively early into the lessons that my parents realized I had a bit of a knack for music. As much as I hated practicing while the timer was going, I loved sitting at the piano on my own time and trying to work out songs I'd heard on the radio or my parents' tape collection. I'd use my allowance money to buy toy instruments (the Fisher Price saxophone and clarinet were my favorites) that I'd actually learn to play. And if my parents happened to be enjoying some much-needed peace, quiet, and relaxation, I'd dutifully enhance their tranquility with the silky-smooth stylings of my toy drum or tambourine. (There was much disagreement between me and them as to what constituted "tranquil.")

When I was five, my parents took me to see *Chariots of Fire*. It was the first movie I'd ever seen in a theater. Although I was much too young to understand any of the plot beyond "that guy is really fast," the classic opening scene with the men running down the beach to Vangelis' iconic score was the most musically profound experience of my young life.

I wanted to play *that song*.

(I also decided right then and there that I wanted to be an Olympic sprinter and silently vowed to never run anywhere ever again without my head back and eyes closed like Eric Liddell, which I attempted immediately upon exiting the theater into the mall. While my dad was occupied tying my sister's shoe, I knelt down into a sprinter's crouch, surveyed the gallery for the clearest path through the mall crowd, then took off at the breakneck-iest pace I could muster. As soon as I got up to top speed, I threw my head back and shut my eyes . . . and a few seconds later crashed face-first into a wall calendar kiosk, sending puppies, horses, and Norman Rockwell scenery flying in every direction—bringing that Olympic training session to a disappointing, head-pounding conclusion.)

As soon as we got home, I hopped on the piano and started picking out the notes to the *Chariots* theme song. It's an incredibly simple melody—far less complicated than some of the lines we had to repeat in our lessons—and it didn't take long to figure out.

But both of my parents were stunned. I didn't really see what the big deal was. Playing by ear essentially only requires two things: remembering the melody you heard and knowing what the keys (or buttons or strings) on your instrument do. That's all there is to it.

By age six, I'd graduated up to private lessons with Jan McDaniel, the pianist and musical director for Wichita Falls' Backdoor Theater. Under his tutelage, we began focusing on classical music and music performance. Since he came from a theater background, Jan's number one rule was: *If you make a mistake, keep playing.*

If you're accompanying a singer, either of you is liable to flub a line or miss a note from time to time, but the other person is going to carry right along. *Don't dwell on the mistake.* If you don't acknowledge it, the audience probably won't even notice. He must've repeated that maxim a dozen times per lesson, drilling it into me like it was a Fundamental Truth of The Universe.

If you make a mistake, keep playing.

Around that time, I'd started to idolize the pianist at our church, David Arinder, and dreamt of one day playing on a huge stage just like him. I idolized him right down to his unique hairstyle, insisting on an identical haircut on my first trip to the barber, who was a little baffled as to why I wanted short hair around the sides and absolutely nothing on the top. Confused, the barber ended up just giving me a crew cut, which I hated with a passion and cried about for days.

(Mom informed me later in life that David's "hairstyle" that I was so enamored with was actually garden-variety male-pattern baldness.)

With Jan's help—and after getting clearance from the church—we worked out an arrangement to one of my favorite gospel songs for me to perform in front of the entire congregation one Sunday morning. We timed it to coincide with Mother's Day, allowing me to dedicate my first public performance to Mom while the ushers collected the offering.

When the time came during the service for my solo, my six-year-old-self bolted down the aisle like an amped up *Price Is Right* contestant, mounted the steps to the stage, and took my seat at the nine-foot concert grand piano that was usually reserved for David. My feet dangled six inches off the floor. I squawked into the microphone, "This is for you, Mommy!" and launched into my piece, playing and singing my heart out.

On the ride home from church, my parents commended the performance profusely and mentioned that I didn't appear to be the least bit nervous.

Nervous?

It had never crossed my mind to be nervous. I'd seen kids in the school play or church Christmas play forget their lines as soon as they stepped in front of the audience, so I was familiar with the concept of stage fright. But it was conceptual rather than experiential for me. Whereas their attitude seemed to be: *Oh god, everyone's looking at me, please get me outta here!* Mine was more like: *That's my stage, and you're going to have to drag me off it with one of those canes-around-the-neck like in the cartoons.*

Nerves were for people who either weren't properly prepared for the occasion or were too self-conscious to be comfortable in front of a crowd. I was neither. I had more confidence than any six-year-old in the world was entitled to, and I simply *did not make mistakes*. That's all there was to it.

My next public performance was notable for consisting almost entirely of mistakes and not much else. It was my very first piano recital. Jan had booked one of the performance halls at our local piano retailer to showcase all his students one Saturday afternoon. I'd been practicing the piece I was to be performing for several months and knew it like the back of my hand.

Once again, I couldn't wait for my turn to get up there and show off. When it was finally my turn, I strode up to the piano, sat down with a great flourish, smiled at the audience . . . and then stared blankly at the piano keys with absolutely no idea what song I was supposed to be playing. It was like one of those weird moments where you're hanging out with one of your best friends, and suddenly, for a split second or two, you can't recall their name to save your life. You know you know it, but all the brain neurons that bring it to your attention have stepped out for a coffee break.

I looked over at Jan, hoping he'd offer me a clue as to what I was doing up there. He just smiled and nodded as if to say, *Feel free to start playing any time now*, which was definitely encouraging but not in any way helpful. So, I went back to staring at the keys, hoping something would come to me before the building closed for the evening. Or their lease ran out.

After what seemed like an eternity—but was probably no more than 30 seconds—it suddenly rushed over me like a tidal wave of what I was supposed to be playing, and away I went. The neurons were back from their coffee break. Unfortunately, it must have been incredibly good coffee that day because they all decided to go back for a refill a few seconds into my performance. One moment I was cruising along in full control, and the next I was as lost as a penguin in Times Square.

If you make a mistake, keep playing.

So, I kept playing.

For a *while*.

Quite a long while, actually. I had no idea what I was playing, but I played it anyway. Any scale/chord combination I'd ever practiced, bits and pieces of melodies I'd worked on previously, riffs I recalled from the radio . . . anything that came to mind. I was grateful these did come to mind because what I was *supposed* to be playing most certainly did not. The piece I was slated to do only lasted about a minute and a half start to finish, but I was generously into the third minute before I even had a notion that I ought to be wrapping up this train wreck. The problem was that I had no idea how to end it. It was like hurtling down a ski slope with no ability to stop. You either fight to stay on your feet and ride it all the way to the bottom or bail out before you hit a tree and hope for the best.

I wasn't a fan of the tree option, so I just kept going until my original song eventually returned to me. I awkwardly segued back into the intended tune, hastily wrapped it up, and then stood and took the most exaggerated bow I could come up with.

I walked back to my seat and sank into my chair beside Dad. "What in the world was *that?*" he leaned over and whispered. They'd listened to me practice that song hundreds of times and knew 98% of the notes I'd just played were not on today's docket.

I shrugged my shoulders. Not out of indifference, but because I genuinely had no idea. For a million bucks, I couldn't have played them again. The last five minutes were definitely getting filed in the Life's Great Mysteries drawer.

I knew Mom was going to be furious, and I was dreading the car ride home. I was sure I'd get an earful about not being disciplined or diligent enough in my practice and probably a lecture about how much those piano lessons cost, for good measure. She loved to inform me how many starving kids in Africa could probably be fed with whatever money I happened to be wasting at any given moment. I also knew Jan was going to be embarrassed by my dumpster fire of a recital, or, heaven forbid, *disappointed,* which would be infinitely worse.

When the last kid had played, Jan walked up to the front of the room and thanked everyone for coming. As everyone began filing out and milling around, he made a beeline straight for us.

Here it comes.

"Wow, what happened up there? That was pretty cool!"

Not the words I was expecting.

"It was?"

"You betcha! You did exactly what we worked on," he beamed, offering me a high-five.

My parents both looked confused.

"You've been working on that in secret?" Dad wanted to know.

I had to come clean. "No, I forgot what I was supposed to be playing, so I just started making up stuff until I remembered where I was."

Jan continued to explain, "I told him that if he messes up, just keep a poker face and keep going. Of course, I meant to continue the same song he was already playing, not slide into an improv solo. But I think it worked out great. Nobody in the room besides the four of us knew anything had gone wrong, right?"

I nodded.

"Well, don't feel bad at all," he instructed. "You should be incredibly proud of that performance."

Jan shook my parents' hands, said goodbye, and left them a piece of parting advice: "Take this kid out for a banana split."

That lesson stuck with me for life.

No matter what happens, just keep playing.

As long as you act like whatever you're doing is exactly what you're supposed to be doing, the audience will never know the difference.

As we got older, Mom never missed an opportunity to trot out my sister and me like a couple of show monkeys. If we had dinner guests, we had to play for them. If we went to someone's house who happened to have a piano, we had to play something. Annual Christmas party? You better believe Mom would pass out carol sheets to everyone in attendance (whether they felt like singing or not) and make me lead the group in a merry yuletide sing-along.

When I was about nine, Mom announced over dinner one evening that she'd arranged for Kyle and me to perform together in church at an upcoming service. Kyle was to sing a solo, and I'd be playing for her. It was a popular Amy Grant song that we both knew well, and I didn't anticipate it would take much work on our part to get it ready.

After dinner, I grabbed the cassette tape the song was on and took it to the piano. A half-dozen passes through it, and I was ready to roll. I knew Kyle knew the song—I'd heard her sing along to it countless times. This was going to be a cakewalk.

I hollered for Kyle to come join me at the piano, and she bobbed in a few moments later. When she was ready, she gave me an emphatic nod to begin, and I played through the intro. Right away, she missed her cue and started singing two beats too late. I started over. This time, she came in early. I tried again, mildly irritated. Late again, by a full measure this time. We were off to a bad start.

"What's wrong?" I asked her.

"You're playing too fast," she snapped.

"No, I'm not."

"Yes, you are!"

I rolled my eyes and started once more, playing exaggeratedly slower. She didn't bother to come in at all that time. I pounded the piano keys in frustration.

"What's your problem?" I yelled at her.

"What's *your* problem?" she screamed right back.

This was going really well.

We tried a handful of more times with similar success, and I decided I'd had enough.

"You're the *worst* singer in the whole world!" I told her.

"You're the meanest *person* in the whole world, and I'm telling on you!" she answered and ran off to the kitchen.

Five minutes later, I was grounded and sitting in my room sulking. *Stupid sister got me in stupid trouble, and* she's *the one who doesn't even know the stupid words to the stupid song that stupid Mom is making us do at stupid church.*

I was righteously indignant.

The good news was that we had three weeks to get our act together before we had to perform. The bad news was that we couldn't manage to get through the entire song a single time without finding something to bicker about.

The problem, as any nine-year-old could tell you, was entirely *her* fault. Of that, I was sure. She would beg to differ, naturally, but she was only seven—seven-year-olds didn't know anything.

Everything came to a head the week before our performance. My parents had invited several families from church over for a Saturday cookout, and Mom informed us that we still needed to rehearse, company present or not. I was mortified at the idea. I tried every bargaining tactic in my arsenal to get out of it, to no avail.

"We'll practice *twice* as long tomorrow," I promised.

"Nope."

"We'll practice *three times* as long tomorrow!" I pleaded.

"Sorry, Charlie."

"But she's going to embarrass me in front of *everyone!*" I started crying.

Mom wasn't biting. "You've got 15 minutes to change your attitude and get your butt in there on the piano, mister!" And that was that.

I didn't know what to do. There was no way I was going to rehearse with Kyle with everyone there, especially not in front of Kari and Becky—sisters who were the same age as Kyle and me, and two of our best friends. As I saw it, there was only one realistic option on the table: I would have to run away from home.

Fifteen minutes.

That did not leave much time to dilly-dally.

The first part was figuring out where I was going to go, which was easy. Grandpa always took me toy shopping whenever I saw him— usually once a year—and he was good about stocking me up with Skittles and M&M's. Plus, he lived just right up the road from us. In St. Louis.

I went and grabbed Dad's fold-out map of the continental United States from the glove box of our Volkswagen bus, spread it open on my bedroom floor, and tried to gauge the distance from Wichita Falls, Texas, to St. Louis, Missouri. It looked to be about 650 miles. So, walking was out of the question. I'd have to ride my bike.

The next step was to load up my school backpack with everything I'd need for the trip. I packed as light as I could, just the most basic of necessities: toothbrush, change of clothes, bathing suit (Grandpa's apartment had a pool), souvenir canteen from Frontier Land at Disney World (it really worked), plastic bow-and-arrows with the suction cup tips (in case I had to hunt for food), three apple cinnamon-scented candles (in case it got dark, or cold), lasso (in case of stray horse), baseball mitt (in case . . . reasons), all the money in my piggy bank (just over seven dollars, mostly in nickels), my Swiss Army knife, a compass, three of my favorite Transformers, a pack of markers and a *G.I. Joe* coloring book, and my stuffed bear, Andy.

Nothing but the bare essentials.

Andy Bear was almost two feet tall and definitely wouldn't fit in the backpack. So, I cinched him to my chest with a bungee cord (not like a BabyBjörn or anything—that would be ridiculous. I made sure he was facing *out* so he could enjoy the scenery on the trip).

I was trying to figure out how to sling my bow over my shoulder with a backpack on and a giant bear strapped to my chest when Kyle barged in with Kari and Becky in tow. She stopped in her tracks, surveyed the room—stuffed bear tied to my torso, bulging backpack with arrows poking out, open map of the US—and eyed me suspiciously, as if I were up to something.

She could, on occasion, be quite astute.

"What do you think you're doing?" she demanded.

I didn't beat around the bush. "I'm running away."

"Where to?"

"St Louis. I'm going to live with Grandpa."

She let that sink in for a moment, then turned and whispered something to the girls. They whispered back, and a deadly, serious discussion ensued in hushed tones. A minute went by, and they finally looked up and turned to me. "We're coming with you."

As much as I would've liked some company on the trek, this seemed highly impractical. For starters, Grandpa had never met Kari and Becky, and I thought it might be a bit awkward if I showed up at his door unannounced with two complete strangers. Then I remembered that Grandpa was, like, totally cool, so he would probably be fine with it.

Secondly, Kyle was stringently averse to physical exercise of any sort, so I knew I couldn't count on her to ride her bike the whole way to St. Louis without a ton of complaining. That meant I was going to have to tie our Radio Flyer wagon to the back of my bike and tow them. There was only room in the wagon for two people, so they'd have to take turns while one of them walked. That seemed doable. I told them to go pack and meet me in the garage in five minutes.

I wasn't feeling absolute confidence in my hunting prowess, so I quickly ran and made four peanut butter and jelly sandwiches for the trip. Hopefully, that would tide us over, at least until we hit Oklahoma. Waurika was only about 40 miles away.

I threw the sandwiches into a lunchbox along with some grapes and a few juice boxes, filled up my canteen, and hurried off to the garage. The girls were already there, laying out blankets in the wagon for padding. I saw that Kyle had packed a suitcase—no telling what was in it—and that she'd also thought to fill a baby stroller up with several of her dolls.

Leave it to her to pack a bunch of frivolous crap.

I grabbed a ten-foot section of rope and quickly annexed the wagon's handle to my bike seat. I slung my backpack over the handlebars, shifted Andy Bear to my back, stuck the lunchbox in the bottom of the baby stroller, and positioned Kyle and Becky in the wagon with Kyle's suitcase sitting upright in her lap. Kari would be on stroller duty for the first leg.

I wheeled my bike out of the garage and looked back at our group. "Everybody ready?"

"Yep!" came the reply.

And away we went.

The street we lived on dead-ended at a two-lane road that was usually deserted. We made a left at it, possibly heading north, and then it was only a mile and a half to US Highway 82. It was exhilarating.

St. Louis, here we come!

I hadn't thought to figure out how long this little excursion was going to take. Our family made the drive every summer, and I knew it was about 11 hours by car. Being on a bike and towing a wagon, I estimated that it would easily take at least twice that long, possibly even three days.

The faster you pedal, the sooner you'll get there, I thought to myself. Also, *those girls are really heavy.*

I hollered over my shoulder to ask if anyone was hungry. Everyone was. So, just a shade under eight minutes into our cross-country expedition, we pulled over and polished off every bit of food I'd packed. Then we set off again.

We'd been gone for about 45 minutes and had made it over a mile down the road when Mom came flying up behind us in our van, honking frantically. Kari and Becky's mom was with her, and they both appeared unhappy about something. No telling what. Actually, it would be more accurate to describe them both as three levels beyond hysterical.

As it happened, they were irate that we'd run away from home. Without telling anyone. Moms get weird like that, I guess. They threw all our gear into the van, hauled us in by our ears, and drove us straight back to the house. Then they sat us all down on the couch and, for the next 30 minutes, alternated between tears of joy, tears of rage, bear hugs, and throttlings.

Our dads ambled in from the backyard, nonplussed to see what all the commotion was about.

"Oh, you found them," Dad observed calmly, as if we'd been playing hide-and-seek in the yard. "Where were they?"

"They were two miles down the road, on the side of the highway!" roared Mom.

Dad cocked his head to the side and looked at me. "What were you doing way down there?"

"We were going to St. Louis," I told him.

"St. Louis, huh?" he chuckled. "That's a pretty long way."

"Yeah, well, I had a map *and a compass*." I held them both up and waved them as proof for everyone in the room to see.

Dad nodded thoughtfully. "Good thinking, son." Then he turned and walked back outside. No blood, no foul. He'd let Mom handle this one.

When Mom finally calmed down and her senses returned to her, she decided the whole thing was more amusing than anything else. We weren't dead, and that's mostly what mattered. And she rewarded our efforts by allowing us to wait until everyone left hours later before making us rehearse, which had been the whole point all along.

Score one for the children.

By Tuesday, we were nailing the song, and we continued to run through it a dozen times a day. We got up extra early that Sunday morning and ran through it a half-dozen more times before leaving for church. Then we arrived at church before anyone else and did a few more run-throughs for sound check. We were as ready as we were ever going to be for our big moment.

When the moment came, we took the stage together, and I made my way over to the piano. Kyle positioned herself at center stage, microphone in hand, gave me a nod . . . and then promptly forgot everything we'd worked on for the past three weeks.

Rather than coming in early or late after the intro, she opted for "not at all," so I played through the entire first verse as an instrumental solo. Then I circled back around to the intro to give her another shot at it, but she was of the same opinion for the second pass as she was on the first. Again, it was a no-go. I was seething inside.

One more musical solo through the verse, one more pass through the intro, and *this* time Kyle decided to join the performance and grace us all with her voice. She started with the words to the second verse.

I decided she would have to die . . . or at least be sold into slavery, as was commensurate with certain parts of the Old Testament.

We made it through the first chorus without event, and I wondered if she'd elect to sing the words to the first verse—or the third—in place of the second since we'd just done that one. Instead, she went with the artistically ambitious choice of singing the second verse again.

Nope, slavery is too good for her. Definitely death. Ideally involving a multitude of alligators.

For the third verse, Kyle decided to sing the first verse, and for the bridge, she decided that she was done singing for the day. So, I soloed it out while she stood there, swaying side to side contentedly, and we were met with a standing ovation from the congregation. As we made our way back to our seats, the people nearest the aisles offered their hands and told us what a fantastic job we'd done.

If only they knew this was the last time they'd ever see her alive.

We plunked down between Mom and Dad, who offered congratulations and pats on the knee.

"Great job, you two," Dad whispered.

"I'm going to kill her," I whispered right back.

"We'll talk about this later," answered Mom, apparently of the opinion that the middle of church was not the time or place to discuss the merits of siblicide.

The four of us sat there in silence: our parents beaming with pride and exchanging nods with other members of the congregation, me simmering with rage, and Kyle seemingly oblivious and/or indifferent to all of it. I wondered how many weeks of allowance it would take to hire a hit man and if there were any to be found in the Yellow Pages.

I vowed to never perform with anyone ever again.

Upon moving to China, Mom wasted no time finding us a piano teacher. The Foreign Affairs Department at our school connected us with a stern little woman who looked to be in her late 30s—which meant she was probably 85—and assured us she was the best piano teacher on campus. I can't remember her name, but she made Nurse Ratched from *One Flew Over the Cuckoo's Nest* look like Mister Rogers.

Being over there, one of the first things that struck me was that there were absolutely no parallels between teaching in America and teaching in China. Whether it was in the classroom, sports field, or piano lessons, the teacher/coach-student dynamic was unlike anything I'd ever experienced—or even *heard* of, for that matter—in the States.

The guiding philosophy seemed to be that a student who was performing at a suboptimal level could be humiliated into greatness. Students who received any grade below an A on an assignment were forced to stand up in front of the entire class and be verbally berated by the teacher until they broke down in tears. On the surface, this didn't seem like the best way to teach algebra.[21]

As far as what was expected from kids in general—and students in particular—the Chinese operated on a different wavelength. It wasn't uncommon for children to spend 6-8 hours a day practicing an instrument, and I found myself consistently in the presence of five and six-year-olds who could play me under the table. It became inescapably apparent that 30 minutes of practice a day wasn't going to cut it. Not with Ms. Ratched and her Yardstick of Doom. An hour-a-day minimum was the new mandate.

As far as I could tell, Ms. Ratched's philosophy of piano instruction consisted entirely of whacking my knuckles with her dreaded yardstick whenever I failed to play with my fingers properly curved. But what she lacked in physical restraint and people skills, she made up for in not being able to speak any English other than counting to four.

---

[21] On the other hand, this was 5th grade, and we were all studying algebra, which was about three years ahead of where American students were in math. So, maybe there was a method to the madness after all. Perhaps abandoning Common Core in favor of public shaming is the missing ingredient to improving our dismal world ranking in education.

A typical lesson involved opening up a piece of classical sheet music and attempting to sight-read it while she smacked the pages with her stick and counted out the beat: "One, two, three, four. One, two, three, four. One, two—" *Whack!*

It was miserable (which wasn't a compelling point of consideration for Mom), but it was also ineffective (which was). Ms. Ratched lasted about two months, and then we looked elsewhere.

I'm not sure what strings my parents pulled to land our next teachers, but they came as a pair: So Mei and her husband, Mr. So. He was the conductor of the Changsha Symphony, she was the symphony's pianist.

They were the antithesis of Ms. Ratched. Both were other-worldly musicians, mild-mannered and soft-spoken, had a passion for teaching, and spoke English. The only similarity they shared with any other teachers I experienced in China was a strict insistence on not deviating from playing exactly what the composer intended. Interpretation was heavily frowned upon, and improvisation was non-existent.[22]

While there was no creative development to speak of at this time, the technical proficiency grew by leaps and bounds. Culturally, the Chinese did not believe in coddling, and they exemplified the idea that people live up to the expectations society sets for them. (It wasn't uncommon to see a seven-year-old boy driving a herd of a dozen 1,200-pound water buffalo to market unsupervised.) Musically, there were some very high expectations set for us, and we did our best to meet them.

The payoff came when the city held its annual kids' talent show, and thousands of children of all ages turned out to audition for one of

---

[22] This was a characteristic that permeated Chinese culture—partially a remnant of the homogenizing Cultural Revolution and partially owing to the sheer size of China's population. In a country of more than a billion people, individuality was seen as a detriment to society rather than something to be celebrated. Fitting in maintained the status quo—nobody wanted to be the nail that stood out above the others, for it was the first to get hit. Even art classes in school operated this way. If we were drawing or painting, the objective was to reproduce an object at the front of the room as accurately as possible. Any artistic liberties were met with the paper wadded up and thrown in the trash by the teacher and being forced to start over.

its two-dozen spots in the showcase. My parents both had to teach, so I was accompanied downtown by one of Dad's students, Jetty. [23]

There were musicians of every imaginable instrument, singers, dancers, gymnasts, jugglers, and bizarre cultural acts that defied description.

I auditioned with Beethoven's *Für Elise,* chosen because it seemed to be one of the most popular songs in China. Every restaurant, store, and hotel lobby in the country had a recording of it. Although it was technically more of a beginner's-level piece, I thought it might ingratiate me to the judges by playing something that was universally beloved. Perhaps it was solid reasoning, as I made it through the first round.

Sitting in the audience afterward and watching the proceeding hopefuls file out to the stage one at a time for the judges, I quickly observed that I was hardly the best pianist they had to choose from. Far from it. Per usual, there were a handful of kids, maybe half my age, who could've been headlining their own symphony orchestras.

I watched for another hour or so, and then disaster struck. Another kid was performing *Für Elise.* Moreover, he was performing it in its *entirety.* The full song[24] was comprised of three sections, and I'd only bothered to learn the first two. Even being a novelty act as the only foreigner in the building didn't seem like enough advantage to edge out this competition. Why would any judge pick someone who only knew two-thirds of a song over someone who knew the whole thing? Round Two was the following day, so I went home anticipating that tomorrow would be the end of the line for me.

Since we were required to repeat the same performance in the second round, I figured I needed to do something drastic to

---

[23] The Chinese loved adopting Western names and would often ask for help choosing one. Naturally, the missionaries would invariably select something from the Bible, which was just as well. Left to their own devices, the Chinese would assign themselves what they imagined were English names, but were very often nothing more than random nouns in the dictionary with a "y" attached at the end. Jetty was one of these.

[24] Yes, I'm aware that the correct term for a bit of music that doesn't contain any words is a "piece," not a "song." However, Beethoven did originally write lyrics for *Für Elise,* so I'm right and you're wrong, and I win a point.

differentiate the parts of the song that I actually did know from the other kid playing my piece. This was going to require some gratuitous *interpretation*.

The Big Taboo.

One thing all of the pianists had in common was their perfunctory body language. They sat rigidly at the bench and played robotically, emotionless, and expressionless. They might have been animatronics sitting at a player piano. If I couldn't outperform them technically or content-wise, at least I could infuse some passion nobody there had seen before. I'd throw all my eggs into that basket.

Jetty and I arrived at the auditorium early the next morning, checked in with a woman walking around with a clipboard, and took a seat, waiting for my name to be called. This time, they had each type of act grouped together so the judges could evaluate all of the singers or all of the pianists in a row. The kid playing my song got called up before me and proceeded to replicate his note-perfect performance from yesterday. Technically perfect, but boring as hell.

One thing every performer, regardless of what kind of act they were doing, had in common was a completely demure demeanor. They walked up to the stage and back with their heads and eyes down. The only indication they gave that they were even aware other people were in the room was to nod at the judges to affirm that the name read off the list was their own.

When my name was finally called, I bounded up to the stage, waving at everyone I could make eye contact with like I was running for mayor of the talent show. Before seating myself at the piano, I stopped at center stage, looked straight at the judges, and said in my best Chinese, "Ni hao ma?" *How are you?* "Thank you all for having me back. It's so good to see everyone again!"

The entire auditorium erupted with laughter. Since it wasn't a very witty joke, I assumed the laughter was for the silly, culturally insensitive American acting wildly inappropriate.

If you guys thought that was bad, just wait until I start playing.

As the laughter subsided, I seated myself at the piano and began. Stevie Wonder was one of my musical idols, and I thought this particular performance called for some of his signature side-to-side rocking. Or rather, *all of it.* It was a body motion that made a lot of sense for a Motown entertainer in the 1970s, feeling that "Superstition" groove deep down in his soul, but probably not so much for a minor-key bagatelle from the early 19th century. Especially since I'd never practiced it before. To the judges and audience, it probably looked like I was being electrocuted.

But I was determined to make them *feel* something (or at the very least, show them that *I* was feeling something), and my best idea of how to do that, other than flopping around like a wind sock in a tornado, was to introduce a dynamic range to the song that Beethoven himself could've heard.[25]

It started barely audible and then got loud.

Startling so.

If there were any hearing-impaired people in attendance, they were treated to a very pleasant and lovely performance. Everyone else was treated to the aural equivalent of getting a flashlight beamed at their eyes while wearing night vision goggles. And that was *before* we arrived at where the third section ought to be.

My solution to the missing segment was to simply repeat the first section but transpose it up a third, from A minor to C minor. This was borderline sacrilege—the musical equivalent of printing a King James Bible with the words of Jesus in purple Comic Sans font.

When I was finished, I stood up and shouted, "Xie xie ni!" *Thank you!* and blew double-handed kisses to the dumbfounded spectators. When I returned to my seat, Jetty leaned over and said, "Au Pei, that was very, very . . . *interesting.*"

Apparently, he wasn't the only one who thought so. When the final 24 names were announced, mine was one of them. The other kid who'd played *Für Elise* was not.

As we left the auditorium, we bumped into one of the judges. He spoke rapidly to us in a Changsha dialect that I couldn't make out. When he was finished, Jetty translated for me. "He says you behave very different from the other children. If a Chinese boy did what you did today, he will probably receive a severe beating when he gets home. But we get bored watching the same thing over and over all day long, and you made us smile inside. I think maybe the other people enjoyed it too, but they're not allowed to admit it. I hope you will play it just

---

[25] A gentle reminder that he was deaf.

like that again at the performance tomorrow. It was very, very interesting!"

After we were expelled from our first school and settled into the next one on the other side of town, So Mei and her husband were too far away to feasibly get to on a regular basis. Even with the closer proximity, it was easily an hour's bus ride both ways. Doubling that commute every week didn't work with my parents' new class schedule. But we ended up with the next best option.

So Mei introduced us to her mother, Anna, who had been So Mei's teacher growing up. Anna happened to live just a few miles down the road from us. And in addition to becoming our new piano teacher, Anna became mine and Kyle's "adopted grandmother."

I don't recall ever arriving at her apartment for a single lesson without being greeted with a plate of freshly baked snacks and hot tea or cocoa. After each lesson, she'd sit between us on the couch and open up old photo albums, regaling us with tales of life in China before the Communist Revolution.

Anna's biggest contribution to our musical studies was insisting that we needed to bump our daily practice up to two hours. That was the bare minimum, in her opinion, that anyone truly serious about their instrument should allocate in their day. That was all Mom needed to hear. Our practice requirements were instantly doubled again. The only silver lining to this new workload was that the school practice hall we were now using wasn't open on the weekends. For the first time since we started taking lessons, we actually got Saturday and Sunday off.

Leaving China offered further respite. Our stops in Hong Kong and Malaysia were too temporary for Mom to bother with finding us a teacher, and there was no available piano to be found to practice on anyway. When we settled in Thailand, we still didn't have a teacher, but Mom located a neighbor with a piano who let us practice at her house to keep our chops up.

When we returned to the States and settled down in Pittsburgh, Mom found us the piano teacher we'd remain with until graduation, Bill Tobin.

Bill was an amazing jazz pianist who had a nightly gig at the local yacht club. I fondly thought of him as the Mr. Myagi of piano for his sometimes unconventional methods that achieved breathtaking results. And also for his propensity to interrupt piano lessons to dole out life lessons. (I was eternally a fan of interrupting lessons for any reason whatsoever.)

He was as interested in how and why people behave the way they do as he was in teaching piano, and he didn't seem particularly inclined to make a distinction between the two. *How* one committed to their practice was a good indicator of one's commitment to school, homework, or a job. Even topics like relationships or parent-child power struggles could be addressed by musical analogy.

By Bill's account, he'd pinpointed about two dozen distinct ways people learn new information, and he was in the process of creating a piano-teaching system that accounted for every different learning style. Be it rote memorization, spatial association, mathematical relationships between notes, colors, shapes, or patterns, he had a knack for deciphering the precise method each student required for optimal learning.

Bill quickly realized my strong aversion to practicing (usually because whatever song he had me working on hadn't progressed as much as it should have after a week of "diligent" practice), but he also took note of my fascination with his keyboard rig that sat behind the piano. Consisting of two synthesizers hooked up to a computer, it was the most intriguing thing I'd ever seen. So, Bill would incentivize me by letting me play around on his keyboards, provided I came to the lesson adequately prepared.

He also indulged my burgeoning fixation on pop music and would order sheet music for whatever song on the radio I happened to be obsessed with that week, again with the caveat that we'd only work on it if my classical pieces were up to snuff. After my parents began questioning some of my daily practice sessions, Bill had to assure them that, yes, I was supposed to be working on Bach and Boyz II Men, or Mozart and Mariah Carey.

Unlike any of my previous teachers (save Miss Birch and Mrs. Crews back in Yamaha), Bill was insistent on improvisation, particularly with the blues. A fairly regular component of our weekly lesson was Bill jumping on his keyboards, setting a synthesized beat, and the two of us improvising together, riffing back and forth. This required learning to recognize when to take the lead and when to hang back in support—an integral part of learning how to play with others and an invaluable lesson for the future.

Another fundamental tool in Bill's teaching arsenal was a focus on music theory—the *why* and *how* aspects of music. He wasn't content to just give you a song and teach you to play it, he wanted you to understand it on a granular level:

Why do certain chords go together instead of others?

What is the mathematical relationship between certain intervals?

Why would a composer elect to have silence—rather than notes—in a particular phrase?

It was the difference between learning how to tell time and learning how the cogs and gears of a watch work.

After three years with Bill, at the age of 16, he decided to ascertain just how much of his instruction I'd absorbed by entering me in the Southwestern Pennsylvania Composer Competition. We had to not only compose an original piece (or *song*, if you wanted to include lyrics), but also transcribe the entire thing by hand.

I was given a blank musical notebook consisting of nothing but staff lines. Every clef, time and key signature, bar, note, rest, articulation, accident (sharps and flats), ornament, dynamic, octave, and pedal indicator had to be penciled in by hand. If I made a mistake, I wasn't allowed to erase—I had to tear that page out and start over. It was an excruciating process that took the better part of six months to complete.

The purpose of transcribing the piece was that, once completed, it had to be sent off to the governing body sponsoring the competition. They would have someone at their headquarters play each piece that was submitted and judge it in-house. A few weeks after mailing it off, the results were published. I'd gotten first place.

The following year, my parents separated. Several months after Dad moved out, I moved in with him.[26] A couple miles down the road from our new place was a music store, Pianos 'N' Stuff, that sold every instrument under the sun. One of my favorite after-school and weekend activities was to head over there and spend hours in the keyboard section, plunking away at the seemingly endless selection of synthesizers and their infinite library of sounds.

Since there was no piano at Dad's house, I practiced every day at the senior center a few blocks away. I desperately needed something to ~~jam~~ practice on at home and lobbied Dad for one of the newest synths I'd just discovered, a Roland E-15. My family had never been one for high-dollar purchases outside of birthdays or Christmas, so I didn't think it terribly likely that Dad was going to spring for a $700 keyboard.

But I dragged him over to the store one afternoon to show him the synth I had my heart set on and give him a little demonstration of its capabilities. As I was playing, one of the store employees approached Dad. "He's been in here just about every day for the last few weeks playing that thing. And all of us working back here are pretty sure he knows every song."

"Every song from what?" Dad asked.

"Every song, *period*. Kid came in here and played some Chopin, some Van Halen, some ragtime . . . and then everything else. We started throwing songs out at him, and he knew *all of 'em*. Damnedest thing I ever saw."

I guess complimenting their kid is an easy way to a parent's wallet because Dad made sure we didn't leave the store that day without that keyboard. I was pretty sure he didn't have the money for it—he

---

[26] If we're being technical, Mom kicked me out of the house. I was supposed to be grounded one weekend—Mom dropped us off at piano lessons Friday evening, and Dad was supposed to pick us up and return us home. But youth group was Friday night, and Dad agreed with me that the reason for the grounding was bogus. So, he took me to youth group instead of taking me home. And then I spent the night at Pete's. When Pete's parents dropped me off the next morning, I was greeted with the sight of Mom's thoughtful placement of all my belongings on the front lawn, which really took an axe to my street cred. Teenage boys are supposed to get kicked out of the house for doing drugs, getting girls pregnant, or sneaking out after dark and hitchhiking to Detroit to see KISS in concert. I got booted for skipping grounding to go to church.

must've put it on a credit card or something—and I thanked him all the way home.

"Just don't let this thing sit in the corner collecting dust," he replied. "I don't want to regret this purchase."

I made sure he regretted it almost immediately.

Bedtime was 11:00 sharp on school nights. At 1:30 a.m., Dad poked his head into my room and told me to turn the music off already and go to bed. I hadn't stopped playing my new keyboard since we'd gotten home, other than to run downstairs and inhale dinner in a shade under four minutes. It was the first time in my life I had every imaginable sound at my fingertips, and my first priority was to go back over every song I'd ever learned and play it with the actual sound from the recording, or as close to it as I could get, anyway.

That's what had Dad up and irritated in the middle of the night—I'd found the perfect drum loop and synth patch for "Axel F" from *Beverly Hills Cop* and was on about the tenth pass through it, pushing up the volume ever so slightly each time.

It was always a bizarre dichotomy—my relationship with the piano. When it came time to practice, I detested it. I dreaded sitting down and setting the egg timer for an hour or two to run scales, chords, arpeggios, and slog through the entire Hannon[27] book every day. I would've preferred to eat glass . . . and then wash that down with a cup of Flint tap water mixed with sharper, dirtier glass. But leave me alone with the piano to do as I pleased, and hours on end would fly by without me noticing.

(It wasn't until years later that I realized the only reason I found the piano so enjoyable was *because* I'd dedicated so much time to the part of it I hated.)

If there was a piano to be found, I'd sit down and play it until somebody kicked me off. It didn't matter if it was at school, church, or in the middle of the airport or the mall. I joined the choir at school to have an excuse to play solos at our annual shows. I signed up for every school or youth group talent show. I played in church whenever they'd

---

[27] Hannon is a finger agility/dexterity book comprised of 40 progressively more difficult exercises. It takes about an hour to play through the entire thing.

let me. My senior year of high school, I volunteered to play at the Oakmont Senior Care home near our house for a couple hours every Saturday morning.

And then came the most glorious day of my life: *high school graduation.* The end of lessons, the end of practice. I solemnly swore to never play another scale again as long as I lived.

That summer was too full of newfound freedom and hanging with friends before we all went off to college to make even playing for fun more than an afterthought. I'd put my time in, and now it was on to a new phase in life.

For college, I'd chosen Palm Beach Atlantic University, a Baptist-affiliated college in West Palm Beach, Florida, to study marine biology. Actually, the beach, tropical weather, and extracurricular scenery (of the 2-piece variety) were my top priorities. If I happened to get an education along the way, I suppose that was a fortuitous byproduct.

Two weeks into college, I made a remarkable discovery. Since PBA was a Christian school, the guys and girls had separate dorms. I'd gone over to the girls' dorm to wait for a classmate to come down for a study group and noticed a piano in one of the side rooms off the lobby. I went in and started playing, and within five minutes, the entire piano was surrounded by an enthralled group of lovely coeds. Coincidentally, it was at this precise moment in time that I came to the sudden realization that Mom was probably a genius. I decided on the spot to rethink my self-imposed retirement from the piano. For all the right reasons, of course.

There was a flyer posted all over campus for upcoming band auditions for the school's Thursday Night Live student-led church service. They played strictly contemporary pop-rock stuff, so I figured I'd give that a shot. I tried out the following week and made the cut. It was my very first band experience, and I stayed with them for the next two years.

Around the time I joined the band, I finally nailed down an appointment I'd been trying to make with one of the guidance counselors since the first week of classes. (To be fair, this delay was the school's fault only to the extent that they'd opted to build their campus a mile from the beach, which I felt was more meritorious of my time and attention than an administrative office.)

Freshmen were all required to take an introductory music appreciation class, and said class kicked off with the professor standing at a piano, informing us that it contained 88 keys and introducing us to middle C.

I wanted to know if there was any way to test out of the class (or, at the very least, find out how many absences I could rack up and still pass).

The counselor agreed to speak to the professor, who agreed to let me drop the class . . . if I could pass the final exam the following afternoon with a 70% or better.

I showed up the next day at noon in my bathing suit, a beach towel draped around my neck, and lathered in suntan oil. I had places to be. The professor handed me the test—three sheets of paper stapled together—and told me he'd grade it when I was done before I left the room. I took a seat in the front of the classroom and penciled in my guesses to such questions as "What are the eight notes on a scale?" "How do you form a chord?" and "What sounds happier—a major key or a minor key?"

The final question on the exam was "Name any five influential classical composers." I saw an opportunity to be an incorrigible smartass, penciled in four names, then walked it over to the teacher's desk and pronounced, "I got a 100."

I paced the front of the room while he sat there grading it, anxiously waiting to deliver my punchline. When he was finished, he stood up and addressed me. "Close, but it's not quite 100. . . You missed one here at the end."

"I did?" I feigned surprise.

"We were looking for five classical composers. You only came up with Bach, Beethoven, Mozart, and Haydn."

"Oh . . ." I paused as I meandered over to the piano. ". . . I guess I forgot . . . whoever *this* guy is," and launched straight into a difficult piece by Franz Liszt, a composer known for his challenging left-hand work. I gave the professor a 30-second taste, flinging suntan oil all over the keys, then checked the time on a watch I wasn't wearing and said, "Sorry, gotta run. You get the point." I turned and smugly strode out.

Told you I got a 100, I thought to myself as I made my way to my roommate's waiting car, aimed straight at the beach.

The next day, the test was waiting for me in my mailbox. At the top, in bright red marker, was a "97." Below it was a brief note:

Nice playing, but attitude could use some improvement. For 3 extra credit points, come back and clean the suntan oil off my piano.

By the time the second semester rolled around, I'd decided to break my old promises to myself and enrolled in piano performance as an elective for reasons that were both noble and . . . lesser so.

On the one hand, I was starting to feel about my last seven months without any practice the same way I'd felt as a kid whenever my parents would get exasperated at all my talking back and say, "Fine, do whatever you want!" Then they'd give me a few days free of any semblance of supervision or guidance: eat as much junk food as I wanted, watch as much TV as I wanted, go to bed whenever I felt like it, etc. The first day or two was glorious anarchy. By day three, I'd start to subconsciously associate the lack of oversight with a lack of caring on their part. Invariably, I'd begin to feel bad about my choices and secretly wish they'd step back in and offer some structure. Better to be constrained than disregarded.

Same deal with the piano. After 15 straight years of day-in and day-out practice, it had become as engrained as any other daily habit. Skipping out on it for seven months felt like going without brushing my teeth for the same period of time.

The less noble reason for it was that I was at school on an academic scholarship that required maintaining a certain grade point average, and I was far more interested in logging beach volleyball and sunbathing hours than classwork and study time. Since PBA didn't offer an International Tanning major, I needed some classes that would all but guarantee A's with the least amount of effort. Piano seemed to fit that bill.

I still enjoyed playing for sheer pleasure as much as ever. If I had time to burn between classes, I'd find my way to the grand piano in the meeting hall above the cafeteria and play for hours in the deserted room.

After signing up for piano classes and familiarizing myself with the music building, I made an even greater discovery than the piano over the cafeteria: the concert grand on the auditorium stage. It was the most pristine-sounding piano in the greatest acoustical environment I'd ever heard. The only problem was that the orchestra, choir, and theater departments kept the stage in almost constant use. There was only one time of day that it was freely available: *after hours.* Not "after hours" as in "after the last class of the day," "after hours" as in "after the building was officially closed and locked for the night."

The basement of the music building had narrow windows up by the ceiling that were at ground level with the campus outside. I'd make it a habit to sneak into the basement during school hours, unlatch one of the windows, and prop it open slightly with an eraser from the chalkboard. Then I'd return after dark and wiggle through the unlocked window and spend as many hours as I wanted playing on a concert hall stage, lit only by a few dim exit signs, in a completely empty building. On more than one occasion, the only indication I had of the time in the outside world was the sound of the first bell ringing the next morning. Somehow, over four years of what essentially amounted to "breaking and entering" for no other purpose than giving private concerts to empty chairs (and whatever phantoms may have lurked in the basement), I never got caught.

By the middle of sophomore year, I'd landed my first regular, paying gig. My girlfriend at the time lived in one of the penthouse suites on the 43rd floor of the beachfront Tiara high-rise on Singer Island, about 15 minutes north of West Palm. Her grandparents owned the condo, but she stayed there during the school year while they were out of the country.

One floor up, at the top of the building, was a restaurant and lounge bar with a breathtaking, wraparound view of the ocean and city, and a gorgeous white baby grand piano in the corner. The lounge was closed during the daytime, so I'd go up during off-hours, open up the sliding glass doors to let the ocean breeze in and perform for whatever seagulls might be hanging out on the balcony that afternoon. If the birds did happen to be out and about on any given day, I'd always start off the impromptu set with a couple tracks from Neil Diamond's *Jonathan Livingston Seagull* soundtrack.[28]

After one particularly long session in the lounge, my girlfriend suggested I talk to the condo manager to see if they had any positions open for a nighttime piano player. I instantly agreed and called down to the front desk to see about getting an appointment. It was a few minutes to 5:00, and he was on his way out the door. He told me to swing by the following day at 4:30.

The next day, I showed up at the Tiara in my best dress shirt and khakis, earrings removed, hair combed (for once) like it wasn't cut and styled with a weed whacker. The front desk security officer directed me to the manager's office, then phoned ahead to tell him I was stopping by.

"What can I help you with?" he asked once I found the right office and poked my head in the doorway.

I took a seat in front of his desk. "One of the tenants upstairs said I should come talk to you to see about playing the piano in the lounge in the evenings. Are there any positions open, or would you guys happen to be looking for a piano player?"

He shook his head. "We had a guy up there a couple years ago, but he didn't work out. Almost everyone that hangs out up there in the lounge is retired. They either couldn't hear the piano to begin with or didn't care for the guy's song selection. He refused to take requests, and after enough complaints from the tenants, we finally let him go. Not worth it to us to pay someone to annoy our residents every night."

"And . . . you don't have any interest in giving it another shot?" I asked.

"Sorry, son. Not at this time. And, to be honest, it's probably not your scene. A bunch of octogenarians sipping gin and tonics and arguing about whose arthritis is worse. You'd probably hate it more than they would."

---

[28] For the record, Neil Diamond was not on any of my playlists at the time. It just happened to be an album my parents played incessantly in China a decade earlier, and it amused me to no end to play seagull-themed songs for an audience of actual seagulls.

I thanked him for his time, hopped on the elevator, and hit the button for the 43rd floor. I got up to my girlfriend's door and knocked. No answer.

Crap, it was Tuesday.

She wouldn't be home from class until 5:45. I checked my watch—4:50. I figured I could go kill an hour up in the lounge until she got back.

I'd been at the piano for about 15 minutes when someone burst through the main doors in a huff. It was a plump, middle-aged woman with an armful of boxes. She was wearing black pants with a white dress shirt, a black vest, and a black apron slung over her shoulder. She heaved the boxes onto the nearest barstool. I stopped playing and asked her if she needed any help.

"Oh, no, I'm fine," she assured me. "You just go right ahead and keep playing. That was lovely."

I started up again as she disappeared behind the bar. A few moments later, she popped back out. "I'm Susan, by the way. This is my bar. Are you our new piano player?"

This was an interesting development. Does she think the people downstairs hired me?

"Maybe I am," I replied coyly.

"It's about damn time!" she snorted. "I've been telling the management for *ages* we need some live entertainment up here, but you think they listen to me? Cheapasses keep telling me they don't want to pay anyone after the last guy, and I keep telling 'em they don't have to pay a damn cent! The regulars want some music, and they all got plenty of money to tip. Management don't even need to be involved as far as I'm concerned."

That perked my ears up. "So . . . these "regulars" tip pretty good?"

"Well, you ain't gonna get *rich*, honey, but they might stick fifty, a hundred bucks in that tip jar over a couple hours."

Fifty to a hundred bucks? For a couple hours?

All my college friends who found time to work were making $8-$10 an hour serving tables or valeting.

"What time do you guys start serving?" I inquired.

"The early drinkers start shuffling in around 6:30. Dinner is served—buffet style—at 7:00. We're usually as filled up as we're gonna get by 8:00, and last call is around 9:00, 9:30. Depends on my mood.

We could probably make it 9:30 if you can play that long. Sound good?"

Could I play for two and a half hours?

I could do that in my sleep.

"Yeah, that sounds pretty doable," I told her.

I got up from the piano and walked over to Susan, extending my hand. "I'm Shane, and it's a pleasure to meet you. Looks like I'm your new piano player."

I'd learned more from *Beverly Hills Cop* than just the theme song. Axel Foley had taught the world that you can get away with just about anything if you act like you're in charge and supposed to be doing whatever it is you're doing, and I took it to heart. The fact that they weren't hiring was not a good reason not to take a job there.

To accommodate my schedule and all the schoolwork I should've been—but wasn't necessarily—doing, we decided I'd play every Tuesday and Thursday night. Susan insisted that dinner was on the house, which meant that in addition to my tips, I'd get a five-star meal two nights a week instead of Ramen noodles or cafeteria food.

The "regulars" turned out to be a delightful bunch as well. If I threw in a Sinatra tune every hour or so, they didn't care what else I played. One of the retirees—a gentleman who'd made a small fortune gambling on Jai-Alai—had a terrific sense of humor and would approach the piano a couple times every evening with a twenty-dollar bill with my name on it if I could seamlessly work "She'll Be Comin' Round the Mountain When She Comes" into whatever song I happened to be playing at the moment, regardless of the style. His only other request was to do it subtly enough that nobody else in the room picked up on it right away and to weave back into the original song before anyone had time to catch on. This amused him to no end. I pocketed an extra 40 bucks a night for it, so it amused me more.

When classes opened the following fall, everyone returned from summer break to discover our favorite hangout strip—Clematis Avenue in downtown West Palm—had just opened up a brand-new entertainment venue: a dueling piano bar called Daddy-O's.

Every Wednesday, half the campus would turn out for College Night, and it didn't take long for my buddies to cajole me up to the stage on a weekly basis to lead the entire bar in sing-alongs to "Piano

Man," "Margaritaville," "Sweet Caroline," or whatever else drunk idiots were in the mood to belt off-key.

The piano bar had an entirely different vibe than any other gigs I'd done. I'd played recitals, church services, talent shows, cocktail parties, weddings, and coffee shops—even made a couple musical guest appearances on Cornerstone Television up in Pittsburgh—but there was something *electric* about the piano bar.

Perhaps it was the direct connection and camaraderie with the crowd. Perhaps it was the sight of a few hundred strangers with their arms slung over each other's shoulders, swaying to the music and singing in rowdy unison. Whatever it was, I'd never experienced anything like it before. But I liked it. I liked it *a lot*.

For the first time in my life, a little bug started creeping into my head that maybe, just *maybe* . . . music, in one form or another, could be a viable life path worth pursuing after college. I was starting to believe I might have the chops to hack it at the next level.

Never tell a young person
that anything cannot be
done. God may have been
waiting centuries for
someone ignorant enough of
the impossible to do that
very thing.

– G.M. Trevelyan

When facing a difficult task,
act as though it is impossible
to fail. If you are going after
Moby Dick, take along the
tartar sauce.

– H. Jackson Brown, Jr.

T-Minus 12 Days

OCTOBER 16, 1999: 12 DAYS TO SHOWTIME

At the moment, the next level I was on was the roof, and I was still desperately trying my Saturday-night-buzzing-best not to fall off of it. In my defense, I had at least made the responsible decision to toss the tennis racket down into the yard so I could address the phone with two hands. Mom had just sprung her audaciously bonkers Concert of the Century masterplan on me, and Chris had agreed to go along with this insane mission. Now I just needed to hook Gavin.

As soon as I hung up with Mom, I called him back and brought him up to speed on her plan to expedite his passport. Gavin was thrilled to be back in the discussion but expressed the same sensible reservations I had about how realistic getting a passport back in one week was: it wasn't.

At all.

He was right, obviously, so all I could do was offer up some lame platitude about missing 100% of the shots you don't take. That was the entirety of my sales pitch. Fortunately, that's all it took to reel him back in.

I decided that I was probably a platitude Jedi and awarded myself an honorary PhD in life coaching.

The next day, Chris, Gavin, and I gathered at my house around noon to figure out what songs we were going to bring to the table. We immediately ran into some problems. Chris thought we should just do every song off the Newsboys' latest album, 1998's *Step Up to the Microphone,* since that was the one they were currently on tour for.

I disagreed with this approach for two reasons: the first being one of purely musical sensibilities, and the second being sheer laziness. To the latter point, I had never listened to *Step Up to the Microphone* in its entirety and was only familiar with the smash hit "Entertaining Angels" from that album. I thought we needed to minimize our learning curve by sticking to tunes we were already familiar with. To the former point, I thought we owed it to the audience to deliver the ten strongest songs we could come up with. If that meant cherry-picking a few older hits, so be it. Besides, the Chinese wouldn't know if the songs had been released last week, last year, or last century. They'd never heard any of it before.

Gavin, vaguely aware that China's access to Western music lagged several decades behind what was current, went the opposite direction and lobbied for some classic rock hits like "Carry on Wayward Son," "Hotel California," and "Don't Stop Believin'." I reminded him that Mom's main purpose for this whole endeavor was the mission outreach aspect of it, not the musical showcase. As much fun as it would've been to cover Kansas, The Eagles, or Journey, we were supposed to be "evangelizing," and those secular apples fell a good long way from our objective. (The Eagles suggestion, however, would turn out to be eerily prescient.)

After several hours of discussion and debate, we eventually settled on five songs culled from the Newsboys' previous albums, then filled in our set with tunes by DC Talk, Jars of Clay, Audio Adrenaline, and, just to keep things weird, Amy Grant. The Amy Grant song—a 1982 release called "Sing Your Praise to the Lord"—didn't remotely fit the vibe of anything else we were doing, but it had a great piano intro that was a lot of fun to play[29], so I insisted on it. I figured with a couple

---

[29] I'd done a solo performance of this song for a musical guest appearance on Cornerstone Television up in Pittsburgh a few years prior.

electric guitars in the arrangement, it might come off vaguely sounding like Styx, not that China would know what they sounded like either.

I was thoroughly satisfied with our selections. All the songs conveyed the message Mom wished to express; all of them were chart-topping, crowd-pleasing hits; and most importantly, they were all fairly easy to learn.

I burned the songs to a disc, made three extra copies for each of us to study, labeled all the tracks with a Sharpie, and set the last copy by the front door to mail to Pittsburgh.

The next morning, Gavin picked me up promptly at quarter after five and we made the hour-and-fifteen-minute drive down to the Miami Passport Agency. Neither of us were under any delusions that he was going to get a passport in time—this was a futile trip simply to pacify Mom's penchant for leaving no stone unturned. Per her instructions, we got there early enough to be the first ones through the door when they opened at 7 a.m. Gavin quickly filled out the paperwork, posed for his photo, and reiterated about a hundred times that we needed this extra-super-mega-hyper *expedited.*

"Where are you guys off to in such a hurry?" the agent wanted to know.

"China," Gavin replied.

"Nice. When are you leaving?" he asked.

"Next Tuesday," I answered.

The agent looked at us in disbelief. "Next Tuesday . . . as in a week from tomorrow?"

"Yep."

"Not a chance," he informed us. "I'm afraid you're going to have to reschedule your trip."

"What do you mean *not a chance?*" Gavin asked. "How close are we cutting it?"

The agent thought a moment and replied, "We always tell people they can expect an expedited passport back in about three weeks."

I was sure that had to be an average, not the quickest. "What's the absolute fastest an expedited passport has ever come back?" I asked.

"They get mailed directly to your address, so I couldn't say for sure. We don't typically handle them after sending off the forms. But I do recall some woman last year who had hers expedited back to our office here—we got it back in 13 days. That's the fastest I've ever seen."

Thirteen days.

Our flight left in eight. We needed it back in seven.

"So, the odds aren't great it gets here by next Monday, huh?" Gavin mused.

The agent looked apologetic. "Son, it would take a miracle."

Since I was the only one of the three of us who had any actual band experience up to this point (Chris had only performed solo or with me accompanying him, and Gavin had never played with anyone), I became the *de facto* bandleader for the faux Newsboys Florida contingent. I only had one hard-and-fast rule: *do your homework and come prepared.*

Rehearsal wasn't the time for learning your parts or figuring out how the song goes. Do that stuff on your own time. Rehearsal was for making sure we were all on the same page with our counts and our cues, that our parts all meshed with each other's, and for working out background vocals and harmonies. As it was, we were going to have our hands plenty full with that. With the constricted deadline, I gave us Sunday night, Monday, and Tuesday to learn the ten songs we'd come up with. Wednesday would be our first rehearsal, after which I'd hand out copies of the songs from the guys in Pittsburgh.

Aside from sheer inexperience, the difficulty factor was compounded by the fact that we had to rehearse without a drummer or lead singer, two fairly integral components of any respectable band, or so it's been explained to me. All we could do was play along with the CD, which we had a tendency to gradually drown out as each song progressed. As anyone who's ever played in a band knows all too well, the only volume a guitarist feels adequately expresses their respective talent is *eleven.* We were blessed with two of those.

We also weren't rehearsing in anything remotely resembling a proper sonic environment; all we had at our disposal was my 120-square-foot bedroom with Spanish tile floor that drenched every note and chord in reverb thick enough to swim through.

Each song would generally start out the same way: with the CD player on max volume and each of us at a level where we could collectively hear what we were supposed to be following. Then Gavin or Chris would start nudging up their volumes to distinguish their parts in the wall of sound we were generating, prompting the other to nudge theirs up a bit further. They'd go back and forth a few times until I could no longer hear what *I* was playing and had to boost my own volume to compensate. By the time the second chorus rolled around, nobody could hear the CD anymore—or really anything, for that matter—and every dog in the neighborhood would be barking like a Cat 5 hurricane was two blocks away. We had to somehow tame the acoustics, or we were never going to make it through an entire song.

I solved this problem by stripping off my bedsheets and comforter, collecting all the towels, pillowcases, and spare blankets in the house, and using them to cover all the exposed tile in my room. I pinned whatever was left over to the wall with thumbtacks, which still left quite a bit of wall exposed. I covered the rest by raiding Nutter's closet, swiping his massive hoodie collection, and pinning those to the walls as well. (I ran out of thumbtacks after the third or fourth hoodie and simply nailed up the remaining 15-20 sweatshirts.) This had the dual effect of dampening the reverb to acceptable levels and making the entire floor slippery enough that any overly energetic movements would send their practitioner crashing to the ground in a heap. After a few such collisions and a broken lamp, both Gavin and Chris decided the now-bare mattress on my bed provided a more stable footing option than the satin-covered tile, and that became their permanent new rehearsal "stage."

Another issue we found ourselves dealing with was the temperature. Even with the AC cranked up, it was amazing how much heat could be generated in a 10x12 room by three guys and all their musical gear. Forty-five minutes into the first practice, we were all soaked in sweat. Chris peeled his shirt off and tied it around his head to keep the sweat out of his eyes. Gavin and I followed suit. And that's exactly the scene Nutter walked into when he got home (early, of course) from work our first day rehearsing together.

(As Nutter later recounted it, he'd heard us from a block away. By the time he pulled into the driveway, it was deafening, and when he opened the front door, he was pretty sure the military was conducting sonic weapons testing in the back corner of our home. He stuffed some toilet paper in his ears and poked his head into my bedroom to discover all the linens in the house coating the floor, his entire prized hoodie collection nailed to the walls like some crackhead Daytona surf shop, and two soaking wet, half-naked sheiks on my bed with electric guitars, belting out *Jesus Freak* lyrics at the top of their lungs. He didn't even bother to ask. He just shut the door, walked back out to his truck, went to his mom's house, and didn't come home for three days.)

Pushing us to the brink were the songs the guys from Pittsburgh sent us. As promised, they'd arrived Tuesday afternoon. I tore open the envelope and shoved the disc into the CD player. We listened to the entire set with growing consternation. There wasn't a Newsboys song in the bunch.

Why wouldn't they include a single Newsboys tune in a Newsboys setlist?

None of us had heard any of these songs before. I couldn't even identify most of the artists. Half of it sounded like some late '70s or early '80s psychedelic rock with Grateful Dead-sounding jam band overtones. Two of the songs were originals—worship songs the singer in Pittsburgh had written—that were probably great for a church service or revival, but not the kind of tunes you'd pick to win over and entertain a concert audience. Our selections couldn't have been more different. They went together like peanut butter and tuna.

In the music industry, professional touring musicians might spend 6-8 weeks in rehearsal before going out on the road with a new act. It's necessary to make a distinction here between acts where all the musicians on the stage are actual members of the band (such as U2, The Rolling Stones, Aerosmith, etc.) and acts where the musicians are merely hired guns for the tour (Michael Jackson, Madonna, Lada Gaga, etc.). In the case of the latter, it's not at all uncommon for artists to hire a different set of musicians for each tour. The musicians are more like freelancers in this sense, playing for whoever will hire them. These are the shows that require months of rehearsals to bring the new [professional] musicians up to speed. We were not professionals. And we did not have months. We had 11 days.

After swapping setlists with the guys in Pittsburgh, we quickly realized we had another problem we'd completely failed to take into account when choosing our songs: nearly half of them didn't have distinct endings. Instead, the song gradually faded out on the recording. That meant we had to come up with our own. In live performances, those endings are usually cued by the drummer. We didn't have one of those. I couldn't think of anything that could possibly make the next week-and-change any more challenging. Thankfully, Chris thought of it for us.

Though Gavin had never played in a band, he was able to read both musical notation and chord charts. Chris, on the other hand, was self-taught and could read neither. While he was a terrific guitarist, he didn't know the difference between a sharp sign and the *pi* symbol. And while he could contort his fingers into implausible shapes to play any chord on the fretboard with ease, he didn't actually know the names of any of the chords he was playing. In fact, he'd come up with his own unique and rather bizarre nomenclature for each chord, which, once I understood, I still didn't understand.

I found this out on the first run-through of the first song we tackled. We'd made it halfway through the first verse when I heard some wonky notes from his guitar. I stopped the song and told him he needed to be playing a D chord there. He looked back at me like I'd just told him to go blattengorf his muxtwurps.

No comprende.

He continued staring blankly at me for a few more moments as he puzzled through it, finally asking, "Which one is D?" Gavin strummed a D chord for him.

"Ah," Chris replied, obviously pleased that he already knew that chord. "I call that one 'E-two-four.'" Gavin and I exchanged quizzical glances.

"Why on earth do you call it that?" I wanted to know.

"Because the top string is an E, and there's no fingers on it," he explained. "The first finger plays on the second fret, fourth string down. E-two-four."

I'd heard of unorthodox, but this was a whole new stratosphere. I was about to launch into a keynote address pointing out that, by that logic, multiple chords would invariably share the same name, then thought better of it and bit my tongue. At present, we needed to find an immediate way to get on the same page and get through the songs, not embarrass someone for their notational ignorance.

We were familiar enough with *our* ten songs that we didn't need chord charts for most of them, but I was going to have to chart all ten of the songs from Pittsburgh. And since Chris, once he got into the groove of a song, had a tendency to close his eyes, I knew I was going to have to yell out the chord changes until we'd gone through the new stuff enough times for muscle memory to kick in. If I was going to be yelling out chords for a few days, I preferred to not sound like Payton Manning barking out play calls at the line of scrimmage. *Omaha! Omaha! D-one-six-niner-G-Whiskey-Tango-Foxtrot-three-blue! Go!* It was much easier to just say "B-flat."

I grabbed a legal pad and handed it to Gavin with instructions to create a cipher for Chris. Together, they were to play through all the chords in all the songs, with Gavin writing down the correct labels for each chord next to Chris' personal terminology. Learning all the proper terms was going to be his homework for the evening.

I have no idea how long he spent poring over it that night, but the next morning, Chris came to rehearsal knowing the proper name for every chord on the guitar, like he'd been studying it his entire life. I was impressed. It was a small victory, but a huge morale boost for all of us. At this point, we'd take any victories we could get.

Every Thursday night for the past year, Gavin and I would drive down to Boca Raton, where Chris' church had a coffeehouse for college kids. If there wasn't a local band on stage, they'd have an open mic night, and we'd hang out for a few hours playing ping-pong or air hockey. The whole event was run by Chris' mother, who served coffee, hot cocoa, or apple cider, and an assortment of homemade cookies and desserts. Mrs. Armfield served as the surrogate "den mother" for all of us who were far away from home. She was an absolute sweetheart with a terrific sense of humor, and we'd hit it off instantly.

As soon as Gavin and I stepped into the building that first Thursday after finding out we were going to China, Mrs. Armfield came running up to us, offering bear hugs and congratulations. "I'm *so* happy for you guys!" she gushed. "Chris has been talking about it non-stop since Sunday. What an *incredible* opportunity! You guys must be so excited!"

I replied jokingly that it was 90% excitement and 10% fear of getting arrested or executed. "They'll probably lop our heads off and mount them on pikes atop the Great Wall," I casually remarked.

"You better return my boy to me in one piece, or *I'll* lop off your head myself," she fired back. We both laughed, and she whisked herself away to grab us a couple mugs of coffee and a plate of homemade brownies.

Gavin, Chris, and I settled down at a table on the outdoor patio and began game-planning our next few days. That day's rehearsal had gone surprisingly well. With the sound issue handled to a manageable degree—and Chris showing up speaking the same musical language as the rest of us—we were able to get through our entire 10-song setlist at least a half-dozen times. Our harmonies were working, and Gavin and Chris were starting to figure out how to play with and off each other.

The biggest issue we were having was that both of them were natural rhythm guitarists, and both tended to play the same parts. This wasn't an insurmountable problem, though, as none of the songs we'd selected had any gunslinger guitar solos to worry about. There were a handful of signature guitar licks that needed to be replicated, and we decided Gavin would handle those duties. I suggested that Chris play chord inversions higher up on the fretboard rather than mirroring Gavin's chords. And if there happened to be some overlap with what they were playing, well . . . this was pop rock. It would help to fatten up the sound. Out of earshot, I told Chris to make sure he knew Gavin's parts since Gavin obviously wouldn't be making the trip with us. No need to rub it in his face.

I asked where everyone was at as far as familiarizing themselves with the Pittsburgh tunes, which I planned on diving into the next day. I'd drawn up chord charts for half of them already, and planned to finish the rest when I got home that night so we'd be ready to roll with them in the morning. Chris reported that he'd been listening to them on constant repeat since he'd left my house Tuesday night. Gavin's reply was somewhat less admirable.

"Dude, I tried to get through all of them one time, but I'm not really feeling 'em," he said dismissively. "Do we really have to do *those* songs?"

"Yeah, we really have to do them," I responded, slightly annoyed. "This is the setlist. You really have to learn these, like 'em or not."

"Then I'm going to have to jet out of here early and go study, I guess," he answered forlornly, like a kid who'd just found out he was going to have to attend summer school instead of going to Disney

World. "I was kind of hoping we could go get some rappelling in downtown tonight, you know? Burn off some stress."

"Dude, we've got the rest of our lives to go rappelling. We've got four days left to nail down this show," I told him. "So, let's buckle down and tackle this like we're cramming for finals, okay? And if you can do tomorrow what Chris did today with the chord names—in fact, just come in knowing *three* of the new songs tomorrow—I'll pack the climbing gear with us and take you rappelling off the Great Wall of China."

That did it. Gavin's face lit up like the Fourth of July.

Oh boy, what've I done?

Before he could press me for more details, Mrs. Armfield approached our table, sat down, and slung her arm around Chris' shoulders. "Sooooo . . .? How are my little rock stars doing? You guys figuring everything out?"

"Oh, absolutely," Gavin replied. "Shane's taking us rappelling off the Great Wall of China."

She cocked her head to one side and studied him, trying to ascertain if this was yet another joke. "Seriously?"

"Yep," I answered without hesitation.

"Is that . . . *legal?*" she inquired.

"Oh, absolutely not," I assured her. "But since we're probably all going to end up in a dank, dark, rat-infested prison cell anyway, we might as well get our money's worth, right?" I offered her my most egregious Cheshire cat smile.

"Hmm . . . In that case, I'd better leave you boys to your scheming." And with that, she sauntered off.

We ordered another cup of coffee and decided to make it our last. Gavin was right—it needed to be an early evening. We all had a ton of work to do that night. I was already thinking about which of the new songs I was going to chart when I got home. But that wasn't all that I was thinking about.

Rappelling off the Great Wall of China.

Could we actually *do* that? I highly doubted it, but it was certainly worth a try. I resolved to pack the climbing gear, whether Gavin came in the next day knowing the songs or not. I would just not tell him that I packed it and then surprise him when we got there. *If* he got there. I figured that would earn me a few favors.

Gavin came over the next morning around 10, bearing three piping hot cups of Dunkin' Donuts coffee. He didn't look like he'd slept a wink. He was also wearing his climbing harness for some reason. I hoped that meant he'd learned the songs.

I went to grab one of the cups of coffee, and Gavin slapped my hand away. "These are mine, dude. Go make a pot in the kitchen."

"Seriously?" I asked.

"Seriously, dude. I haven't slept yet."

I shrugged and walked off to the kitchen. While I was fixing the coffee, Gavin plugged his guitar in and started noodling through the new songs he'd stayed up all night working on. I stayed in the kitchen, waiting for the coffee to brew and listening intently. Actually, noodling would be a poor description. It implies someone vaguely searching for notes without much urgency. Gavin was *playing* the songs. Flawlessly. Five of them.

He learned half *the songs last night?!?*

I figured that entitled him to hoard all three cups of coffee for himself. It still didn't explain the climbing harness. But then, if he was coming in prepared beyond my wildest expectations, I didn't care if he showed up wearing nothing but a Viking helmet and shower curtain.

Chris arrived around 10:30, looking like he'd had a long night too. He immediately spotted Gavin's coffees and went to grab one. Gavin smacked his hand, right on cue. "Those are mine, dude. There's a fresh pot in the kitchen."

Chris gave me a glance, and I nodded to confirm it. "Those are his. Don't ask. There's a fresh pot in the kitchen." I held up my mug for corroboration.

With fresh coffees in hand, we spread out on the floor and set about mapping out our agenda. We had exactly four days until we had to board a flight. We had 20 songs to learn. We already knew 10 of them well enough to play through them together (though not well enough to convince anyone else that we'd played through them as a group more than a handful of times). We had chord charts for the remaining 10. Gavin had half of those down. Chris had learned three of the same songs that Gavin had, and one more that Gavin hadn't worked on. That made 13 songs we could work on today. I figured we could put in a full day's rehearsal and then spend all night learning the remaining tunes. We'd reconvene on Saturday morning with everyone (theoretically) knowing all 20 songs, and that would give us two solid days to make everything gel before we had to start packing. There was little time to waste.

We dove into one of the new songs from Pittsburgh, and 30 seconds into it, one of Gavin's guitar strings snapped on his acoustic. We stopped playing while he fished around in his guitar case for a replacement.

"*Dude!* I don't think I have an extra one of these in here," he informed us after a quick search.

"Are you sure?" I asked. "You looked through *all* of your backup strings?"

"Um . . . I actually, uh . . . I don't have any backup strings."

I took a peek into the compartment of his guitar case he'd just been rummaging through. It was completely empty. "Why were y—?"

Never mind.

I looked at Chris. "You got any extras?"

Chris shook his head sheepishly. "Sorry, man. I'm all out too."

I was perplexed. "Neither one of you has a *single* extra guitar string? Of any sort?

"Nope."

"Huh-uh."

At that moment, I had a sudden vision of the actual Newsboys with their touring setups. In my mind, I could see their racks of guitars—maybe 20 of them—lined up just offstage should they need a quick change or replacement during the show. And here we were with three guitars, with a grand total of 17 strings between them. It didn't exactly scream *professional.* We needed to take a quick trip to the nearest music store.

The three of us piled into Gavin's car and set out on a hunt for some guitar strings. We found the shop we were looking for—a little hole-in-the-wall instrument and gear rental place—a few miles from my house.

"Let's make this quick," I told the guys as we pulled up. "In and out, five minutes tops."

A bell on the front door announced our arrival, and a sound technician came running over to greet us before all three of us had made it all the way inside the building.

"Anything I can help you guys find today?"

"We're just here for some guitar strings," I informed him.

"Yeah, we're heading out on tour to China next week," Gavin needlessly volunteered, despite the fact that he wouldn't be joining us. Gavin loved to talk. And he loved telling the China story to anyone who would listen.

More information than he needs, buddy.

Too late.

"China, huh?" The tech guy seemed impressed. "What are you guys doing over there?"

Aaaannnd here we go. Gavin's just committed us to a 15-minute conversation.

A side room full of keyboards caught my eye. "I'll be right back," I told the group and wandered off as Gavin launched into the tale of our escapades.

Did I say five minutes? Make that 20.

A half-hour later, Gavin, Chris, and the tech guy walked into the keyboard room, where I was busy not looking for guitar strings or paying attention to the time. "Dude, we've got a problem," Gavin announced dramatically. "Like, a *big* problem."

I looked up from the synthesizer I was hammering away on and noted that neither Chris nor Gavin had managed to snag any guitar strings as of yet.

"What's the problem?"

"Tell him," Gavin said to the tech.

"I wouldn't go so far as to call it a *problem,*" the tech began. "I was just asking them some questions about your production setup. They didn't have any of the answers and said you were the guy to ask."

"Okay, shoot," I told him.

"Well, first off, this is the most ridiculous story I've ever heard, and I'm still not sure I quite believe it. If you guys actually pull this off, you'll all be my new heroes. Anyway, I was just asking your buddies here what kind of production gear you were taking with you. Racks, monitors, cabinets . . . stuff like that."

I had no idea what any of that meant. I told him that the venues in China were handling all of the production.

"Yeah, they're handling all your sound and lighting, but what gear are you guys actually taking with you? And how are you packing it?"

I told him I was bringing my keyboard and that Chris and Gavin were bringing their guitars. That was it, to my knowledge. I'd played plenty of coffee shops in the past. You just showed up, plugged in your instrument, and started playing, right? How would this be any different?

The tech looked at us like we'd just stepped off a UFO. "Have any of you actually toured before?"

We shook our heads.

"Do you have travel cases for your instruments?"

I had a soft case with a shoulder strap for my keyboard, and I'd "traveled" with it in the sense that I occasionally packed it into the back seat of a car. As it turns out, a travel case (or *flight case*) is a rugged, foam-filled monstrosity that allows your very expensive instrument to be loaded into an airplane underbelly and jostled around with 500 other pieces of luggage and equipment without breaking in half.

Who knew?

"No, I don't have one of those," I told him.

He nodded sympathetically. "No worries. We've got plenty here to rent. What about mics? Bringing your own, or are they gonna supply them?"

I didn't know.

"How about monitors? Wedges or in-ear?"

I knew what wedge monitors were (the reference speakers on the front of the stage that point back at the musicians so they can hear what they're playing). I had no idea what he meant by *in-ear*. "I'm sorry, can you go over all this stuff with us from square one? Pretend like we're total idiots."

"Shane *is* a total idiot," Chris offered helpfully. "You don't have to pretend anything."

The tech visibly lit up at the chance to introduce a bunch of amateurs to every piece of equipment, gear, gadget, and doodad on the premises—clearly savoring the opportunity to impart his decades of knowledge and technical know-how to a willing and rapt audience. I imagine this was probably the ultimate fantasy of every tech/salesman in the universe—three guys strolling into his shop and saying, un-ironically, "Tell us everything you know about everything under this roof."

Two hours later, I looked down at the legal pad that I'd filled with six pages of notes. I'd asked the tech for something to write on about five minutes into our field trip when it became apparent there was no way any of us were going to remember everything we needed to know. It was embarrassing—mind-boggling, really—how clueless we all were about what we were getting into. We'd simply taken for granted that being proficient at our instruments meant we'd know how to navigate a professional stage setup. It was a knowledge gap on par with the difference between knowing how to drive a car and competing in a Formula 1 Grand Prix. In hindsight, it was probably the most valuable two hours we invested getting ready for the shows.

It turned out that "in-ear" was a monitoring system that does exactly what its name suggests: fits into your ear like earplugs. This allows you to hear not only what *you're* playing and singing but also what everyone else on the stage is doing without all the latency and echo from the room ambience. In the tiny venues I was used to playing, it wouldn't make a significant difference. One or two wedge monitors at the front would be sufficient for everyone crammed onto a stage the size of a kitchen. We still had no idea what kind of stages we'd be performing on, but if they had anything approaching enough room to move around on without sending the bass player crashing into a broom closet, we'd need individual wedge monitors at the very least. *Were these going to be provided?* I had no idea. I circled that bullet point to call my mom about when we got back to the house.

Microphones were another issue we'd given zero thought to. As the keyboard player, I didn't really need to worry about my options since I'd be stationary. But if the guitarists planned to do a lot of moving around while singing, they might opt for a headset mic rather than one on a traditional stand. *Were the Chinese venues providing these options?* Another question for Mom.

I decided not to wait until we got back home and called Mom from the store. I went down my list of questions, which she promised to call her China liaisons about as soon as they were awake. I then explained our need for road cases, and she told me to go ahead and reserve whatever we needed. She asked to speak to our tech guru to ask a few questions and give him a credit card. After 10 minutes, when it became apparent they were going to be on the phone for a while, I ambled back off to the keyboard room.

Forty-five minutes later, the techie returned and handed me my phone. "Well, *that* was interesting," he said. "Your mom's a piece of work."

Tell me something I don't know.

"Everything go okay?"

"Oh, yeah. Fine. We're gonna be in contact until you guys leave. I'm supposed to make sure you boys have everything you need. And she spent the last 20 minutes trying to get me to accept Jesus Christ as my personal savior."

"Yep, that sounds like her."

We thanked him for his time and told him we'd be in touch the next day. We piled back into Gavin's car, and I checked my watch; it was 3:30. We'd just spent nearly four hours in there. A half-block later, Gavin slammed on his brakes. *"Dammit!"* he exclaimed, slamming his hand on the steering wheel and whipping the car around to hang a U-turn.

"What?" Chris and I both asked simultaneously.

"We forgot to get guitar strings."

It was Saturday morning, and three zombies were leaning against the kitchen counter, downing coffee. With yesterday's unexpected field trip to the music store, we hadn't gotten started with rehearsal until late in the afternoon. We ran through the songs on repeat until Nutter finally resurfaced a little before midnight and threatened to kill one—or all—of us if we played another note. (He also offered to kill me, independent of the music, for nailing his entire hoodie collection to the walls.)

So, we disbanded, and everyone went home to learn the remainder of the songs and then reconvene back here at 10 a.m. I'd been the first one to bed at 5 a.m. (after practicing all night with headphones on so as to avoid waking up murdered), Chris had conked out around 7 a.m., and Gavin had pulled an all-nighter. It was going to be a long day.

The good news was that everyone had done their homework on the rest of the setlist. So, the plan was just to run the seven songs we hadn't gone over yet as many times as it took for us to have them down in our sleep, which didn't take as long as you might think since we were practically sleeping on our feet anyway.

I felt particularly bad for Gavin. None of us were saying it out loud, but we all understood the situation. Although he was giving it his all, he was essentially the practice squad. Practice squad guys are expected to show up and work just as hard as the guys who suit up on gameday, maybe even harder. Their job isn't to win games, it's to keep the guys who actually have to take the field sharp. It was beyond admirable—it was pretty freaking inspiring, to be honest. The guy who wouldn't be traveling with the team was putting in the greatest effort. For a second, my mind flashed to the movie *Rudy*. That was Gavin— knowing you're not gonna get the opportunity to suit up, but running every drill and scrimmage with the heart of a starter. It was too bad life wasn't scripted like a Hollywood movie. Gavin deserved this opportunity more than anyone. It wasn't fair.

We ran the new songs hour after hour until a phone call from Mom interrupted our rehearsal. She'd just heard back from China about what gear they would be providing and what we needed to bring with us.

Fortunately, they had just about everything covered. We'd just needed to rent our road cases, a set of backup mics, and a few bulky monitors in even bulkier cases. Apparently, there had been some confusion in translation over the term "monitors," and Mom wasn't certain the Chinese understood what she'd been asking about. Since she couldn't get a definitive answer, she thought the safest bet was for everyone in the band to bring their own wedge. The rental fee for the in-ear monitoring system turned out to be way beyond our budget, so we'd each be lugging around an 80-pound floor monitor. *Just in case.* We'd be picking up all the gear Monday morning, the day before we left.

It was almost five o'clock—still plenty of hours left in the day to cram in plenty more practice. But I decided we could all use a little downtime. There's an odd little quirk about learning a new skill—you start off making incremental improvements, hit a bit of a temporary plateau, and then gradually start to regress. The regression is usually due to overthinking the new task before muscle memory has had time to develop. Further practice at this point usually yields diminishing returns. The key is to notice when the regression starts setting in and to stop and walk away for a period of time. Typically, 24 hours. When you come back to the task, more often than not, you'll find you're more proficient at it than at your best point before you took the break. It's a weird little brain hack that bucks the conventional wisdom of just "powering through."

I figured the best thing for everyone to do was get a good night's sleep, let the day's work sink deep into their subconscious, and then reconvene tomorrow morning to put it all together. I said goodbye to the guys, plopped myself down on the couch, and was sound asleep in under a minute.

The phone woke me up a few hours later. It was Chris wanting to jot down a few last-minute notes about intros, solos, and transitions. Groggily, I sat up to answer what questions I could.

"I've got you on speakerphone. Say hi to Mom," Chris said.

"Hi, Mrs. Chris' mom!" I yelled into the mouthpiece.

"Hello, my other son!" Mrs. Armfield shouted back. "How's everything coming along?"

I decided to take the opportunity to playfully pester her with creative new hypotheses as to how we might be tortured or meet our demise once we got to China. Since I'd already floated the idea of prison and beheadings, I suggested that a firing squad might be in order. Or possibly being shipped off to whatever the Chinese equivalent of a Siberian gulag was. Whatever it was, it would definitely be unpleasant!

When I was done inventing creative ways for the Communists to theoretically end us all, I bid Mrs. Armfield a good evening, answered Chris' song questions, and then drifted off to dreamland.

The downtime and extra sleep had achieved their desired effect: the seven hours we'd put in yesterday had begun to turn into muscle memory overnight, and we were all pleasantly surprised at how much better everything sounded when we dove into rehearsal Sunday morning than when we'd left off yesterday. The nifty little brain hack worked.

We decided to run the entire 20-song setlist, top to bottom, like a dress rehearsal—no breaks, no interruptions. By the end of the fourth run-through, after nearly eight hours, it was apparent that we had our set down as well as we were ever going to get it.

It's generally acknowledged that there are four stages of learning. The first is where you're not even aware of what you don't know. They call this stage Unconscious Incompetence. Stage Two is Conscious Incompetence—where you start becoming aware of the skill and knowledge gaps you've got to overcome. This is where learning actually begins. Stage Three is Conscious Competence—you're able to perform the new skill, but it requires careful attention and concentration. The final stage is Unconscious Competence. At this point, the skill is engrained enough that you can do it without even thinking about it.

We were at Stage Four with our set. The notes were all muscle memory, the counts were subconscious, the song transitions were on autopilot, and the harmonies were an afterthought. This is where things started to get *fun*.

It was hard not to be impressed with the progress we'd made in just a week's time. There was still no telling how everything was going to mesh once we finally met up with the other half of our band, but if anyone had a need for a trio comprised of two guitarists and a keyboardist playing to a CD, we were probably near the top of any list. Top Ten, anyway.

I decided to make that Sunday afternoon our final rehearsal. We were scheduled to pick up our rental gear Monday morning at 11, and none of us had bothered to start packing yet. No need to make our last day any more stressful than it had to be. Gavin and Chris left my house Sunday evening around 5, and I flopped down on the couch to watch some football.

At 10 p.m., my phone rang. I had dozed off on the couch. I glanced at the caller ID—it was Chris.

"What's up, man?" I answered groggily.

"I've got some bad news, brother."

I sat up, suddenly wide awake, trying to imagine what could possibly be wrong.

Silence on the other end.

"I really hate to do this," he finally said, "but I can't go to China."

I exhaled a sigh of relief.

Good one, Chris. You had me going for a split second there.

"Ha-ha. Very funny. For real though, what's up?"

"I'm being for real. I can't go with you guys to China."

"Are you being *serious?*"

"Yeah."

"Swear to God?"

"I swear. My mom's not going to let me go."

"Why not?"

"I think you scared her."

"What are you talking about? What did I do?"

"All that talk about getting locked up or tortured or executed. You got her worried."

"Dude, I was joking! Nothing's going to happen to us. I mean, *probably* nothing's going to happen to us."

"Yeah, it's the *probably* part that she's worried about. Look, I've been arguing with her about this for 2 hours now. She won't budge. I've given her every argument I can think of, and she's not having any of it. She said no."

"Would it help if I talked to her?" I asked.

"I don't know. You can try. But I wouldn't bet on it."

"Okay, I'll see what I can do. Put her on the phone."

A few seconds went by, and then she picked up. "Hi, Shane. I'm so sorry about this," she began before I could say a word. "I know how hard you guys have been practicing, and how much time you've put in, but you just got my wheels turning and—"

I interrupted her, "I was completely joking with you. Honestly. There's nothing to worry about."

"No, I know there's most likely nothing to worry about," she continued, "but I just can't take any chances. He's my son. Please don't be angry at him. You can blame it all on me."

"Would it help if you talked to my mom?" I asked. "I can have her call you in, like, two minutes."

"Unless she can tell me you guys are going to London instead of China, I don't think anyone's going to be able to change my mind. Again, I'm so sorry, but that's my final answer."

A long pause. "Should I put Chris back on?"

"Sure."

"Okay. I wish you all the best of luck, and I'll be saying prayers for you. Here's Chris."

Chris jumped back on. "No luck, huh?"

"Unfortunately, no," I muttered. "Are you sure there's nothing you can do to convince her?" I still couldn't believe he was springing this on us 36 hours before we were supposed to take off. We'd all known Gavin was never a real option because of the passport situation. If Chris was out, the fake Newsboys would be heading to China without a guitarist. That was no way to put on a rock show. This was a bad dream. A worst-case scenario. Or maybe this was one of those divine signals that it really was time to cancel the show. Before somebody got hurt.

"Dude, I've tried everything. I'm sorry," Chris said.

If there was nothing he could do, there was nothing he could do. It was what it was. I was resigned to attempting Jedi platitude mind tricks on myself. At the moment, the only alternative was to confront the impending logistical nightmare this posed to our entire operation, which I didn't want to think about. To put it bluntly, *we were screwed.*

"If it helps, though, I'll drive you guys to the airport and pick you up when you get back," he offered.

"I'd appreciate that, thanks." I wasn't sure what else there was to say. I needed to call Mom and Gavin and inform them. "I'll give you a shout tomorrow." I hung up.

We. Are. S.C.R.E.W.E.D.

I called Mom first. She didn't share my opinion that this was an insurmountable disaster, which I supposed should've come as no surprise. If she didn't think the entirety of a *real* band canceling was sufficient to derail her concert, why should she fret over a mere 17% of a *fake* band jumping ship? That was hardly an insurmountable obstacle. The show must go on, and it would go on whether there were six of us or five of us.

Or worse.

I decided to finally address the elephant in the room nobody wanted to talk about: *Gavin's passport.* If the show indeed must go on, it wouldn't actually be going on with five of us—it would be with just *four* of us.

We'd been avoiding the subject like it was a no-hitter going into the ninth inning, and we didn't want to jinx the pitcher by mentioning it in the dugout. But we were down to our last day. If his passport didn't arrive tomorrow—and it was ridiculous to believe it would—we'd have no guitarist. It was, as Mom put it, in God's hands.

I called Gavin next and broke the news.

"Dude, that *sucks!*"

I agreed.

"What are you guys going to do? You know I don't have my passport, right?"

Yes, we were vaguely aware.

"We leave on Tuesday!"

Couldn't get anything past Gavin.

"That's still the plan," I said.

"Are we still picking up the gear in the morning?"

Indeed, we were.

"Do I have to learn all of Chris' parts?"

That would be incredibly useful . . . if he could also grow an extra pair of hands.

"Not just yet," I told him. "Let's see what happens tomorrow, and then we'll worry about how to deal with his parts."

"Cool, dude. I'll see you in the morning!"

My, he sounded chipper.

I didn't want to be in the same county as him when his mailbox turned up empty the next day.

Gavin met me at my house the next morning, and we drove over to pick up our gear. Our tech guy had everything waiting for us by the front door when we arrived, and there was a small contingent of his colleagues waiting to help load it up and bask in the general lunacy of what their equipment was getting itself into. We could've easily handled the gear ourselves—which we were going to have to do anyway as soon as we got to the airport—but the tech had spread the word around the store. Everyone in range wanted to get in on this little piece of history/notoriety-in-the-making, even if it was just to lug a travel case a dozen feet to our vehicle.

We got back to my house around noon and unloaded everything into the living room. I looked at Gavin. We both knew what came next. It was time for him to head home and check the mail, which should've been delivered while we were out. I offered to ride along for the 25-minute drive to his place, but he quickly and firmly vetoed that idea. He didn't offer an explanation, but he didn't need to. If I were in his shoes, I wouldn't want anyone around either when the mailbox turned out to be empty.

A half-hour later, I got the call.

"Dude." That was it.

He sounded deflated.

I could barely muster any words myself. "No mail?"

"Just some junk."

Silence.

I let out a big sigh. "I . . ." I trailed off. Even if I could think of something to say—which I couldn't—what would be the point?

After a long pause, Gavin finally broke the silence: "At least there's one little piece of good news."

"What's that?" I asked weakly.

"If you expedite a passport, they don't send it via the post office."

I wasn't sure why this was good news, but *okay*. "Are you sure about that?"

"Yeah."

"How do you know?"

"Because they send it FedEx."

"How do you know *that?*"

"Because . . ." he paused for dramatic effect: "I'm holding a FedEx envelope in my hand with my passport inside of it. *DUDE, I'M GOING TO CHINA!!!*"

How in the world did that passport get here in seven days?

It didn't matter. At the eleventh hour, it was going to be Gavin instead of Chris. The "Newsboys" were going to have a guitarist after all.

All you need in this life
is ignorance and
confidence, and then
success is sure.
– Mark Twain

From Russia with Luck

RUSSIA, SUMMER 1993

If we were going to go off and cause an international scene, one thing I had working in my favor was that it wouldn't be the first time—I had a bit of previous experience stirring up international trouble.

Back in 1993, I'd gone on a six-week mission trip to Russia with an evangelical youth organization called Teen Mania. And suffice it to say that no part of their regularly-scheduled teen mission program included hookers, mild aggravated assault, a bit of prison time, and a personal kerfuffle with one Mikhail Gorbachev as part of the itinerary.

Those were just my own flourishes.

The gist of the Teen Mania international program was that they'd assemble teams of 20-30 kids, aged 13-20, and each group was assigned a handful of adult supervisors, of which my group did not have enough.[30] The actual proselytizing was done by way of a 17-minute choreographed play that was supposed to be an allegory of the Gospel

---

[30] Editor's Note: The amount of adult supervision was, in fact, *more* than enough for this group. At least in theory. The problem turned out not to be the size of the group, but the author's inclusion in it.

story, albeit one that featured pirates, clowns, cowboys, a bunch of mimes, a samurai, and a sacrificial sea captain. (It was a very *loose* allegory.) The entire production was set to music, with a pre-recorded voice narrating the plot in the native language of whatever country was being ~~invad~~ visited.

Each day would consist of going out into the city with a PA system and setting up anywhere we could find room to operate a 30-person production: parks, bus stops, street corners, whatever. After the play, we'd go out and mingle with the gawkers and—with the help of our handy translator—try to convert them. If you're having a hard time envisioning this outreach, just picture a large group of average American teenagers . . . dressed like the Village People . . . trying to win souls for Jesus in a Russian subway station via choreographed sword fights and interpretive dance. Just like Paul discusses in 3 Corinthians.

Thousands of kids from around the US would descend upon the Omni hotel in Miami for a 3-day crash course—meeting our teams, learning the choreography, and then jetting off for whichever one of the several dozen countries Teen Mania sent groups to that we'd signed up for. My sister went off to Thailand, and I headed to the recently former Soviet Union. With my learner's permit.

That will be important later.

There were actually three separate teams traveling to Russia together—almost 100 of us in total—and the trip from Miami to the Moscow dorm we'd all be staying in was memorable for a number of reasons.

The first leg, from Miami to London, was on some reputable, name-brand airline where the doors and wings stay attached the entire flight. At Heathrow, we switched over to Russia's Aeroflot for the flight to Moscow.

Stepping inside the Aeroflot plane, we were first greeted by the captain—who was slightly red-eyed and appeared a bit wobblier than you'd prefer your commercial airline pilot to be—and, turning into the main cabin, immediately confronted with a spray of . . . steam? Mist? Vapor? *Something* was spraying out of the ceiling on either side of the aisle the entire length of the cabin. Whatever it was, it was dense enough that you could barely make out the head of the person directly in front of you. From the shoulders up, the plane looked like a set piece from Ridley Scott's *Alien*. Like, at any moment, the Alien Queen might spring out of one of the overhead luggage bins and bite off someone's face.

Once we found our seats and buckled in without a Xenomorph attack, it was time to be on our way. The plane powered up (or whatever planes "do"—I have no idea how you turn on a commercial jet. Keys?) and immediately began shuddering and groaning like the old pipes in an abandoned insane asylum in a horror movie. Not your typical airplane noises, is what I'm saying. The tremors intensified, the rumblings deepened, and just when it seemed like the convulsions couldn't possibly get any worse without the plane coming apart, a 3-inch screw fell out of the foggy upper regions of the fuselage and landed in my seatmate's lap. I was no airplane mechanic, but I was pretty sure that was a bug, not a feature.

Thinking fast, I pushed the call button for the flight attendant, handed her the errant screw, and explained its troubling origin story with what I felt was the appropriate amount of urgency: all of it. She listened politely, took the screw, thanked me for my alertness, shuffled back to the front of the cabin, and . . . threw it in the trash.

Okay, not how I would've handled that.

I decided that if the plane was going to disintegrate around us, it would be better if it happened while we were rolling down the tarmac than soaring through the clouds. And if it didn't fall apart before we took off with the screws literally coming loose, I figured it could probably survive another 4-hour flight intact, so there was no point in worrying about it.

If a problem can be solved, there's no point in worrying about it. If it can't be solved, worrying about it won't do any good anyway.

By the time we landed in Moscow, the fog or steam or alien vapor at the ceiling had completely dissipated, allowing us an unobstructed view of our definitely inebriated captain being helped off the plane by the co-pilot and a flight attendant, too drunk to stand on his own two feet.

This was a promising way to kick off a mission trip!

We were greeted at baggage claim by a 20-something college student, Victor, who would be our translator for the trip. We collected our luggage, then Victor led us down the amusement-park-ride escalators[31] to the subway to catch the shuttle to the campus we'd be staying at. Thirty minutes later, we disembarked and exited the subway station into urban Moscow. From there, it was a 10-minute walk to the dorm that would be our home for the next six weeks.

As we walked, I took in the surroundings. Other than all the signs being in Cyrillic, there wasn't much to indicate this was a foreign land. Well, perhaps the build quality of the university buildings we were passing. They reminded me a bit of China. It was summer, so there weren't a lot of people to be seen moving about the campus. We crossed the street and walked past a bus stop where a lone young woman was waiting. A *stunningly* attractive lone woman in a bright red miniskirt, the likes of which are hand-stitched by the Devil himself for the sole purpose of wreaking havoc on the minds of teenage boys.

I smiled and gave her a slight nod as I walked past, full of 15-year-old swagger. She returned my gaze with an icy stare that was equal parts uninterested and unamused.

Note to self: Russians do not appear to be an overly friendly people.

When we reached our dorm, the group leaders pulled out a sheet of paper and began assigning people to floors: leaders on the first floor, girls on the second floor, guys on the third. We were free to choose whoever we wanted to room with. I picked a buddy, and we elected to drag our suitcases up the stairs rather than wait in a line of 60 people for the one working elevator.

Reaching our floor, we found a room that hadn't been claimed yet: two beds, two desks, two sets of drawers—a typical college dorm. We set about unpacking, folding, hanging, putting things away, and settling in.

We'd been in the room for maybe 15 minutes and had just about finished putting everything away when a consternated male voice suddenly boomed out from the lobby, echoing up the stairwell and

---

[31] The Russian subway escalators are truly something to behold. The entire Moscow subway system is situated at depths of up to 84 meters (276 feet) below ground level, or the height of a 27-story building. The escalators into and out of these stations are immensely long—some of them measuring over 430 feet—and were often absurdly fast to the point of being dangerous. A teenage adrenaline junkie on a budget could get an entire afternoon's worth of thrills riding up and down Moscow's subway escalators.

down the halls, *"DID SOMEONE HERE ORDER A PROSTITUTE?!?!"*

Now *that* was something you didn't hear every day on the mission field! Intrigued, everyone on our floor bolted down the stairs to find out what kind of Christian brothel we'd inadvertently booked ourselves into.

Reaching the ground floor, we found our team leader and Victor in a heated argument with a giant bear of a man and a stunningly attractive woman in a bright red miniskirt that looked vaguely familiar. All four of them were shouting over each other—Red Skirt and the Bear in Russian, our team leader in English, Victor in a mix of both in a vain attempt to translate—and gesturing wildly. The woman took a deep breath and briefly looked up from the fight. Our eyes locked.

"Eto on! Eto on!" (That's him! That's him!), she yelled, pointing in our direction.

We all stood there confused, unsure exactly who she was pointing at or what she was saying. When none of us budged or offered a response, she strode across the crowded lobby, stopped directly in front of me, and jabbed a pointed finger into my chest: *"Eto on! Eto tot samyy!"* (It's him! This is the one!")

Okay, now we knew she was upset with me for some reason, but we still didn't know what she was yelling about. Having singled me out, she recrossed the lobby and resumed her side of the fiery debate.

Finally, Victor said something to the Russian duo that quieted them down long enough for him to turn and explain to our team leader—along with the 100 of us standing there gawking—what was happening. "She says that *he* . . ." Victor pointed at me, ". . . hired her. And now she wants her money."

"Nobody hired anybody for anything!" our team leader insisted furiously. Then, "Shane, what did you say to her?"

I raised my hands and shrugged, obviously confused: "I didn't say anything to her."

"Nothing at all?" Victor inquired.

"No. Not a word. All I did was smile at her when we walked past."

Victor clearly didn't like that answer and growled something in Russian. He thought for a moment, then addressed our team leader: "It is all a big misunderstanding. It is a cultural thing. I will explain it to everyone after they leave. But they are not leaving until she is paid."

Our team leader was incredulous. "We are Christian *missionaries.* We're not paying off a prostitute just to make her leave!"

Victor looked sheepish about what he was about to say. "I'm afraid that if she does not get paid, her friend here," he gestured at the Bear, "will make things very unpleasant for you."

"Unpleasant, *how?*" our leader demanded.

Victor looked at him quizzically as if to say: *Have you honestly never seen a crime movie in your life?*

"Unpleasant as in, it will be good fortune if he only breaks one arm."

Our leader stood there, dumbfounded. We could see his brain furiously attempting to process the current situation, one that had certainly never come up in the Youth Missions Team Leader Training Manual. *Pay off a prostitute for services unrendered, or have her hulk of a pimp rip my arms off in front of all my kids . . .*

I felt a little sorry for him, almost as if I had somehow contributed to his present predicament.

Eventually determining that a life lived with arms was preferable to the alternative, our leader turned to Victor, sighed, unzipped his fanny pack, and took out a roll of bills. "How much?"

When they were gone, Victor gave us our first lesson in Russian culture: *Do. Not. Smile.*

The Russian people are incredibly warm and friendly, he explained, but smiling at strangers is simply not done. If you smile at someone for no apparent reason, like Americans are so fond of doing, people here will think you are either crazy or a fool. If a man smiles at another man, it will be taken as a challenge to fight. And if a man smiles at the kind of woman who happens to be for sale, he is signaling that she's hired . . . all without saying a word.

Okay, so now we knew.

Russia was going to be a ball.

A couple weeks passed without the kind of incidents that belong in this book, but that's just because I was saving up.

The first incident was "my fault" only in the sense that you definitely couldn't blame it on anyone else, and nothing at all would've transpired if I hadn't picked an inopportune time to make a joke. Other than that, it absolutely wasn't my fault.

As I mentioned, there were three different teams in Russia. We were all doing the exact same production, so we'd go our separate ways in the morning and then meet back at the dorm in the evening. One day, after we'd finished our final street performance for the afternoon, we bumped into one of our fellow teams in the subway station and rode back to campus together. It was a total chance encounter, as Moscow is the largest city in Europe, and our team leaders usually planned their itineraries together to make sure we weren't crossing paths throughout the day.

The subway was packed, but at one point, a buzz of commotion could be heard from the opposite end of our car. Nobody could tell what was happening while we were packed in there, but the commotion continued on the platform once we exited several minutes later. It was still impossible to tell what was going on, but then several people started shouting for help and gesturing at a woman in apparent distress.

In less than a minute, a half dozen police were wading through the current of people towards the woman, barking commands in Russian and scanning the sea of bodies for anyone who looked suspicious, of which we provided an abundant supply.

As I mentioned, this street performance we were doing meant everyone was in costume with their faces painted. The chief bad guy in the production was the Pirate King, who wore a do-rag and an eye patch and had a huge scar painted down the side of his face, creating a fairly menacing look. And since the show's big climax featured an elaborately choreographed sword fight, the Pirate King also carried a length of gray PVC pipe with one end wrapped in black tape for the handle. It was basically a harmless, two-foot-long piece of hollow plastic, although that wouldn't be the first impression your brain settled on if you were, say, a cop scanning a crowded subway platform for a potential mugging suspect. Which is exactly what the cops trying to reach the woman in distress were doing.

As soon as the police arrived at the platform, our translator Victor began yelling out to us what the cops were shouting—*Did anyone see who did it? Did anyone see who did it?*—at which point I began craning my neck around to see if anyone was doing anything suspicious. As one of the police officers pushed past me, I jokingly thumbed over my shoulder at the other team's Pirate King a few people behind me and said, "It's him!"

As we would later learn, the commotion on the subway had been due to an elderly woman getting mugged, and she'd stepped off the car clutching a bloody cloth to her head with a cadre of do-gooders surrounding her to provide assistance until security showed up. Security promptly showed up in search of an antagonist, which is when the Spirit led me to single out a fellow teenage missionary, albeit one dressed like a pirate and carrying what appeared at first glance to be a club of sorts.

Not getting my humor, the Russian cops immediately pulled out their *real* batons and pounced on the Pirate King, beating him nearly senseless before a scrum of cowboys, mimes, a samurai, and a circus clown dove in and tried to shield his limp body.

The Pirate King spent the night in the hospital and was released the next afternoon with fresh stitches in his head and plenty of bandages to give his costume a much-improved air of authenticity. At least that's how I saw it.

The team leaders saw it as I had essentially invited a near-death beating upon one of my fellow travelers for no discernible reason, so they sat me down without dinner and gave me a several-hours-long scolding/lecture/Bible study session in which I hungrily learned several dozen different reasons how and why aggravated assault is neither a Fruit of the Spirit nor a laughing matter, most of which I already knew. Or at least could've guessed.

Since the whole ordeal was an accident and a big misunderstanding, I was quickly forgiven. The following weekend, when they had to negotiate my release from jail, was an entirely different story.

Saturdays were our designated free days, and we were permitted to do pretty much as we pleased so long as nobody went anywhere on their own and each group had a teen leader (a member who was at least 18 and had signed up for a leadership position). Most weekends, a free day would involve groups of 10-20 of us heading out to landmarks like Red Square to sightsee and snap some pictures of Saint Basil's Cathedral or Lenin's tomb. On this particular Saturday, a dozen of us decided to hit up the markets to do some souvenir shopping. A few teen leaders joined our group, including my buddy Heath, who, at 20, acted as my big brother on the trip.

Since we were venturing off without a translator, Victor scrawled some directions on a sheet of paper to a famous souvenir shopping district about an hour from our campus. We found the location without much trouble and then split off into smaller groups as different stores and vendors caught our eye. It was a huge, outdoor tourist trap of a market, made up of crisscrossing streets, side streets, and alleyways, lined with stalls selling every kind of trinket, knickknack, and bauble under the sun.

Several hours later, I had countless bags full of pins, patches, keychains, flags, nesting Matryoshka dolls, hand-carved wooden chess sets, a few watches, a couple old Soviet military uniforms, several decorative daggers and knives, and an embarrassing number of oversized Jean-Claude Van Damme movie posters.

As the day wore on, kids slowly trickled off and headed back to campus until, around mid-afternoon, it was just Heath and me left at the market. And that's when I saw it.

The sword to end all swords.

I knew enough about swords to know this one was out of place here. Most of the distinctly Russian-looking swords we'd seen since we'd arrived were curved, single-blade weapons, like the Russian Sabre or the Cossack Shashka. This looked more like a Chinese Tai Chi sword—straight-edged and double-bladed. The blade was not the usual kind of unsharpened stainless steel most souvenir or decorative blades were made of. This had clearly been a working blade at one time, one that had lost its edge but had the capacity to be sharpened. It had an *old* feel to it. The entire scabbard was a whitish-silvery mother-of-pearl that shimmered in the sunlight. It was hands-down the most gorgeous sword I'd ever laid eyes on and would go perfectly with all the other exotic weaponry from China and Thailand I had hanging on my walls back home.

I had to have it.

I began haggling with the vendor, but even though all the souvenirs at the market seemed hilariously underpriced, it quickly became apparent that this one was probably going to be out of my price range. The seller offered us a price of $200 US. I had about $40 left in my wallet. I asked Heath if he had anything on him that I could borrow, promising to pay him back when we got home to the States. He fished around in his pockets and came up with $50 for me. I offered the seller our collective 90 bucks, but he shook his head furiously and refused. With no other options, I apologized and said I'd have to pass.

We started walking away, but the shopkeeper ran up to us and grabbed my arm, pointing at my watch. It was a $15 Seiko from Target. He wanted my watch, Heath's watch, my backpack, and Heath's belt. Those four items, along with the $90, and we had ourselves a sword. He had himself a deal.

To this day, I couldn't tell you how or why Heath went along with it. He just gave up his watch, belt, and his last 50 dollars so that I could bring home a sword. It's not like we were neighbors back home and could take turns displaying it in our rooms. We'd just met on this trip. I didn't even know what state he lived in. We'd just hit it off during orientation back in Miami, and he'd taken me under his wing. It was some next-level generosity to indulge me and trust that I'd somehow pay him back.

With the Purchase of the Century complete—and both of us completely out of money—we decided to call it a day and head back to campus. We made the 15-minute walk back to the nearest subway station and descended the psycho escalator, then plunked ourselves down on a bench in the middle of the subway lobby to see if any stragglers from our team showed up so we could all ride back together. Before long, we recognized a group of familiar faces descending the escalator, and I waved them over with my sparkling new sword.

No sooner had they joined us than a pair of police officers approached our group from the other direction. One of them gestured at my new sword and said something in Russian. I shook my head, indicating we didn't understand, and simply said, "English."

One of the cops spoke something into his radio, and a minute later, another officer appeared beside them. "Excuse me," the new officer greeted us. "Where did you get this sword? May I see it?" Beaming with pride, I handed it to him.

He looked it over admiringly, sliding it halfway out of the scabbard to inspect the blade, then handed it to his colleagues, who both did the same.

When they were all done looking it over, the first officer repeated himself, "Where did you get this?" I couldn't help but notice he showed no inclination of handing it back to me.

"We got it at the big market down the street," I said, pointing vaguely towards the escalators we'd come down.

The officer nodded and conferred with his two colleagues for a moment before turning back to us. "Okay, you will take us there now."

I looked at Heath quizzically, who just shrugged back at me. What else were we going to do?

We told our fellow team members to head back to campus without us, assured them we'd be fine, and told them to let the leaders know we were probably an hour behind them. Curfew was 6 p.m.. It was currently 4:30.

Then, with the English-speaking cop still clinging tightly to my prized possession, Heath and I led the three officers back to the same market we'd left not 45 minutes ago. Or at least where it *had* been 45 minutes ago.

Now, there was nothing there.

We were standing in the middle of an alley that had been lined with vendors the entire length less than an hour ago. Now, the whole street was deserted. It was like a scene from a movie. Everyone had rolled up their wares, pulled the shutters, dropped the awnings, and wheeled off their carts like nobody had ever been here.

"I swear, this street was packed a little while ago," I told the officers.

Heath nodded in agreement. "Yeah, it most definitely was."

The three men looked skeptical, not that I blamed them.

"You are *sure* this is the street where you found this?" the first officer inquired once more, waving my sword at me just in case I'd forgotten what souvenir we were all discussing.

I'm pretty freaking sure.

"Yeah," I told him, "I'd bet money on it."

If I had any money left.

The officer thought for a moment and then said, "Okay, so now we will take you back to the subway."

And give my sword back, thank you very much.

I would not be getting my precious sword back, thank you very much. Instead, the officers walked us back to the subway station, down to the lobby where they'd first approached us, and then marched us through a security door beside the main ticketing booth. Now we were in the backrooms that were off-limits to the regular subway crowd. We went down a long, dingy corridor, down a couple flights of stairs, through several more winding hallways, and finally stopped in front of a massive sliding door that looked designed to stop a tank. One of the cops hit an intercom button on the wall, a horn sounded, a red light over the door flashed, and the giant steel door slid open.

And just like that, three police officers and my sword led Heath and me into Russian jail.

The first thing they did was confiscate all of our souvenirs. I didn't see where they took everything, and I had no idea if we'd ever see it again. I'd never been arrested in my home country, let alone Russia, so I had no idea how this was supposed to work.

You know exactly how this works, you idiot. You've seen movies—they're about to ship you off to a gulag in Siberia.

They didn't fingerprint us, take our mugshots, or do any of the other things I knew from television. Instead, they walked us down a sterile white hallway to a submarine-type airlock door with a giant rotating handle that looked like a steering wheel. The guard spun the wheel until the door swung outward, motioned us inside, and then shut the door behind us without a word.

Now, I know what you must be thinking: *Oh my gosh, you poor kids! You must have been terrified! This must've been the most horrifying experience of your entire lives!*

Please push that nonsense out of your head, *tout de suite.*

On the contrary, this was officially the Single Greatest Moment of my life! Getting thrown into a Russian jail—and potentially sent off to Siberia—was straight out of the books or movies! This was Hardy Boys stuff. It was *Goonies* stuff. It was straight-up Indiana Jones stuff!

This was a PROPER adventure!

I was so giddy at the prospect of all the potential impending Hollywood plotlines that it took me a full five minutes to notice that Heath looked about ready to wretch and/or pass out. He'd gone a weird color combination of white and slightly green and appeared to be in shock.

I quickly guided him to a bench, made him sit, and told him to lean over and put his head between his knees. That should get some blood flowing back into his thinker. Once I was sure Heath wasn't going to pass out on me, I turned my attention to our new digs.

Our cell—or whatever it was—was a long, narrow room with a single bench running the length of one side, a single toilet and sink opposite the bench at the back. Everything, from the walls to the floor to the ceiling to the bench and door, appeared to be coated in a layer of white paint. There were no windows—not so much as a peephole in the door. The ceiling was about 10 feet high, with an industrial-sized air duct running the length of it. I quickly determined that was how we were going to escape.

Pleased that our Russki captors had not scrimped on the requisite escape-air-duct trope that was so vital to every proper prison break, I shared the good news with Heath. He didn't share my enthusiasm.

Understandable. I suppose getting tossed into a foreign jail wasn't everyone's idea of winning the lottery.

Or maybe the problem was that Heath simply hadn't processed the specific logistics of our escape yet. So, I explained it to him: *If he stood up on the bench and then I got up on his shoulders, I could probably reach the air duct and haul myself up on top of it into that 12-inch gap between the top of the duct and the ceiling. I would just lay up there in hiding until someone came to check on us. They would open the door, only see one person inside, and walk all the way to the back of the room to make sure nobody was hiding behind the toilet. While they were back there peeking into cracks, I would silently drop from the top of the air duct [like a ninja!] and dart out the wide-open door.*

That's exactly as far as I'd gotten with the plan, and in hindsight, it seems like I'd possibly left out a few key elements. To Heath's credit, we made it as far as Step 2: *I got on his shoulders*—before realizing there was absolutely no way for me to pull myself from there up onto the air duct. Our escape plans were dashed.

This was turning out to be the worst prison stint ever. Not because conditions were *bad*, but because they were hopelessly *boring*. Since there were no windows or clocks, and we'd both given away our watches to acquire the sword, there was no way to gauge time. Had we been in here 20 minutes? Two hours? Did anyone know we were in here? When were we getting out? *Were* we getting out? How long was the train ride to Siberia?

We couldn't hear any sounds from outside the room. No guards. No fellow inmates. Nothing. Just a silent, white, concrete cell, where time stood perfectly still. It was maddening.

After what felt like an eternity, an idea popped into my head, and I decided to try something: I took off a shoe and banged it against the door in the familiar "Shave and a Haircut—two bits" pattern. Within seconds, a guard came and opened the door.

"Da?" he asked, staring down at me.

I quickly opened my wallet and pulled out my driver's permit, holding it out to his face so he could clearly see that whatever it was, it was foreign. "American!" I told him, "VIP!"

His eyes registered surprise, and he motioned for me to follow him out into the hallway. I looked back at Heath and gave him a thumbs up.

The guard led me around on a hunt until he found who he was looking for—a guard who spoke English. He said something to his colleague, then motioned for me to pull out my "VIP card" again. Once again, I waved it and declared, "American, VIP!"

The new guard looked me over and replied, "It is nice to meet you, American comrade. How may I help you?"

I had prepared to tell him the one and only fact I knew [from television] about us Americans when we get arrested: that we are entitled to a phone call.

I knew Miranda Rights weren't a thing in Russia, and I also knew phone calls weren't a Miranda Right anyway, but there was no harm in trying. What did I have to lose?

"I'm an American VIP," I said firmly, "and I know my Miranda Rights. I get to make a phone call."

The guard looked nonplussed. "You want to make a phone call? Of course, you may." He said something in Russian, and the guard who'd brought me out of my cell led me down the hall to a private room containing a single desk with a phone. He flipped the light on, ushered me inside, then pulled the door shut and left me alone.

Surely it can't be this easy.

I wasn't about to start arguing. Instead, I started debating who to call. The US Embassy? The Consulate? Teen Mania headquarters? Chuck Norris?

I finally decided to call Mom.

Moscow was eight hours ahead of Pittsburgh, and my best guess was that it was sometime between 5-6 p.m. where we were. That meant 1-2 a.m. for Mom. She always turned her ringer off at night, so I didn't expect her to answer. I put through the collect call and was surprised to hear her actually pick up on the other end.

"Hi, my guy!" she said in her familiar greeting. "To what do I owe this honor in the middle of the night when everyone is supposed to be fast asleep?"

"Oh . . . um . . . well . . . I, uh, got arrested, and now I'm in jail in Moscow."

My mom had never been known for her laid-back, even-keeled approach to out-of-the-blue, earth-shattering news, of which this middle-of-the-night revelation that her 15-year-old son had just been incarcerated in Russia qualified. She instantly had a million questions, none of which were of the helpful variety. *What had I done? Were they treating us well? Was I getting plenty to eat? What was the name of the jail?*

She didn't give me a chance to answer any of the questions she was firing off a mile a minute. I couldn't even get a word in edgewise. I just sat there quietly for several minutes with the phone up to my ear while she frantically talked herself in circles in panic mode. But while she was babbling on, I suddenly remembered that Victor had written down the phone number to our dorm on the same sheet he'd written the directions to the market. Just in case we got lost.

At that moment, I heard the guard's footsteps start down at the end of the hallway and realized I might not have much time left in the phone room. "Mum, I love you, but I think I hear the guard coming. I have to go!"

I hung up the phone.[32]

---

[32] While some kids called home every week because they got homesick or had worrying parents, regular check-ins weren't our family's style. After we all said our *goodbyes* at the airport, the next planned chat was when we got picked back up at the airport. The sword incident occurred about halfway through our 6-week trip, and it didn't dawn on me to give Mom a courtesy call to let her know I was okay once I'd gotten out of jail. As she tells it, I just yelled, "Mum, they're coming. I have to go!" and then hung up and left her in the dark for three weeks, wondering what became of me. She later confessed that this incident prompted her to explore the legalities of justifiable homicide.

I quickly dug Victor's directions out of my pocket and dialed the number at the bottom. After a few rings, an American voice answered. "Hello?"

I forgot to ask who I was speaking to. "Hey, this is Shane from Team 2. Can you please find out if our translator, Victor, is there and put him on the phone? Thanks!"

A few minutes later, he picked up. "This is Victor."

"Hey, Victor, it's Shane," I said casually. "Heath and I are in jail, and I'm not sure what's happening. Any chance you could help us?" I explained to him what had happened and gave him our last known whereabouts—the subway station near the market he'd written down the directions to. After telling him everything I knew, Victor told us to sit tight and to try not to worry. He would do what he could.

I hung up the phone, opened the door, and waited for the guard to take me back to our cell. On the way back, I happened to catch a glimpse at a clock on the wall—7:15.

After what felt like days, our cell door opened, and Heath and I were led to a conference room with an executive table in the center. Seated at the table were Victor, one of our assistant team leaders, and an older gentleman I didn't recognize.

The guard motioned for us to sit, and then Victor introduced us to the stranger with him—our attorney. The man spoke broken English, so Victor translated as he explained the situation to us:

As it turned out, the sword we'd been apprehended within the subway was no garden-variety souvenir for tourists. It was a genuine, 19th-century cultural artifact that had recently disappeared from the Kremlin Armoury Museum and had thus been placed on a national watch list.

I was furious.

Not that some underhanded street vendor had taken my watch, backpack, and the last of my cash for some illicit, black-market contraband—that didn't even cross my mind. I was furious that I'd most likely gotten *myself* noticed by waving it over my head like an idiot trying to get our friends' attention.

If I'd only waved my arms instead, I'd probably be back at the dorm sleeping right now with my new sword![33]

Since we were teenagers on a mission trip and obviously not international arms dealers, the whole thing was chalked up as an honest mistake, and we were going to be released. But they were going to require us to sign a confession before they let us go, which I was more than happy to do. If I wasn't going to get to return home with an actual Russian Empire sword, at least I'd have the street cred of having signed a confession admitting to possessing one stolen from the Kremlin.

It was an acceptable consolation prize.

We got back to campus around two in the morning and found our two team leaders waiting up for us. They told us to go straight to bed and that they'd debrief us first thing in the morning. By "us," they meant "me" because the next morning they sat me down alone for a come-to-Jesus talk.

Teen Mania was a Christian youth organization—it was explained to me—and as such, their summer mission trips did not attract the type of youth that anyone in their right mind would typically describe as "troubled." In fact, in the seven years and more than 20 trips they'd both led, they'd never had to reprimand another missionary teen for so much as breaking curfew. But now, in the span of just three weeks, I had managed to hire a prostitute whose pimp was ready to tear our team leader's arms off, landed a fellow traveler in the hospital with a police-induced concussion, and gotten tossed in jail for walking around with weapons stolen from a Soviet museum. Nobody at Teen Mania had ever been trained on how to deal with the level of nonsense I seemed to attract.

None of it had been intentional, of course, but I apologized nonetheless, vowing to be on my best behavior for the remainder of the trip.

I very nearly almost made it.

---

[33] Such is the thought process of a 15-year-old. It would probably be 20 years later before it dawned on me that getting caught with it on the subway immediately after leaving the market was infinitely more fortuitous than if they'd discovered it in my luggage at the airport, trying to take it out of the country.

DESPERADOS

Our itinerary in Russia was to spend four weeks in Moscow, a full week in Saint Petersburg, and the final week back in Moscow. Now, we were on the tail end of our stint in the gorgeous, cultural mecca formerly known as Leningrad and had the day off.

Our team leaders had booked an outing for the entire team to do together: we were going to catch an afternoon performance of the "World Famous Saint Petersburg Something Something on Ice," which I'd never heard of before. How famous could it possibly be?

This better not suck.

The stupid ice ballet—or whatever it was—was inside a huge facility about the size of a professional hockey arena. Our group occupied eight full rows near center ice, less than a dozen rows back from the ice itself. I settled in next to Heath, prepared to be bored out of my mind, and waited for this frozen ballet snooze-fest to commence. Then the lights came down, the music came up, and the greatest thing I'd ever witnessed came flying out onto the ice from the far tunnel.

The first act was three men dressed in traditional Mongolian garb, and they were each spinning a *bō* staff, the weapon of choice of my favorite Teenage Mutant Ninja Turtle.[34]

For as long as I could remember, the *bō* had been my favorite martial arts weapon, and learning how to twirl one was up near the top of my teenage bucket list, sandwiched right in between "get a yellow Lamborghini Countach" and "marry Cindy Crawford."

Whatever concerns I'd had about sitting through two insufferable hours of *Tchaikovsky on Ice* were immediately waylaid by these three whirling dervishes and their impeccable ninjitsu choreography. I was completely mesmerized. And, in that moment, there was room for only a single thought in my brain: *I must find those guys and get them to teach me their secrets!*

For every boy since the invention of the universe, every stick, pole, broom, mop, bat, pipe, and wrapping paper tube under the sun was a potential *bō* to be spun, twirled, waved around (and ideally whacked against a friend's head). But there was a technique to it. Much like

---

[34] Bonus points for knowing his name is Donatello, and he wears the purple mask. Double bonus points for knowing that *bō* is actually the Japanese word for *staff*, so "*bō* staff" literally means "*staff* staff" and is therefore redundant.

nunchucks, the *bō* could be enthusiastically flourished by any amateur so as to look vaguely threatening to someone who didn't know any better, but actually spinning them as intended required quite a bit of practice and proper technique. I had never learned the technique.

We are finally going to remedy that today.

The Ice Ninja performance was over in less than three minutes, and then another act came out, and for a million-gazillion dollars, I couldn't tell you what it—or any other act that afternoon—was. The only thing that mattered right then and there was that *there were three expert* bō *masters under the same roof as me!* And I was going to find them.

After an hour or so, the lights came up, and a voice announced over the loudspeakers in Russian and English that there would now be a 15-minute intermission.

"C'mon!" I yelled at Heath. "Let's go find those guys!"

Heath sighed in resignation and rolled his eyes. "Fine, lead the way."

I figured we needed to get as low down into the building as we could—surely that's where the dressing rooms or locker rooms would be. We made our way out to the main concourse and then started scanning for elevators or stairs. There were plenty that went up, but none that appeared to go down. As far as the general public was concerned, this was the bottom floor.

Obviously, it couldn't be, which just meant that we had to keep looking. We walked up and down the concourse, testing any doors we came to to see what was on the other side. Before long, we found one that opened into a stairwell. We ducked inside and followed it down two flights to the bottom. Emerging from the stairwell, we found ourselves in a narrow, carpeted hallway lined with office doors. Probably an administrative level. At the end of the hallway were a pair of elevators. And on the wall between them was a single button: *down.*

We called the elevator, stepped on, and observed that there were two floors below us to choose from. I picked the bottom one. When we reached the bottom, the elevator opened into a barren, concrete hallway that curved around the wall into the distance. Twenty yards to our left, another hallway bisected the one we were standing in. We approached it and turned the corner. *Now* we were getting somewhere!

The hallway we turned into was also concrete and bare, though a red carpet was rolled down the length of it, dead-ending at a massive set of ornate double doors. Two hulking giants in three-piece suits and sunglasses stood on either side of the door. There was a faint sound of classical music in the air.

The second we rounded the corner and spotted the behemoth guards at the other end, Heath nudged me and whispered, "Okay, I'm thinking we should probably turn around."

"No way," I whispered back. "Let's go see what's down there."

"With those guards standing right there? Are you out of your mind?' (I was, probably. But Heath didn't need to know that.)

I was still feeling my oats from securing phone privileges in jail by flashing my driver's permit. If it had worked once, why not try it again? "Pull out your license," I told Heath. "Follow my lead."

And with that, we marched down the hallway, straight up to the towering guards blocking the door (as we closed the distance, I couldn't help but notice they were both wearing earpiece radios as well), and held up our driving credentials. "Americans, VIP!" I declared in the most commanding voice I could muster, which wasn't much.

Without even taking them out of our hands or leaning in for a closer inspection, both guards turned simultaneously, pulled open the double doors, and gestured us inside.

It was still the middle of July, and Heath and I were both dressed like normal teenage tourists on summer vacation: athletic shorts, t-shirts, and sneakers. Decked out as we were, we stepped through the doorway . . . and into a cocktail party.

There were maybe 40 people milling about what appeared to be a swanky lounge area. There were men in suits, women in elegant dresses, and a number of people in the kind of eccentric ensembles that announced they were almost certainly celebrities. In the far corner, a man in a tuxedo sat behind a baby grand piano.

I guess that was the music we'd heard wafting down the hall.

I had no idea what we'd just stumbled into. I also didn't care. Because on the far side of the room, in an animated conversation with a small group of people, stood one of the guys from the opening performance. He was still wearing his Mongolian warrior costume.

Jackpot!

This is what I'd come down here for. Unfortunately, I had just exhausted the entirety of my plan. I had no idea what to do next. Walking directly up to the guy and smiling seemed like a bad idea.

Dressed as we were, I didn't need any help looking like a crazy person. And I definitely didn't need a *ninja master* thinking I was looking for a fight. And so I just stood there like an idiot, dumbfounded, looking around the room and praying for a sign.

There!

On the near side of the room, next to the bar area, leaning against the wall, was a push broom. Just a normal, wooden-handled push broom like we used every day in shop class—the kind where the handle unscrewed from the base of the broom, leaving you with a perfect . . .

I didn't pause to think or question. The Universe had just presented me with a gift horse, and I wasn't about to start looking around in its mouth. Or something to that effect. I walked over to the broom, unscrewed it from its base, walked up behind the Mongolian ninja master, and tapped him on the shoulder.

He turned to look at me, did a doubletake, and appeared confused, unsure what was happening. I made a conscious effort not to smile. *"Privet! Rad tebya videt."* It was one of the few phrases I'd learned in Russian—*Hello, nice to meet you.*

I held the broomstick up in front of me and pointed at him. "You—" I pantomimed spinning the stick. "Show me—" I said in English, pointing at myself. He was staring at me intently, as if trying to solve a puzzle.

This wasn't going well.

I began to repeat the same series of gestures that he hadn't understood the first time when he suddenly appeared to get it. A look of realization flashed across his face, and he nodded. I offered the broomstick to him, and this time he took it out of my hands. Taking a few steps backward, he motioned for everyone around him to back up and clear some space, and then launched into a short routine—the staff an almost invisible blur of speed. When he was finished, half the room burst into applause.

He started to hand the stick back to me, but I shook my head and indicated I wanted him to show me in slow motion the hand-over-hand technique that generated all the speed. And for the next several minutes, I got a personal tutoring session on the weapon I'd fanboyed over for years from a bona fide *master.*

I was in heaven.

I was so enthralled that I completely disregarded the first tap I felt on my shoulder. Whatever Heath needed, it could wait. I slowly started the technique again and felt another tap.

Not now, Heath. I'm about to get the hang of this.

A third tap came, and I snapped without even turning to look at Heath. "Dude, chill out! We can leave in just a second."

The voice that responded did not belong to Heath. "Who *are* you?" It was a deep, heavily accented Russian voice.

I did not have time to start meeting people. I needed to milk every last drop of tutelage I could get from this moment before we had to return to our seats. "My name's Shane. It's great to meet you," I said hurriedly, before focusing yet again on my stick.

I was about to begin the technique again when the hand fell on my shoulder once more and rested there, heavy. "Who *are* you, mister Shane?"

Now I was annoyed. This private *bō* lesson was the pinnacle of my entire existence—my *raison d'être*—and some pushy weirdo behind me was trying to get all existential with me. Or maybe he was hitting on me? No telling what kind of weird stuff some of these oligarchs were into. I decided it was probably time for us to bail.

Ignoring the creepy guy behind me, I thanked my new instructor profusely, *"Spasibo, spasibo!"* handed him the broomstick, and made a beeline for Heath, who was still standing in the middle of the room where I'd left him.

"Happy now?" he inquired.

"Oh my gosh, man. This made my entire trip!"

"Well, congratulations then. Now, let's get back to our seats before they send someone off looking for us."

And with that, we retraced our steps through the bowels of the arena, up to the main concourse, back to our group's section, and squeezed past our fellow team members to our seats in the center of the row, just as lights began to dim.

Perfect timing.

It was about five minutes into the second half of the show when we noticed a bit of commotion down at the end of our row. Standing in the aisle, a contingent of five or six men in dark suits were whispering with two ushers, who had pulled out pocket flashlights and were sweeping them up and down our section. They appeared to be looking for someone. Curious, most of our group turned our attention from the ice to the impromptu search party happening in the aisle to our right.

After a few moments of scanning, one of the flashlight beams came to rest on my chest. The other one settled on Heath. One of the men in the suits pointed directly at us and then motioned with his finger for us to come over. Slowly, we stood up and started squeezing over bent legs back to the aisle. Out of the corner of my eye, I caught our team leader—two rows back—drop his face into his palm and shake his head. I knew that expression well: *What have they done now?*

Heath and I reached the aisle and were soon joined by our disgusted team leader and Victor.

"What's going on?" our team leader demanded.

The men said something to Victor, who relayed it to us. "They want to know who he is," he said, nodding at me.

"Why? Did he do something?" our team leader wanted to know. "Shane, did you *do* something?"

Possibly. A good rule of thumb was—when in doubt—I had probably done something.

The men said a few more words to each other, and then Victor turned and stared at us, puzzled. "They are saying Mikhail Gorbachev wants to know who he is," he said as he nodded in my direction once more.

Mikhail Gorbachev?

The former leader of the Soviet Union?!?

Why? How? Wha—?

I had no explanation.

Flummoxed, I assured Victor I had no clue what they were talking about. The men chatted another minute, and then Victor asked, "How did you get into the bottom-level club?"

"Um, well, we were just walking around and found it by accident, and then we showed our IDs, and they just let us in," I answered matter-of-factly.

"Wait, what club are you talking about?" our team leader chimed in. What's the 'bottom level?'"

Victor went back and forth with the men in suits another round, then finally turned back and gave us all the explanation we were so desperately seeking.

"There is a very exclusive VIP club at the bottom of this building. *Very* exclusive. Very few people even know it's down there, so it's unclear how they found it or how they got in. There is a very strict dress code. These men said Shane and Heath entered the club—in violation of the dress code—and then Shane found a pole and began roughhousing with one of the show's performers. They appeared to be good friends. Mr. Gorbachev is in attendance downstairs and observed all of this. He was curious who this is," he said, tapping me on the forehead.

"So, he sent over this man right here," Victor continued, nodding at the Suit still holding the flashlight, "to inquire about Shane's identity. But Shane dismissed him several times and then left."

Oh boy.

It hadn't been a creepy oligarch trying to cart me off to a bathhouse. Mikhail-freaking-Gorbachev had sent over his personal assistant to find out who the heck the foreign teenager in the Umbro shorts was and why he was waving a broom handle around their Top Secret, Ultra VIP club. And I'd just casually waved him off like he was a homeless guy trying to squeegee my windshield at a red light.

I was pretty sure that personally insulting the former leader of the Soviet Union wasn't anyone's idea of "being on my best behavior" after getting out of jail, so now it was time for the million-dollar question:

How much trouble was I in?

Amazingly, inexplicably, I was in . . . *none.*

Gorbachev and his men had been amused more than anything, not offended. They came looking for us purely out of curiosity. Were we the rambunctious children of some famous celebrity? The sons of diplomats? Some obscenely wealthy oligarch's spoiled grandkids they should be pampering and pretending to tolerate?

Nope. None of that.

Just an idiot teenage tourist from America with a one-track mind for Ninja Turtle weaponry. End of story.

Did I learn a lesson in all of this?

Absolutely not.

Wait, no. I learned that I had an uncanny aptitude for getting into implausibly surreal situations, and an equal or greater knack for getting back out of them mostly unscathed. Even on an international scale.

Impersonating rock stars in China for a few days would be par for the course.

I think on some level, you do your best things when you're a little off-balance, a little scared. You've got to work from mystery, from wonder, from not knowing.

– Willem Dafoe

Courage is knowing it might hurt, and doing it anyway. Stupidity is the same. And that's why life is hard.

– Jeremy Goldberg

Flying Blind

OCTOBER 26, 1999: 2 DAYS TO SHOWTIME

stared out the window of the plane and watched the ground fall away beneath us. Within minutes, we were out over the Atlantic Ocean, heading north for New York. As promised, Chris had driven us down to the Ft. Lauderdale airport, where he planned to be waiting when we returned.

If we returned.

Our first stop was a layover at LaGuardia Airport. We'd rendezvous there with my mom and the rest of our bandmates from Pittsburgh before continuing on to Beijing. Touching down three hours later, we collected our carry-ons and set out on a scavenger hunt through the airport for the rest of our team.

After 20 minutes of winding through terminals, Mom spotted us and waved us over to their luggage encampment. The obligatory hugs and kisses ensued, and then she turned and began making introductions.

Dean Baktay, our lead singer, was 35 and looked exactly like a high school math teacher. I'd been mildly acquainted with Dean from church back in Pittsburgh many years ago—he and his wife had come over for one or two of Mom's Christmas parties—and vaguely recalled seeing him on stage with the worship team on a few occasions. I knew our church didn't exactly hold *X-Factor*-level tryouts to score a spot on the worship team, so I didn't know if that was a good sign or bad.

Budd Kelly, our bass player, was 40, making him the de facto godfather of the band. The best way to describe Budd would be: picture a bass player. Got it? Whatever you're picturing, you're probably right. Skinny as a rail with straight black hair halfway down to his waist, Budd was the guy you'd take one look at and then be shocked to find out he *wasn't* a bass player.

Dean and Budd had toured around Europe together playing music back in the 80's. When Mom called Dean and asked him to go find some musicians who were up to this task, Budd had been his first call.

His second call had been to Jeremy Diehl, our drummer and the youngest of the group at 19. Dressed in baggy pants with tons of zippers, a wallet on a long chain that hung by his side, a baseball cap, and a Rage Against the Machine t-shirt—he looked the part too. It probably didn't hurt that he had a pair of beat-up drumsticks poking out of his back pocket.

For our part, Gavin and I had decided the night before to test the highly unscientific hypothesis that 90% of being a rock star was *looking* like one and had dressed in our best approximation of what that might be: ripped jeans, leather jacket, rings on every finger, and sunglasses indoors. It was our notion of what Axl Rose would wear if he could only afford Goodwill. We had every intention of staying in character for the entire week, regardless of how uncomfortable and impractical these get-ups were for a 14-hour flight. This was method acting at its finest, and we were fully committed.

All told, we did a pretty fair job of resembling a collection of musicians. What we definitely did *not* do was resemble a collection of musicians from the same band. Or from the same genre. Or even from the same era, for that matter. We looked like Mom had just walked into a random Guitar Center on a Saturday afternoon, collared whatever five guys happened to be standing closest to the front door, and told them they were now a band. Just as long as everyone could *play*, I supposed it didn't matter.

Once all the introductions had been made and pleasantries exchanged, conversation turned to how everyone's rehearsals had progressed. Gavin had brought along an acoustic guitar as a carry-on, so we decided to pop it open and go over a few spots that required group harmonies. We formed a circle and sat down. And there on the floor in the middle of LaGuardia Airport, less than an hour before we were to board our flight for Beijing, the "Newsboys" had our first practice as a full band.

Fifteen hours later, we were in a practice circle again, this time in Beijing. And we had a small problem. Checking in for our connecting flight to Changsha, Gavin discovered his boarding pass was gone. He'd had it in his hand coming off the plane, which meant he'd dropped it somewhere between there and here, which meant it was . . . somewhere in the Beijing airport, which was only slightly smaller than Rhode Island.

"Well, let's go retrace our steps and look for it," Mom said. It was "only" a 20-minute walk back to our arrival gate—through thousands of people—so this was most likely a fool's errand. We were looking for a needle in a haystack. But what other option did we have? My guess was that it was probably stuck to the bottom of some businessman's shoe and halfway to the Hyatt by now.

Mom, Gavin, and I hoofed it back to the gate, scanning the concourse floor the entire way, to no avail. Then we *re*-retraced our steps back the way we'd just come with even lower expectations. Mom spotted a guy standing off to the side of the flow of traffic, sporting a black blazer but not carrying a suitcase, and decided that combo meant he must work at the airport. Because if you're at the airport and don't have a suitcase, you work there. Everyone knows that. Mom walked over to him while we waited impatiently and asked, "Do you speak English?"

"Yes," he replied.

"Do you work here?" she inquired.

"I'm sorry, I don't work here. Can I help you with something?"

"Do you know where I would need to go or who I would need to talk to if we lost a boarding pass?"

"Is this it?" The man reached into his blazer and pulled an errant ticket out of his inner pocket.

Mom looked at the name on the pass: *Gavin McLaughlin.*

"Yes, that *is* it!" Mom exclaimed. "How did you get this?"

The man shrugged and handed it to her. "I saw it on the ground and picked it up."

She ran back over to us, waving it in the air. "Found it! That guy in the black jacket had it."

Of course he did.

It didn't appear her ongoing streak of airport dumb luck was in any danger of running out.

"Now don't either of you try to convince *me* God's not pulling the strings here!"

I had to admit, those were pretty long odds. Of the 150,000 passengers that traversed the monolithic Beijing airport on a daily basis, Mom randomly selected the *one* guy who'd stumbled upon Gavin's boarding pass."

It was possible she wasn't completely insane.

By the time we made it back to our gate, it was too late for Gavin to check in for the connection. He was going to have to wait for the next available flight. I volunteered to stay behind with him.

It was a two-and-a-half-hour flight to Changsha, and the next flight out didn't leave for three hours. That meant the group going ahead of us would be on the ground in Changsha for about 30 minutes before we even took off.

What would they be walking into? Would there be a welcoming party, or would they be on their own to collect all their belongings and find their way to the hotel? Would we even be able to cram all our gear into a taxi if we had to? These were all questions nobody had bothered to ask, let alone answer, before we'd left. "We'll figure all that out when we get there," Mom had offered.

We'll figure it out.

Gavin and I watched the rest of our group make their way to the departing gate—the same one we'd be leaving from later that afternoon—then found ourselves a table at the nearest café. We ordered a couple coffees, pulled out a travel chessboard, and spent the next couple hours passing the time until the armed guards from the beginning of our story approached us, questioned us, and then led us away.

he officers had just marched us through a private doorway marked SECURITY: NO ENTRY and down a narrow hallway that stopped dead at an imposing steel door. One of the guards took a badge out of his jacket and pressed it to a security pad on the wall.

Where were they taking us?

My heart threatened to pound out of my chest as I had a sudden flashback to Moscow. At least in Russia we'd had the luxury of being blissfully unaware that we'd done anything wrong while being herded through the labyrinthian subway backrooms to our jail cell. Now, I was acutely aware that we almost definitely deserved to end up wherever it was they were taking us.

Moments later, the door swung open from the other side. It opened into a stairwell, and the officers led us down several flights until we arrived at the bottom floor and another steel door. The same officer placed the same badge against a matching security pad. The door made a clicking sound, and the officer opened it for us, motioning with his head for us to go through. I glanced over at Gavin. He didn't say a word, but his face said that he was either trying to pass a kidney stone or he'd suddenly contracted a bout of swine flu.

Instead of an interrogation room, torture chamber, or rat-infested dungeon, the security door opened into the bowels of the airport, a massive, sprawling complex of conveyor belts, maintenance trucks, and hundreds of workers. Luggage carts darted everywhere, carrying their payloads of suitcases to or from their assigned planes. To our right was an empty golf cart. One of the officers motioned for Gavin and me to climb in the back rear-facing seats, while two more hopped in the front and started it up. A third officer stepped up on the rear foot platform, holding onto the roof for support and blocking our exit should either of us attempt to jump off the back and make a run for it, which I was definitely contemplating.

The cart took off, expertly weaving through the maze of people and machinery. The ride was actually kind of fun. I mean, if you could get past that whole "abducted by the Communists" bit. We exited the bay doors into the sunshine and zoomed out onto the tarmac. I couldn't begin to fathom where we were going. Eventually, it pulled to a stop next to a small puddle-jumper plane that didn't look much bigger than a private corporate jet. A mobile stairway led up to the main door. At the top of the stairway stood two armed soldiers at attention.

The officer driving our cart motioned for us to exit and then pointed at the stairs: "This is your plane." Once again, it was not a suggestion.

I didn't know what was happening or why, but none of the scenarios flashing through my head were ideal. This was most definitely not "our plane." *Our plane* was parked back at the terminal with the rest of the civilian aircraft, a big "China Airways" logo painted down the side of it. Gate D23, I think it was. *Our plane* was one you boarded via those jetway loading bridges connected to the gate whose number matched our boarding pass. *Our plane* was absolutely not some unmarked jet a quarter mile from the terminal, crawling with heavily armed soldiers who had no interest in boarding passes. But being out here didn't give us very many options, so Gavin and I took a deep breath and climbed the stairs.

The plane sat about 40 people, and every seat was filled except for two in the first row. As I waited for Gavin to stow his backpack, I quickly surveyed the other passengers—every one of them in military garb or black suits that said they were with the government. There were a handful of officers whose shoulder epaulets proclaimed them three- or four-star generals. By the looks of it, we were on a plane with an upper-level contingent of the Chinese Communist Party. I sat down beside Gavin and whispered one instruction into his ear: "Don't say a *single word* the entire duration of this flight."

By this point, I wasn't even convinced the plane we were on was headed for Changsha. A scenario—a very ugly scenario—had crept into my mind, and the longer we were in the air, the more I became convinced of its reality: the group ahead of us had arrived in Changsha and had been apprehended going through Customs when they turned out not to be the group of people the Chinese were expecting to show up. The Customs agents had notified the Beijing airport to be on the lookout for the two remaining members who were planning to catch the next flight out.

This would explain the three officers huddled together in the airport, stealing glances at us. It would explain why we had been escorted out of the terminal by members of the military. And it would certainly explain why we now found ourselves not on the commercial airliner we were scheduled to board, but on this tiny craft filled with high-ranking government personnel.

Our group had been busted before we'd even made it out of the airport, and now The Government was showing up to "make an example" out of us. There would probably be a huge press conference of some sort.

What did you think was going to happen screwing around with the CCP, you idiot? Play stupid games, win stupid prizes.

They'd probably trot us out in front of the cameras and maybe force us to read some kind of contrived, prepared statement acknowledging our crimes and guilt. And then what? Prison? Torture? Execution? Or would we be lucky enough to merely get expelled from the country and barred forever? I hoped it would be the latter, but I wasn't feeling terribly convinced. I suddenly noticed I was sweating profusely.

I looked over at Gavin, who looked uncharacteristically damp as well. He was sitting up straight as a rail, clenching both armrests as if we were experiencing a pocket of major turbulence, of which there was currently none.

There was a surreal quality to the flight, like the kind of dream you don't want to end, where you find yourself disappointed when you finally wake up and confront the dreary reality that you didn't actually find buried treasure and can't actually fly. Not that this flight was *enjoyable* by any means—it was whatever the opposite of that is. It was that I wanted the plane to stay in the sky forever because touching down would be waking up, and whatever was going to happen down there was going to be supremely unpleasant.

There was also an odd sensation of time as we flew—it seemed to simultaneously fly by at light speed and stand perfectly still. Not knowing where you're going, why you're going, or how long it's going to take to get there makes the passage of time interminable. On the other hand, once the plane began its unmistakable decent, it felt like it came entirely too soon. *It was time to face the music,* I thought, smirking at my own ironic, gallows humor pun.

The plane finally touched down and lazily made its way towards the terminal. Out the window, I could see a small crowd of a few dozen people gathered on the tarmac in the distance, along with a row of a dozen or so black sedans and SUVs. As we drew closer, I observed that the crowd was cordoned off behind a length of red ropes and that at least half of the crowd was wearing or holding large, media-style cameras. I spotted at least three TV cameras perched on shoulders. It would seem my worst-case scenario had turned out to be spot-on.

I hate it when I'm right.

The plane came to a halt in front of the gathered crowd. As a stairway was rolled up to the door, a man from the back of the plane made his way down the aisle and stopped at our seats. He was dressed in a black suit and sunglasses and sported an earpiece. China's equivalent of the Secret Service.

The man looked down at us and said, in a tone tip-toeing the line between unfriendly and threatening, "Do not move until everyone else has exited this plane. Do you understand?" We both nodded. Without another word, he went and assumed a position at the front of the plane, hands behind his back, facing all of us.

The doors opened, and our fellow travelers began filing out. I tried catching the crowd's reactions to the disembarking passengers out of my peripheral vision, unwilling to swivel my head even *just a hair* for fear of disobeying Secret Service Guy, who was still frozen to his spot with his gaze trained on us. Oddly, the crowd was displaying no reaction at all to the men disembarking.

As the final passenger exited the plane, Secret Service turned and fell into step behind him. We watched as the entire contingent made their way to the waiting vehicles, climbed in, and inexplicably drove off. The crowd still had not moved.

The only ones left on the plane were the pilot, copilot, and two flight attendants. I wasn't sure if our instructions meant we also had to wait for them to exit before we were allowed to move or not. If we moved and we weren't supposed to, would the crew radio our departed government captors and inform on us? Were the crew members secretly *spies*? *Was this some kind of test?* We had no idea. So, we continued to sit, unmoving.

After several minutes, a puzzled-looking flight attendant came over and said, "Please, if it's not too much trouble . . . please to exit the plane now."

She certainly didn't seem like a spy.

Idiot, that's exactly what a spy would want you to think!

I had a point. I would show these Communist spies that I could not be had so easily. I was onto them and their little spy games. I didn't budge.

A few awkward moments passed, then the attendant cleared her throat and repeated, this time with a hint of concern, "Please, it is necessary you must exit the plane now." She looked uncomfortable.

"Dude, I think she wants us to get off the plane," Gavin whispered out of the corner of his mouth. I was tending to agree and decided to take my chances. We stood, collected our backpacks, thanked our crew members, and stepped off the plane. The waiting crowd below went berserk.

Gavin and I stood frozen at the top of the stairway, trying to make some sense of what was happening. This was the press conference I was sure was coming, but not in any way I'd imagined it. These people—all media folks—were cheering, waving, filming, photographing, and shouting questions over each other. It was like a mini-Beatlemania.

A jovial middle-aged man ran up to the base of the stairs and waved us down excitedly. "Come, come! You come with me now! I take you to hotel!" We descended the stairs.

At the bottom, our host grabbed both of our hands and shook them frantically. Then, remembering his manners, he released our hands and bowed repeatedly. Then, immediately forgetting them again, he grabbed us both in bear hugs. He released and gave a few more frenetic bows, seemingly unsure of the proper greeting etiquette, and determined to try them all on until one fit. Since he wasn't military or carrying a machine gun and marching us off to parts unknown, he could've given us Eskimo kisses for all I cared.

The jovial stranger turned and said something I couldn't understand to the gathered media crowd, which prompted a large round of applause. Then, grabbing both of us by the arms, he turned and led us to our ride, the only vehicle that hadn't departed in the caravan—a black stretch limousine. As we ducked into the limo, Gavin and I gave a big wave to the crowd, eliciting another huge round of cheers and applause.

Inside the limo, our host introduced himself. His name was Mr. Wu, and he was one of the chief organizers of the concerts.[35] Seated next to him was a young man about our age whom Mr. Wu introduced as Adam. He would go everywhere with us while we were in Changsha, serving as our translator. Mr. Wu directed the driver to the terminal, escorted us through a series of private hallways and elevators up to Customs, and then back down to the limo.

As we drove, Mr. Wu and Adam brought us up to speed, filling in all the blanks that had been wreaking havoc on our minds: The city of Changsha had been advertising and promoting the Newsboys concerts for several years at this point, and it was now the biggest news in the entire city. While the group ahead of us had received a welcoming committee of their own, it was a much smaller contingent made up mostly of members of the Cultural Affairs Department. When they showed up a couple members short, the city media got wind of it and turned out to welcome the two stragglers. We'd been redirected from our commercial flight to the one we'd found ourselves on, not because anyone was in trouble, but because that tiny plane would be disembarking on the tarmac, providing ample room to form a welcoming committee and snag some arrival footage for the evening news. The fact that everyone on our flight was military or with the government was merely a coincidence.

Gavin and I slid down into our seats as relief washed over us. We were both emotionally drained. But now we were back on the emotional rollercoaster, going from potential political prisoners to celebrity rock stars in the span of 10 minutes. It was a lot to take in.

I asked how it was that everyone in the city knew about our shows, and Mr. Wu casually pointed out the window. To my horror, I saw a giant banner spanning an entire intersection. At least 60 feet wide, it read, "Welcome Newsboys!" and featured the five faces of the *actual* Newsboys. And it was far from the only one. I counted at least a dozen more intersection-spanning banners en route to the hotel; banners— several stories tall—draped the sides of buildings; and sandwich boards announcing the shows dotted every sidewalk we passed. You couldn't look 50 feet in any direction without being confronted by giant

---

[35] It was only in the research for this book that I realized this was the same Mr. Wu Mom had been corresponding with all those years.

advertisements featuring faces that definitely did not belong to any of us. But if Mr. Wu had noticed that none of the people he'd picked up from the airport were the same people whose likenesses decorated his entire city, he gave no indication. Perhaps Mom was actually right: *we all look alike to them.*

The limo pulled up to the front door of our hotel—a luxurious five-star establishment—and a dozen attendants immediately flocked over to help us unload two medium-sized backpacks. The rest of our luggage and gear had already arrived with the other group on the earlier flight and was waiting for us inside.

We found our bandmates and Mom lounging on couches in the lobby. Everyone was exhausted. I could think of nothing better than to crawl into bed and sleep for two days, so it was disheartening to hear Mr. Wu announce that we should all go freshen up and meet back in the lobby in an hour to go to dinner.

We found our rooms, changed clothes, and then gathered in the room Dean and Budd were sharing to talk strategy and get into our first (and only) band "fight," if you could call it that. Dean started it by pointing out, very sensibly, that our first show was the following evening, and we'd never had a group rehearsal. That was something that we might want to remedy ASAP.

He had a valid point. It wasn't very often you'd find a band disagreeing with the notion that having at least *one* rehearsal under their belt before their first show was kind of important and necessary. But I felt like his priorities were somewhat misplaced. As I saw it, we had a far more pressing issue on our hands that needed to be addressed: whether or not we were all going to adopt fake Australian accents for the rest of the trip.

I'd seen enough spy movies to know that it was usually a trivial misstep that blew someone's cover: an inopportune hand gesture or an improperly used bit of slang. The last thing we needed was to get busted for something as careless as "sounding American."

"Australian accents?" Dean seemed confused. And slightly annoyed once he realized I wasn't joking. From the expression on his face, you'd think I'd just suggested we skip rehearsal to get drunk and do Chinese calligraphy with our toes. He immediately opined this was a silly idea and a ridiculous waste of time.

"Why Australian?" Budd wanted to know. "British accents are great for a band. Or, you know, maybe even German? That would be cool too."

German?

I wasn't sure what was happening. Were we just naming countries we were aware of? Sure, maybe the accents weren't as important as rehearsal, but why did these two seem so oddly confused by the mere suggestion of it?

Gavin, to his credit, saw the impeccable wisdom in my reasoning and was on board. Jeremy didn't care one way or the other. 2-2. We needed a tiebreaker.

It seemed only fair that, since this was my idea, I got to have Jeremy's vote since he wasn't using it. I took it, cast it for the "aye's," and just like that, we were the winners.

Budd seemed a bit skeptical and voiced some concern that this might not actually be how the democratic voting process worked. He and Dean decided to abstain from any further votes or discussions about fake accents. With the two of them out—along with Jeremy—I held a silent run-off vote in my head, winning in a landslide 3-0. Gavin and I would be the only authentic Aussies in our Australian band.

Having reached a verdict, I was suddenly confronted with a mildly inconvenient realization: I didn't actually know how to do an Australian accent. I tried a few phrases out loud, but the closest I could manage was something that sounded vaguely Cockney.

"Dude, you sound like Oliver Twist," Gavin smirked. *"Ello, gov'na!"*

This was going to require some work. I had no frame of reference for the accent other than having seen *Crocodile Dundee* maybe a decade ago. And the only line I could recall from that movie was, "That's not a knife . . . *this* is a knife!"[36] I could at least nail that line in what seemed like a passable accent to my ears. The only problem was that I couldn't foresee a wealth of scenarios that would necessitate an American keyboardist in town to sing about Jesus to be arguing with any locals about the size of cutlery. I didn't even have a knife with me anyway, big

---

[36] Turns out this is another one of those famous movie quotes that everyone remembers slightly wrong. The actual quote was, "That's not a knife. *That's* a knife."

or otherwise. If the situation presented itself, I was going to look like a total idiot. I resolved to buy the first sword I came across.

While I was busy planning how to arm myself with Ming Dynasty weaponry in order to justify the only line of dialogue I could convincingly pull off as an Aussie, the rest of the band had started doing actual band stuff like assembling the setlist and planning tomorrow's rehearsal.

I decided I should probably join them.

Hey man, if we're gonna
wear uniforms, man, you
know, let's everybody wear
something different.
– Anthony "Man" Stoner, *Up in Smoke*

The Newboys

OCTOBER 27, 1999: OPENING NIGHT

The next day we had our first actual rehearsal as an actual band on an actual stage with actual instruments and an actual sound system. And we couldn't have picked a more opportune day for all those actuals to coincide because our first actual performance unveiling our talents to the world was actually that evening.

We were slated to do two performances in Changsha: the first at Hollywood East, the city's largest nightclub (or *discotheque*, as they called it), the second at Changsha's prestigious Hunan Theater the following night. Today's rehearsal was at the club we'd be playing later that evening.

The club itself was large—a two-story affair that appeared to double as an arcade, as retro video games dotted the interior with no apparent rhyme or reason.

Awesome. I've always dreamt of screaming Jesus music at foreign nightclubbers playing Donkey Kong.

The two levels of dance floors were surrounded by stadium seating and a bigger stage than anything I'd ever played on. It was covered in speakers, monitors, and gear racks, with cables of all shapes and sizes littered across the floor. For a million dollars, I couldn't have told you what went where, why, or how—or what any of the equipment actually did. When I'd do little college shows or coffee shops, the setup was pretty straightforward: set up keyboard stand, place keyboard on stand, plug in power cord, plug in audio output cable, start playing. I could go from sidewalk to first verse in three minutes.

It was into this baffling array of stage equipment that we, along with the Chinese hosts assigned to help us, began hauling in the piles of gear we'd shipped over from the States. Several stagehands and sound guys made their way down from the mixing board upstairs and sprang into action—moving, shuffling, stacking, organizing, arranging, rearranging—while we stood around nonchalantly, pretending we understood any of what was happening. To my untrained eye, it looked like a whirlwind of productive activity. To Dean and Budd's more experienced estimations, not a whole lot of anything was being accomplished.

As eventually became apparent, the club's sound guys weren't familiar with the speakers, cables, and racks of various gadgets and doodads we'd brought from home and weren't sure how to integrate them into their club's sound system. But the deeply ingrained Chinese concept of "saving face" would not permit our colleagues to admit to us the embarrassing fact that they had no idea what they were looking at. To acknowledge as much would've been a humiliation.

So, the best thing they could come up with to hide their ignorance was to just keep rearranging everything on the stage, kinda like when a kid doesn't want to eat their vegetables and merely shuffles them around the plate in the hopes of fooling Mom and Dad that some broccoli was going down. Unfortunately, the joke was on them, as Gavin and I knew less about what we'd brought with us than they did.

It was a breathtaking scene to behold, and we were all bearing witness to comedy gold. Five Americans pretending to be a band, hopelessly lost in a sea of equipment we'd never even used once, and trying our best to save face with our Chinese production crew by allowing them to take charge. They, in turn, had no idea what they were taking charge *of* and were trying their best to save face with us by expertly rotating the bewildering array of equipment around the club, which we all took to mean they knew exactly what they were doing.

Forget about crashing and burning because the Communists heard one too many *God* lyrics and cut the power off. At this rate, we'd be lucky just to figure out how to plug any one thing into any other thing on the stage and successfully turn the power on.

It was O. Henry-esque.

Fortunately, Budd came to the rescue.

He probably could've come to the rescue a whole lot sooner, but for that awkward fact that we barely knew each other. We had no idea if there was a pecking order, and if so, what the order might be. Nobody wanted to speak out, step on anyone's toes, or do anything that might be construed as trying to "take charge." Despite being the elder statesman, Budd was the most reserved, soft-spoken, and demure. He wasn't about to suddenly start barking orders.

So, in an effort not to offend anyone, Budd stood politely in the corner, staring at the idiotic scene of frenetic confusion unfolding in front of him until someone happened to ask if he had any ideas or suggestions.

As a matter of fact, he did.

He had all of them.

Turned out ol' Budd was a gearhead with a full recording studio in his basement and several decades' worth of music knowledge hiding under that long hair of his. He began directing the hoopla on the stage, coordinating the sound and lighting guys, cutting and splicing cords and cables until everything we'd brought was tied into everything they'd supplied, putting all of our minds very much at ease.

A short while later, the head of production flashed us a thumbs-up sign, "Okay, everything is good, yes? Please to check your sound now. Okay!"

The five of us made our way to our instrument stations. I powered on my keyboard, selected a meaty synth sound, and hit a power chord. The club's cutting-edge sound system was deafening in the very best possible way—the kind that melted your face off. Playing in my bedroom with just a keyboard amp all those years, I'd never dreamt my humble synth was capable of such a sound.

Perfect.

The entire building immediately descended into sonic anarchy as all five of us simultaneously set about testing the limits of our brand-new setup by diving straight into our favorite riffs from our favorite tunes, which—it cannot be emphasized strongly enough—were not the same tunes.

Budd set the groove with some funkadelic bass line straight out of the '70s, Jeremy launched into a Nirvana drum solo, Gavin hammered out a Dave Matthew's Band lick, and Dean belted out something I didn't recognize, but sounded like Sebastian Bach doing vocal exercises reading a hymnal. I tied it all together with Van Halen's "Jump."

The output approximated the sound of several Super Bowl halftime shows dueling for audio supremacy amidst a squadron of fighter jets crashing into Valhalla. It was pure, unbridled, unadulterated chaos.

And it was glorious.

After a couple minutes of madness, the sound guy indicated that we should stop playing and sound-check our instruments one at a time. This novel approach struck me as immensely practical, and I couldn't wait to get back to Florida and share this new, professional "insider technique" with my other music pals.

Once we were all checked, Dean suggested we run straight through the entire setlist, making notes along the way of what we needed to go back and work on. The show opener was a Newsboys song called "Not Ashamed," and it was one I had some trepidation about Chinese officials paying too close attention to the lyrics of. It started:

I'm not ashamed to let you know
I want the light in me to show
I'm not ashamed to speak the name of Jesus Christ

Not very subtle.

Remember, the Chinese were under the impression that we were a harmless pop/rock band with innocuous lyrics. They were in for a rude awakening before we finished the first verse of the first song in the set. I could already picture Communist Party officials rushing the stage and frantically yanking power cords out of the wall barely a full minute into our show.

Jeremy counted us in with his drumsticks, and I kicked off the opening keyboard riff. The entire band joined in, and it was, surprisingly . . . *good.*

The Newboys

None of us had any idea what to expect from each other or the collective group, so hearing ourselves for the very first time plastered big dopey grins on all our faces as we made wide-eyed looks at each other.

We're actually doing this!

Any concerns I'd had about the quality of musicians I'd be sharing the stage with were squashed instantaneously. Jeremy was a beast on the drums, with clockwork precision and mind-boggling fills. Budd's bass might as well have been plucked straight out of George Clinton's funk band. Dean's vocals belonged in any '80s hair band of your choice—take your pick. And he played guitar, so we'd have two guitarists after all.

How in the world did Mom find these guys?!?

The boys from Pittsburg had definitely done their homework. Mom stood frozen in the middle of the dance floor, beaming as she watched a decade's worth of work materialize right in front of her. When the first song ended, she and everyone else in the club broke into applause. If any of the sound guys understood what we were singing, they didn't give any indication.

It's a good thing we started off on a high note because things quickly went downhill after that. Halfway through the next song, Budd's power went out at his station. Not on just his amp—on everything he'd brought with him.

Though I didn't know it at the time, Budd was one of those musical genius types who could play literally anything. He could've done this gig on the drums, guitar, or keys—whatever. It turned out that the keyboard was actually his main instrument as well, but he'd volunteered to play bass because that's what Dean and Jeremy needed for their rehearsal time in Pittsburgh. But since bass players are notoriously relegated to the back, he'd worked up a song showcasing his versatility that had him pulling double duty on lead vocals and keys. He'd brought along a full-sized keyboard of his own, along with three sound-module racks and various amps for all of it.

Every bit of it went dead.

We all quit playing to see what was going on, and the sound guys rushed down to the stage to help him figure it out. Budd took the opportunity to channel my old piano teacher, Jan, and remind the rest of us that if something like that happened during the live show, *just keep playing.*

Eventually, the sound guys determined that a loose power strip had just pulled out from the wall, and then we were back up and running. We got to roughly the same spot in the song again when all of Budd's power went out a second time. As instructed, we just kept playing while Budd tried to figure it out. The same offending wall socket from before was the culprit, so Budd grabbed the cord and tossed it over to Jeremy—who had brought an electronic drum kit—and signaled him to plug it in wherever he could find an empty slot. Jeremy complied while keeping both feet and his right arm banging on the kit. Budd's station roared back to life . . . for about two seconds. There was a loud *pop* that cut through the music and made everyone in the club jump a foot in the air, and then a faint smell of smoke. This time we all quit playing.

"Uh-oh, my bad," Jeremy said sheepishly.

"Why, what happened?" asked Budd.

"I, um, I think I plugged it into a 220."

Yeah, that would be a problem.

Everything we'd brought over from the States was wired for 110-voltage, and everything in China ran on 220. Someone had somehow missed a switch on one of the adaptors and just fried all of Budd's gear six hours before showtime. And unless someone had a DeLorean handy that went 88 mph, there wasn't much we could do about it.

Budd and the sound techs set to work cutting and splicing and seeing what they could salvage, and eventually got his amps and one of the sound modules back online. The other two modules and his keyboard were dead as nails.

This meant we were either going to have to scrap his big showcase tune or . . . figure something out. I offered to let him use my keys for his solo, but we quickly determined that wasn't going to work. He'd brought a full-size, 88-note keyboard—and needed every one of those notes—mine was only 66 keys.[37] Plus, he was running his keyboard

---

[37] At this point, I should probably disclose that my grand touring rig consisted entirely of the single Roland E-15 Dad bought me all those years ago—an entry-level synth with built-in speakers. (Built-in speakers are the first giveaway that a keyboard is not a professional-level instrument.) It wasn't much to look at, but it had all the sounds I needed to get through our 20-song setlist, and I knew the instrument like the back of my hand. It did what I needed it to do.

through the sound module, so the only way we could make it work was if we sat up both of our stations on top of each other and played elbow to elbow, which would look ridiculous.

If we couldn't get our musical act together, there was a better chance we'd get tossed in jail for failing to convince the government we were actual musicians than because we were singing about God.

"Does anyone know where we can get another keyboard?" Mom yelled out from the middle of the dance floor to no one in particular.

"Somebody translate that for me!" she added, also to no one in particular.

Adam the translator heard her cries for help and sprang into action. A half-hour later, a full-sized keyboard was delivered to the club—one of our hosts had sent someone over to the theater we'd be playing at the next night and ordered them to locate a keyboard and bring it back.

Crisis averted. The show would go on.

About an hour into our rehearsal, we were interrupted by a television crew who showed up to conduct an interview nobody had mentioned we'd be doing. The five of us sat down at the front of the stage, leaving room in the middle for our interviewer, one of the local television news anchors.

If we'd had time before we left the States to do anything other than learn the songs, some topics someone might have thought to earmark for discussion should we find ourselves doing a TV interview were:

1. Do we have a designated spokesman for the group so we don't end up shouting out conflicting answers to easy questions?

2. Are we going with fake Aussie accents or not?

3. For that matter, what country are we pretending to be from?

4. Do any of us know how long we're supposed to have been a band?

5. What's the name of the band member we're each pretending to be?

6. What's the name of the *band* we're pretending to be?

That wouldn't have been the complete list by any means, but it would have been a terrific place to start. Because smack-dab in the middle of this interview is when I finally realized for the very first time that the guys from Pittsburgh had no clue that, as far as China was concerned, we were *supposed to be the actual* Newsboys. Mom had never bothered to tell them. (If you haven't figured it out by now, she's a "big picture" gal, not a "details" person.)

The only reason I happened to be aware of what we were up to was because she'd kept me vaguely in the loop due to my highly esteemed position of being related to her via DNA. In her desperate scramble to find musicians, she hadn't conveyed aany of these "minor details" to Dean when she'd called him the day before she'd sprung this on me last week.

Dean was under the impression that we were just going over to China—no big deal—because someone had canceled and China needed a replacement. But China was *not* aware that anyone had canceled, and they certainly had no idea we weren't the same band they'd spent half a decade trying to bring over that the US Government had vouched for. They thought they were getting superstars, and that's what we were supposed to show up giving them. I was flabbergasted.

At least this finally explained why the Pittsburgh guys hadn't included any Newsboys songs in their set and why Dean and Budd were so baffled at my suggestion about adopting Australian accents. They didn't know anything about anything![38]

In my head, I started trying to piece together this comically absurd web of deceit Mom had constructed to get us to this point:

- She'd gotten Communist China to agree to host a Christian concert without realizing it was Christian.

- She'd gotten the Newsboys to agree to perform without letting them know that China didn't know they were a Christian band.

- When the Newsboys backed out, she didn't bother to tell China she was showing up with a completely different band than the one they'd booked and promoted and were expecting.

- She hadn't bothered to inform three-fifths of the replacement band that China didn't know they weren't the original band they'd booked.

---

[38] When I interviewed Budd for this book, he told me he hadn't even heard the Newsboys mentioned at all until the flight to Beijing.

And now we had to do a tap dance through a TV interview while I was putting all this together in real time.

Thanks a lot, Mum!

Nobody wanted to be responsible for blowing our cover by not knowing a basic piece of trivia about our own backstory, nobody wanted to accidentally contradict another bandmate's answer to a question we all should've had the same answer to, and we were all hyperaware that Mom was needlessly complicating the whole situation by serving up little white lies that served absolutely no purpose whatsoever other than to make our task even more difficult than it already was.

Case in point: all the posters, banners, flyers, and marketing materials all over the city featured the press photo of the actual Newsboys that Mom had sent Mr. Wu years ago.

"No biggie," Mom said. "I've already told them it's very common for famous bands to shuffle members, so that's why we might not match up perfectly with the marquis sign out front."

Okay, fair enough.

"Also," Mom continued, "They all think we all look alike, so just pick the person on the poster you look the most like, and try to mimic their look while we're here to create a resemblance."

Hold on. What?

Mom was starting to overcomplicate things with contradictory stories. Were we supposed to put on hats and glasses and trim our facial hair to pass ourselves off as whichever person we most resembled in the poster? Or were we supposed to admit we weren't *in* the poster because the band rotated members? Pick one or the other, Mum, but we can't say both.

"Oh, and one last thing," she added, "We're calling ourselves the *Newboys,* not the Newsboys—we'll just say there's a typo on their posters."

HUH?

I mean, how do you even go about unpacking that doozy? What is even the point of it? You're supposed to tell lies to get *out* of trouble, not wade neck-deep *into* it!

There was absolutely no reason for this whopper. It didn't even make sense. China had just spent half a decade booking the Newsboys; we showed up pretending to be the band they booked, and then, just so nobody had to lie about who they were on a poster, the plan was to tell them we were actually an entirely *different band* than the one they booked . . . a band whose name was off by one letter?

It would be like if China had booked U2, and then someone showed up wearing wrap-around shades pretending to be Bono, using an American accent, and introducing themselves as UToo.

It boggled the mind.

(Mom later tried to explain her rationale for trying to call us the *Newboys*: "Well, you're a *new* band, and you're all boys, so . . . *Newboys!*" Yes, it was even dumber than my reasoning for wearing a New Kids On The Block shirt.)

Being such a ridiculous idea, it would naturally make sense that the six of us wouldn't be able to agree on how to proceed, and so we just went about our business in total disagreement about what our band name was and what country we were from. This was going to be problematic because it was an idea conceived in Mom's head, and once conceived there, she did not relinquish ideas easily. Or readily. Or eventually. Or at all, if we're being totally honest.

Nope, Gavin and I were determined to keep masquerading as the Newsboys; Mom, Dean, and Budd were going to tell everyone we were an altogether different band called the *Newboys*, and everyone in China could work out for themselves who they thought we were.

It was going to be a fun week.

(This trip was Jeremy's first time on an airplane, and he'd decided on the flight over that he absolutely loved Asian women. Since this whole discussion had nothing to do with Asian women, Jeremy had no interest in having an opinion one way or the other. He just wanted everyone to shut up so and finish rehearsing so he could go talk to girls.)

And so began a weird cat-and-mouse game between news reporters anxious to get some soundbites from us and a group of guys equally anxious about being accepted by our hosts, yet cognizant of the fact that the only way we might let them all down was by answering any of their questions honestly.

Of course, there was always that other tried-and-true tactic of answering with such blatant honesty that nobody would think for one second that we were telling the truth.

"How long have the five of you been playing music together?"

The Newboys

It's really hard to pinpoint. These guys are all so much fun, and time definitely flies when you're having fun. It almost feels like we just got together yesterday.

"How does it feel to know you are only the second western rock band to ever perform in China? Do you feel any pressure?"

It's an incredible honor to be here—we truly feel like the luckiest guys in the whole world. With so many famous bands out there to choose from, it seems very surreal that it would be us. But yes, there is a little bit of pressure.

"How do the people back home feel about your visit? Are they very supportive and filled with pride for your accomplishment?"

Oh, I think that all our friends and family back in Americ— I mean, Austra— I mean, you know, wherever we're from—are even more surprised than we are that we're here. Everybody is just really shocked that it's us instead of, say, Aerosmith.

More media outlets were trickling in by the minute. Some patiently waited for their turn with us. Others strode right into the middle of ongoing interviews and interrupted to ask whichever "Newboy" was closest to plug their radio station or hawk the same orange soda the entire city seemed to have an inexplicable infatuation with.

Whatever.

I didn't care who wanted us to say what about which. The way I saw it, we were a bunch of nobody's on a one-week loan from Everydayville, America. I was just thrilled to have news crews pointing cameras in my direction without any crimes actively in progress. If they wanted me to swear up and down that we kept our voices sharp by gargling strawberry-scented panda urine, I was down for it. No one had ever interviewed me about anything—ever—other than maybe for a minimum-wage position at Red Lobster.

All I knew was that this was the biggest, brightest spotlight any of us had ever been thrust into. I couldn't speak for the other four guys, but I fully intended to milk it for all it was worth for as long as it lasted.

Or die trying.

Yeah, or that. We'd made it through Customs, and we'd survived a partial soundcheck, but we had yet to sing any of our brazen lyrics in the direction of anyone from the Chinese Communist Party, who still didn't know what we'd be singing about. We weren't out of the woods by a long shot. Practically speaking, we hadn't even made it *into* the woods yet. That moment of truth was just a few hours off and closing fast.

Aware that the clock was ticking, we began dropping hints that it was time for us to get back to rehearsal, but we were looking forward to seeing everyone back here that night. The news crews took the hint and began packing up, but not before one last radio station roped us into one last plug in unison: *"We're the Newboys/Newsboys from ~~Aust~~ America, we LOVE Mandarin Cola, and you're listening to Channel Four Radio!"*

We finally got back to rehearsal and made it through a few songs when Dean decided he didn't like something about the sound coming through the club's system. We took another 45-minute break while he and the sound guys tried to sort out whatever it was that was bugging him. They finally got it to his liking—which, for a million bucks, I couldn't tell you what was different about it—and we plowed through as many more songs as we could.

Eventually, the clock ran out on our rehearsal, and it was time to go back for dinner and get ready for the show. We'd made it through exactly half of the setlist.

Ten of the songs we would be performing later that night had never been rehearsed a single time as a band. Whatever surprise the audience expressed about the visiting act from overseas, we'd be sharing it right along with them. We had no idea what was going to come out.

The club was already packed solid when our limo pulled up to the front doors an hour before showtime.

Did I say the club? I meant the block. The block the club was on was packed solid. So was the block across the street. And the blocks on either side. It looked like Mardi Gras. Despite knowing exactly what we were being dropped off to go do, it still took us a minute to realize that this mass of people had turned out to see *us*. It was insane.

As soon as our ride came to a stop and we started to get out, the crowd went berserk. Pure pandemonium. I wasn't alive for Beatlemania, but I've seen the footage—the boys from Liverpool would've been envious of the greeting we received.

It was a short distance from the curb to the club entrance—maybe 20 feet—but they'd rolled out a red carpet and lined it with velvet ropes, which were lined with paparazzi blinding us with a thousand flashbulbs. Security ushered us through the crowd and into the churning *discotheque.*

It was like stepping into Studio 54 in its heyday.[39]

Thumping techno music pummeled our ears as we entered. The entire club was a fever dream of neon, strobe lights, disco balls, fog machines, and carpet that glowed under the blacklight and looked like it had been filched from Chuck E. Cheese. Some sort of Cirque du Soleil act was dancing on the stage. The place was packed wall-to-wall in what was surely a fire marshal code violation several times over.[40]

We were led up to the second floor to an open VIP room with a few couches to lounge on, and several hostesses rushed off to get us drinks.

Everyone in the vicinity of our lounge area was trying to press into the room to gawk at the foreigners, yell a *hello*, and maybe snap a picture. For the most part, they were successful since the security guards hired specifically to keep them from doing that were also busy doing it themselves. Tonight, the inmates were running the asylum.

We had a million last-minute questions about introductions, set lengths, intermissions—all the fine details a tour manager and stage manager would typically work out in advance. Unfortunately, our tour manager was Mom, the stage manager didn't speak English, and it was so obscenely loud that Adam couldn't hear what any of us were asking him to translate, let alone convey the translation back to anyone. So, we were forced to try figuring it all out with a game of bilingual charades instead, everyone agreeing to pretend like any of us knew what anyone else's pantomimes actually meant.

We finally caught a break when the DJ cut the music for a city government official to take the stage to announce our presence and that we'd be on shortly. There was a burst of applause, whistles, and cheers before slowly dying down as he segued into a meandering propaganda speech about unity, friendship, breaking down cultural

---

[39] Or so I imagine. I wasn't around for that one either.

[40] If you've ever seen those YouTube videos of people being packed into trains, subways, and buses like sardines, you're aware that many Asian cultures have a much different sense of personal space than we Americ— I mean, we Aussies do. ~~In the Sta~~ Where I'm from, a club this size might be coded for a 400-person capacity. This club was probably holding three times that.

barriers, East-West relationships, yada yada yada. The important thing was that the music was temporarily off, and we could actually hear ourselves talk.

The first thing we did was confirm that everyone in both the band and production crew had understood all the important charades and pantomiming from earlier, which, naturally, nobody had, and we had to start over. Once everyone was done communicating all the last-minute details, Adam asked us if we had any final questions. I suddenly thought of one I should've thought of earlier.

Is there a back door exit from the stage?

Nothing about this gig has been typical so far. In a normal club gig, the band and crew would load in from a back or side door attached to the stage. When we showed up for rehearsal earlier, we'd brought everything in through the front. And any band worth their salt certainly wouldn't have made their grand entrance through the front doors in the middle of a DJ set where everyone could see them; they'd have snuck in the back unnoticed and made their grand appearance on the stage.

The only door we'd used so far was the front door. I needed to know where the other exits were located should we need to bolt out of there like the Von Trapps once all the officials in the audience realized what we were singing about.

Adam had a brief, animated discussion with two of the stagehands, then turned back to us to deliver their answer. "Yes, there are three exits at the back of the building. But because you are very famous now, the club owner is anxious that some troublemakers maybe try to sneaking into the club. So, he chained all the doors shut for your protection. He personally guarantees your safety!"

Terrific.

We were locked in.

When the official was done speaking, the DJ made an announcement that elicited another round of cheers. Adam beamed at us with two thumbs up: "He says the Newsboys will be on in a few minutes and—" The music kicked back in, drowning out the end of his sentence. I hoped it wasn't something important.

The next twenty minutes felt like an eternity. The flight from Beijing had been nerve-racking enough, and that's when we were just *assuming* the officials surrounding us knew what we were up to. There would no longer be any assumptions. In precisely 1,200 seconds, every last person in this building would know exactly what we were all about.

Chris and his mom may have been on to something.

After what seemed like either an eternity or three heartbeats, the music died down and the lights dimmed.

This was it.

I don't remember walking down the steps from the VIP lounge to the stage. It was the kind of mental haze brides and grooms frequently describe after the wedding ceremony—everything suddenly went dark, they were in a fog, and then their faculties returned to them just in time to catch the minister saying, "You may kiss the bride." I'd placed one foot on the top stair . . . and then I was standing behind my keyboards with no recollection of how I got there.

Someone at center stage said something into the mic—English? Chinese? I couldn't tell—and the crowd erupted in a roar. The stage lights were blinding. (I would later find out it was Dean, alternating between English and Mandarin in a bilingual salutation he'd planned for the crowd.)

To my left, I heard Jeremy shout out the count-in with his drumsticks: *ONE, TWO, THREE, FOUR!* I hit the opening synth rift, and we were off to the races.

If I'd consulted the Vegas bookies on the over-under on how many minutes into the set we'd get before they pulled the plug and hauled us all out of there, I'd have bet the house on the 5-minute under. And I would've lost the house.

The thing about rock shows at a significant enough volume in a smaller indoor venue is that it's often incredibly difficult to make out anything the singer is singing. And that's when the singer's singing in your native tongue. Sure, you can make out enough to sing along with the band . . . *if* you happen to already know the song and lyrics in advance. But go out to a local rock show for a band you've never heard of before, take a notepad and pen, and see if you can transcribe anything from the stage with more than 20% accuracy. Good luck.

The sheer, distorted volume we were playing at, coupled with the language barrier, meant nobody in the building understood a single lyric out of our mouths. The crowd who was there for the show was enthralled. They were dancing and clapping—along for the ride. The officials who were there to monitor the show were beaming, pleased that everyone was behaving themselves.

For their part, the crowd was as into it as we could've hoped for. As soon as we realized that no one was coming to cut the electricity, we could actually relax and focus our energy on performing, which was not a thing we had any prior experience doing. At least not on this level. We'd devoted every waking second to making sure we knew the *music*; it had never dawned on any of us to maybe rehearse the *performance* aspect of putting on a show.

But we'd all seen enough music videos to know there were certain signature "moves" that signified one as a bona fide rock star, and we were each fully committed to doing our closest approximation of what we thought a person in the actual position we were pretending to be in would be doing if they weren't actually pretending.

Gavin struck The Stance every guitarist in a '90s band was contractually obligated to pose in—legs wide apart, weight fully forward on the front leg, bouncing up and down with the beat. I'd never seen him strike that pose before in his life—it's a hellacious workout on that left quad—so good for him. Bud thrashed his waist-length hair in circles. Jeremy twirled his drumsticks in the air every chance he got. Keyboardists aren't exactly known for their stage moves, so I just mimicked the only keyboard player I could conjure up an image of who had a distinct playing style: Stevie Wonder. That meant eyes closed, head back (eerily similar to my disastrous *Chariots of Fire* sprint through the mall), rocking side to side with a big dopey grin on my face.

The last time I pulled this move, I was also in this city, out of my element, trying to win over a crowd. Small world.

Dean was all over the stage, kneeling, jumping, and working the crowd with call-and-response showmanship. The crowd ate it up.

The Communist Party had a vested interest in keeping all aspects of social life as orderly, structured, and controlled as they could manage. Showboating and flamboyance were deeply frowned upon in every aspect of society. Even the popular, mainstream bands in China performed with a subdued, reserved energy that would've been better suited for the *Ed Sullivan Show* than MTV.

"Tame" was probably the operative word to describe Chinese pop culture entertainment at the time. Compared to what the Chinese audience was accustomed to, we were the equivalent of The Who's famous (or infamous) performance on *The Smothers Brothers* back in 1967.[41]

We weren't detonating any bombs or destroying any equipment, but we might as well have been as out of place as we were.

When the concert ended, everyone who was even remotely involved with the affair—city officials, hosts, translators, promoters, sponsors, booking agents, tour guides, the guy who ran the banana stand across the street (probably)—was brought on stage, given flowers, and handed the microphone to say a few words. Once every official south of Mongolia had taken a turn on the mic, we all milled around shaking hands, slapping backs, and hugging like we were at a theatrical wrap party and not center stage in a nightclub, surrounded by partygoers who were ready to *dance*.

The sound guys made it a point to come over to us and let us know they really appreciated the show. They couldn't quite put their finger on what it was about our act, but something had definitely made an impression. They said it hadn't just been different, it had been . . . *special*. The head sound guy told us he'd been at the club for five years and had learned more in an hour that night from Dean and Budd than anyone had taught him in his half-decade there prior.

---

[41] At the time, The Who were already well known for their destructive stage shows. Tom Smothers had apparently caught The Who's act earlier that summer at the Monterey International Pop Festival, was a witness to the instrument-smashing climax to their performance, and was an admirer of the spectacle. Booking them for the *Smothers Brothers Comedy Hour*, Tom encouraged them to treat their instruments as they saw fit. According to Hollywood insiders, drummer Keith Moon took this as a personal challenge. He situated a small cannon filled with theatrical flash powder next to his kit that he'd detonate at the end, but under union rules, he wasn't allowed to fill it himself. Moon bribed a stagehand to grant him access to the cannon before the show, and he allegedly stuffed it with ten times the legal amount of gunpowder you're allowed to use on a soundstage. The resulting explosion shook the entire studio and filled it with smoke. Pete Townshend's hair caught fire, and he later said his hearing was never the same again. Moon himself was injured as the blast blew apart his kit, slicing his arm open with metal shrapnel from the cymbals. The studio audience and the television audience at home were equally shocked. Google "Keith Moon drum explosion" to relive the epic moment.

The DJ turned on the music, which meant that we could no longer hear ourselves, so all of us stepped outside to the front of the club to finish our congratulations. Before we could get a chance, a sea of partygoers from inside the club poured out the door, encircled us, and practically dragged us back inside. They had come out that night to dance; they were *going* to dance, and any visiting foreign rock stars they could get their hands on were jolly well going to dance with them.

We finally rolled back into the hotel sometime after 3 a.m., exhausted, drenched in sweat, but mostly just relieved to still be alive and un-incarcerated. We had passed our first test—successfully convincing an entire concert audience that we were the internationally acclaimed rock band their city had been relentlessly promoting for the last six years.

Were we good?

Um . . . define "good." We were definitely *loud.* And loud covers a multiple of sins. Talking to Dean and Budd years later, I think what we all agreed on was that we were five incredibly proficient individual musicians who had never played together before and had never collectively rehearsed half the songs we performed . . . and it showed. Had anyone in the country ever heard the actual Newsboys (or even a decent college band), we might've gotten booed off the stage. But we were a complete novelty, and China thankfully had no frame of reference. That made us rock stars.

But we'd also dodged a bullet. The Cultural Affairs Bureau still had no idea what we were singing about, our hides saved by the club's acoustics.

Tomorrow's show would be an entirely different ballgame.

You know, my girlfriend had a theory. She said at some point in your life, you find a use for every useless talent you ever had. It's like connecting the dots.
— Dr. Dakota Block, *Planet Terror*

We can't always choose the music life plays for us, but we can choose how we dance with it.
— Unknown

Desperados

OCTOBER 28, 1999: SHOWTIME

The next morning, we gathered around a dining table in the expansive lobby, enjoying a continental breakfast and reliving the glories of the previous night. The five of us concurred that while nobody back home would've called the performance great, it still went better than we had any right to be. Yes, the acoustics weren't ideal, and the sound crew could've been more experienced, and it was pretty obvious we'd never rehearsed half the songs, and Jeremy blew up most of Budd's gear. But everyone's musicianship was on display, the crowd was energized and into it the entire night, and nobody ended up in jail.

Between the crowd's energy and our own adrenaline, we'd somehow managed to coax a performance out of ourselves that I hadn't dreamt as remotely possible the week before. Most importantly, our hosts seemed delighted by it, which is all that really mattered. But, as we were about to find out, everything we had going in our favor last night that kept the show from being an absolute trainwreck was about to be tossed out the window and flipped on its head.

The auditorium where we were slated to play that evening was in walking distance from our hotel, so after finishing our meal, our hosts collected us and led us the block and half over to get the lay of the land and start setting up.

Arriving in front of the building, I couldn't help feeling completely in over our heads. This was no middling nightclub or amateur venue; it was an honest-to-God concert auditorium with marquees and lights and ticket booths.[42] Oh, and pictures of "us" *everywhere*. But if the exterior induced a sense of sudden-onset imposter syndrome, we were ill-prepared for what was waiting inside.

We entered the lobby and made our way across the ornate carpet, past the concessions, and up to the giant double doors that opened into the auditorium proper. A doorman greeted us with a smile and pulled open the doors. I took two steps inside and froze in my tracks.

Dumbfounded.

Awestruck.

I'd never seen anything like it in my life.

To welcome us, they had brought down the house lights to show level and turned on what appeared to be every stage light at their disposal. The drums sat high on a riser at the back of the massive stage as three spotlights swept back and forth and a pre-programmed laser show danced around the entire theater. It was truly breathtaking.

This is all for us?

It was like that scene from Spike Lee's *He Got Game* where Ray Allen's Jesus Shuttlesworth is being recruited by Tech University. While touring the school, he's taken down to the basketball arena's courtside seats and then treated to a mock game-time introduction featuring a light show and intro music as the public address announcer introduces his name, and the jumbotron over center court shows a career highlight reel—all standard fanfare for college or NBA players, but a completely foreign welcome for a meager high school prospect.

Welcome to the big time.

It was almost too much. I'd been to my fair share of concerts in the past. Just three months prior, four buddies and I had rented a van and drove from West Palm Beach to Rome, New York, for the Super Mega Dumpster Fire that was Woodstock '99, so the kind of stages

---

[42] The venue was on par with any major city's primary theater for Broadway-type productions: floor-level seating divided by aisles and sections, and balcony seating overhead.

they set up for celebrity musical acts was still fresh in my mind. The stage I was gawking at was for *those* people, not us. We played in church services, coffee shops, and piano bars.

Once the shock wore off, I strode down the center aisle, taking it all in, and climbed up onto the stage. It was enormous. I'd thought last night's stage was impressive, but you could easily fit a dozen of those onto this one. My humble little single-keyboard setup was going to look woefully pitiful out here. On most of the stages I'd ever played on, you couldn't knock a mic stand over without hitting three other people in the band. Here, it was doubtful I could javelin toss a mic stand from the keyboard station at stage right all the way to the bass player on the opposite side. Curious, I wandered off backstage in search of an aerodynamic-looking mic stand to test the theory.

Ten minutes later, I still hadn't found a suitable mic stand, but I had discovered something infinitely more interesting: two very expensive-looking, full-size synthesizers stood up on their ends and stacked against each other in a maintenance closet. I didn't know who they belonged to or what they were used for—or if they even worked—but I fully intended to commandeer them both tonight. Purely for the optics.

We still had the keyboard we'd borrowed—from this very venue— the night before. For tonight's performance, we decided to stack the two keyboards at my station to make my setup a bit more impressive-looking, and then Budd would just walk over and slide in next to me when the time came for his showcase song. At no point was it discussed what I would do when he took over my keys. I didn't play any other instrument, so I guess the plan was for the two of us to camp out behind the keyboards while I just nodded along, wishing unironically for a tambourine.

Now that I'd discovered two more synths in the closet, I could set up a very impressive 4-keyboard station that actually looked like something worthy of a professional. That is, if I could find a stand for them to sit on. I searched all over the theater and couldn't find anything. So, I decided to pull a power move.

Calling one of the stagehands over, I explained that I seemed to be missing a keyboard stand and asked if there was any way we could maybe borrow one from the club we'd played at last night. He walked off to radio somebody and returned a couple minutes later to let me know it was being handled. Thirty minutes later, one of the sound guys from the night before delivered it to the stage, thanking me for "allowing him the opportunity" to be of service once again.

This was going spectacularly. Last night, we had to borrow a keyboard from the theater we were now at to play at the club, and now we were at the theater using their own keyboard and asking to borrow a stand from the club we'd used the borrowed keyboard at. I submit to you that it doesn't get any more professional than that.

Unfortunately, the stand he'd brought over wasn't multi-tiered, which meant I'd have to forego one of the new-found synths. It was all just as well, as it turned out neither of them worked. Since I wouldn't actually be playing either of them anyway, I selected the one that had the most impressive array of buttons and knobs as the decoy, angling it slightly away from my functioning boards so I'd have somewhere to stand and something to pretend to be doing when Budd came over to do his solo.

My new setup complete, I hopped down from the stage, made my way to the first row of seats, sat down, and surveyed my handiwork. If I'm being perfectly honest, it looked . . . *good*. There was a two-tiered rack of keys facing the audience, and a third set of keys turned at an angle. Sure, it was a nonfunctional synthesizer that wasn't plugged into anything, but nobody else was going to know that.

Optics. That's all that mattered.

I was sitting there admiring it and taking it all in when Budd came flying across the stage out of nowhere, on his knees, and crashed into the drum riser, knocking the whole front of the riser a foot or two off-center. Jeremy, now angled slightly towards the left of the theater, gave him the same look I usually gave the dog whenever it came tearing through the house for no discernible reason and slammed face-first into the back door.

Why did you just do that?

As I was discovering, another part of Budd's ethos was to have as much fun—and put on as much of a show—as humanly possible. Since he was using a wireless bass tonight, that gave him free rein to roam wherever the spirit moved him. Apparently, the spirit had preemptively moved him to see how far he could slide if he took a full running start from offstage and then hit his knees right before coming out from the curtains. This first test run looked like a solid 30-foot slide and would've gone even farther had he not slammed into Jeremy's drum platform.

"I wanna try that!" Gavin exclaimed.

"You might want to change your pants first," Budd advised, nodding at Gavin's ripped-to-shreds jeans, "unless you don't mind leaving some of your knees behind in China."

"Budd, stop screwing around, and let's start moving these empty cases off the stage," Dean suggested.

"Roger that," Budd answered.

Jeremy hopped down from the elevated riser and dragged it back to center. I'd already moved all my cases offstage and out of sight, so I was content to sit and observe the final cleanup.

Since the drum riser had a black floor-length skirt all the way around it, Budd decided to store his cases under the drums. He grabbed an empty bass case and slid it across the floor towards the riser and out of sight. A second later, we all heard a loud *THUNK!* followed—several seconds after that—by a deafening crash that reverberated through the entire auditorium.

What the—

Budd walked over to the riser, lifted the skirt, and peered underneath it.

"Whoa," he said. "You guys should come check this out."

We all came over to have a peek at whatever had impressed Budd, and . . . *Whoa* indeed.

The drum riser had been set up over one of those mechanical floor lifts that theatrical productions use whenever someone has to appear out of nowhere in the middle of the stage. However, the lift hadn't been raised back to floor-level for some reason, and we were all staring into an uncovered, 40-foot elevator shaft that Budd had just flung his guitar case to the bottom of.

"Hey, maybe we could do that knee-slide thing somewhere away from the drums tonight?" Jeremy proffered.

He had a decent point. Had the spirit moved Budd to generate enough additional velocity to move the platform another 10-12 inches, it would've knocked the back corner leg of Jeremy's drum riser into the bottomless pit.

I wondered if Budd would want us to keep playing if our drummer suddenly vanished in the middle of "Shine." The visual of Jeremy suddenly getting swallowed up by the earth made me laugh out loud. We were like a cross between Bon Jovi and The Apple Dumpling Gang.

Once the stage was all clear and yet another crisis averted, we sound-checked and ran a few songs.

Houston, we have a problem.

Last night, the sound had been deafeningly loud—almost distorted—but somehow muffled at the same time, making it impossible for anyone to understand anything that was being sung. This, on the other hand, was a concert hall with top-notch acoustics and a professional audio crew who knew exactly what they were doing. Dean's voice cut through the mix, clear as a bell, almost pristine. There was a zero percent chance we were going to make it through our entire setlist that evening without a few people picking up on some of the lyrics. What happened at that point was anyone's guess. It was out of our hands.

We wrapped our mini-rehearsal and headed back to the hotel with several hours to kill. A couple of the guys wanted to shower; Jeremy wanted to take a nap. I still hadn't given up on the idea of a sword, so I set off on foot to find one—no destination in mind and no idea where to go looking. Sometimes, aimlessly wandering around a foreign city was its own reward. That day, it would have to be enough because I returned to the hotel a couple hours later still swordless.

I t was finally here.

The moment of truth.

We made our way down to the lobby a few minutes before our scheduled rendezvous time with our hosts and translator. All of us were fidgety with nervous energy. There was a grand piano in the lobby next to the dining area, so I went over and started tinkering. A Chinese businessman dining at a nearby table stopped eating, walked over to the piano, gave a nod of approval, and said, "Billy Joel?"

That was all I needed to hear.

I plunked out the opening riff of "Piano Man" and was soon joined around the piano by the rest of the band. By the time we reached the first chorus, a number of Chinese guests had joined us as well, everyone belting out the familiar lyrics as one:

Sing us a song, you're the piano man
Sing us a song tonight
Well, we're all in the mood for a melody
And you've got us feeling alright

There's something magical about sports and music that unite perfect strangers otherwise separated by language and culture. Whether it's kicking a soccer ball or sharing a refrain, I'm hard-pressed to think of any other examples that so easily bridge international gaps. When you share one of those moments with someone, it's as if both parties are saying, *I know I don't know you, and maybe we don't understand each other, but at least here's something we have in common.* Sometimes, that's more valuable than hours of conversation.

When the song was over, everyone in the lobby applauded, and everyone around the piano hugged it out like the ball had just dropped on New Year's Eve. If things went sideways at the show tonight, this would be an indelible Last Supper moment for the memory bank.

We arrived back at the auditorium about an hour before we were scheduled to go on. Backstage was a madhouse of stagehands, production crew, city officials, cultural affairs members, booking agents, venue directors and their staff, the emcee, the opening act, and Lord knows who else. All of them urgently needed to speak with us about something, and since Adam was the only one whose English was good enough to translate, a million different conversations were being shouted over each other with none of us clearly understanding who was saying what to whom.

We did manage to make out a few key points, much to our chagrin. The first, it was pointed out, was that this was an entirely *seated* venue. Unlike last night's show where the audience had been jammed up against the stage, free to dance as they pleased—if they could find room to move—here it was strictly forbidden. The ticket holders had all been firmly instructed to remain seated for the duration of the show, both out of respect for us and to demonstrate their keen aptitude for "orderliness."

The two most disappointing superpowers to unleash at a rock show.

Someone shouted something from the back, and Adam translated: "We have arranged for you to receive the most attentive audience!

There will be no yelling, no screaming, no whistling, no jumping around or commotion, and no . . . boisterousness."

Boisterousness? That's a pretty impressive vocabulary word. Where in the world did Adam learn that one?

"I guess we won't be needing these," Mom remarked, holding up two inflatable beachballs she'd packed to toss out into the audience.

"Nope, probably not a beachball affair tonight, Mum," I told her.

"Well, I'm just gonna blow them up and set them right here just in case," she replied. "You never know."

Yes, mother, sometimes you know.

This was terrific in the most sarcastic usage of the word. In an effort to impress us, city officials had ordered our audience not to do any of the things performers usually rely on the audience *for* in order to make that invaluable connection. In a perfect world, it's a symbiotic relationship—the people on stage feeding off the crowd's energy, the crowd reciprocating it right back at them. How on earth were we supposed to "feed off the crowd's energy" when the crowd had been explicitly ordered not to display any? This was shaping up to potentially be the dullest rock show ever delivered in the direction of other human beings.

Secondly, and to make matters somehow even worse, we were told that the show was going to have a 20-minute intermission right smack-dab in the middle of it.

Perfect. Exactly like no rock show in the entire history of music has ever had.

A freaking intermission? This was a rock concert, not *Les Mis!* It violated every unspoken rule of concert etiquette, especially for an audience who didn't know the music or the band. The hardest part of performing for any audience unfamiliar with your material is winning them over in the first place. Assuming you can capture their attention, the last thing you want to do is bring everything to a screeching halt so everyone can go take a smoke break and grab some popcorn. Instead of coasting on the momentum you've built up, you have to get the whole locomotive back up to full speed from a dead standstill.

If the goal of our Chinese hosts was to make our job as difficult as humanly possible tonight, then kudos to them for nailing it. We'd come over here to *rock* (for Jesus, but still), and they'd all but ensured it wasn't going to happen. We were being effectively handcuffed. For the life of me, I couldn't see how they could make our task any more daunting.

At intermission, they would manage to find a way.

An opening act went on to warm up the crowd. We never did figure out exactly who he was, but he appeared to be a local pop celebrity. Decked out in a baby blue rhinestone ensemble—and rocking a single glove that he'd obviously cribbed from Michael Jackson—he came out and sang a few disco-sounding numbers about unity and friendship to prerecorded tracks. It was. . . interesting.

Finally, the theater lights came down, the fog machine kicked into overdrive (did we really need *that* much fog?), and it was time to take the stage.

We hadn't discussed what we were going to do when we got out there. Would there be an announcement? Was one of us supposed to say something? Was Jeremy going to immediately count us in?

This is probably why bands try to squeeze in at least one rehearsal before they go out on tour—so they don't look like idiots.

Dean broke the silence with that pristine voice of his—weaving through an a cappella vocal riff that hit every note he was capable of hitting, holding out the last note in an impressive vibrato before yelling, "WHAT'S UP, CHANGSHA! HOW'S EVERYONE DOING TONIGHT?" The audience broke into a tepid applause, seemingly unsure if they should even be doing that. Jeremy took that as his cue— *one, two, three, four*—and off we went.

Our opener was probably the song we had nailed down the best. Other than the two songs Dean had written—worship songs that he could sing in English and Mandarin—we were performing all covers. Sonically and production-wise, "Not Ashamed" was the one that sounded closest to the actual album recording, which made it especially fun to perform. Up there on the stage, if you closed your eyes, you almost couldn't tell the actual Newsboys weren't performing around you. *Almost.* Something about it wasn't sounding quite right, though I couldn't pinpoint what. It just sounded . . . *thin.* Like something was missing

Midway through the second song, which was also sounding thin, Gavin made his way over to my keys station and yelled, "Dude, I can't hear myself at all!"

I shook my head and shrugged. He'd been happy with his mix at soundcheck. I didn't know what to tell him. I was about to holler back at him that he should signal up to the sound booth that he needed his monitor turned up when I happened to look over at his guitar stand. There was an audio cable lying on the floor beside it. I looked back at his guitar. There was nothing plugged into it.

That's a new one.

I started laughing hysterically.

He gave me a quizzical look, so I nodded over at the stage where the cable was lying and yelled, "Dude! You're not plugged into anything!"

Gavin glanced down at the empty audio jack on his guitar, shook his head, then casually walked over, picked up the cable, and stuck it into his guitar, just in time for the second chorus. That's what had sounded thin. Our five-piece band of "seasoned professionals" had started the concert of their lives as a four-piece because our lead guitarist had unplugged himself after soundcheck and forgotten to plug himself back in.

The remaining eight songs in the first set went off without a hitch, save for Jeremy's epic drum solo, which everyone heard, but nobody saw because whoever was operating the fog machine got carried away and completely flooded the back of the stage. One moment he was there, and then he was just . . . *gone*, engulfed in a fog bank. Even from 20 feet away onstage, I couldn't make him out.

That's also a new one.

Depending on how he handled flying blind and came out of it, this could either come across as upside-down-Tommy-Lee-level epic or *This Is Spinal Tap*-level bad *a la* when bassist Derreck Smalls gets trapped inside that plastic pod. Jeremy went with Option A, and we all acted like it was all just part of what we'd planned.

The crowd remained seated, politely applauding after each song, but that was the only indication they were even awake. We were pouring everything we had into this performance and getting zero feedback. Did we actually suck? It would've been more enjoyable playing to an empty theater than a full one that was this ambivalent. Suddenly, I couldn't wait for intermission. This was shaping up to be a disaster.

We wrapped the first set and made our way backstage. There was no proper greenroom, but someone had set up a few tables covered in drinks and an assortment of fruit and snacks. I wasn't hungry, but I grabbed a handful of hard candy and stuffed them in my pocket for later. I thought about it for a second and then stuffed the other pocket too. Just in case they didn't have free candy dishes in prison.

I looked around for Mom—she was always good for positive, if not practical, feedback—but she was nowhere to be found. That was strange. She'd set up a video camera front row center in the balcony, so I know she'd been watching intently and would probably have notes for everyone.

At that moment, in the midst of considering that this whole show might be a huge bust, Mr. Wu came over and made a "request" that was less a request and more a demand: when we went back out, would we please open the second set with a song the audience knew?

Why is this country so uncomfortably comfortable making song requests of huge superstars? And us.

We had no idea what songs the audience knew and asked if he had any particular songs in mind. "Yes," he replied. "There are three very famous songs from the West that everyone in China knows. Whichever one you pick will be good."

"We'll do our best," Dean assured him. "What are the songs?"

"Ah, yes, they are: "Leaving On A Jet Plane" by John Denver, "Edelweiss" (from *The Sound of Music*), and "Desperado" by the Eagles. These are all very famous songs, yes? So, you will play one of them."

We all glanced at each other, incredulous.

Is he serious?

Was this Mr. Wu's ill-timed attempt at humor? *Those* three songs were the "most famous" Western songs in all of China? You couldn't come up with a more random selection of tunes. The only thing those three songs had in common was that they were all released several years before three of us in the band had been born.[43]

---

[43] In case anyone was wondering how far behind the rest of the world China's pop culture scene was lagging in the late '90s, there's your answer. "Desperado" was released in 1973, "Leaving On A Jet Plane" came out in 1969, and *The Sound of Music* debuted in 1965. The latter made its first broadcast on Chinese TV in the mid-90s and had been a smash hit with the populace, hence their request for "The Lonely Goatherd" and "Edelweiss."

The Sound of Music was my mom's favorite movie, so I'd been forced to watch it more times than I cared to admit. I could hum the entire melody, but I could only recall every sixth word. Compared to my bandmates, this made me an expert. We quickly tabled "Edelweiss."

"Leaving On A Jet Plane" fared slightly better. John Denver's *Greatest Hits* had been one of the few secular albums my parents actually played growing up. As a matter of fact, I'd learned that song by heart in this very city a dozen years ago. Unfortunately, that was probably also the last time I'd heard it. Nobody else in the band was familiar enough with the tune to try playing it, so it would be up to me to figure it out as a piano solo while also trying to remember the lyrics. Nobody comes to a concert hoping to see a solo band member noodling through a song he's never practiced and hasn't heard in over a decade. That one wasn't gonna fly either.

That left the Eagles.

"Does anyone know the lyrics to 'Desperado?'" Dean asked.

"I think I can remember them," offered Gavin.

"Great. Does anyone know how to play it?" Dean wanted to know.

"Nope," said Gavin.

Budd shook his head.

All eyes turned to me. "What about you, Piano Man . . . can you play it?

I'd never attempted to play "Desperado" before in my life. Nary a stab at it. At the time, outside of "Hotel California," I wasn't super familiar with the Eagles in general. But I could hear it in my head, which had to count for something. Besides, Dean hadn't asked if I *had* played it, he'd asked if I *could* play it. It was a song that existed, so I was pretty sure I could figure it out. "Yeah, I can play it," I told the group.

So, that settled it. We didn't know any of the songs they wanted, but "Desperado" was the one we didn't know the least. And we were actually considering opening the second act of our Christian rock show for an audience that didn't care, performing an unplugged rendition of a secular classic rock ballad that we'd never rehearsed, never so much as practiced, and weren't even sure we knew entirely? Why not just tell Mr. Wu we're sorry, but we don't know any of those tunes? Avoid the humiliation of whiffing hard and falling flat on our faces altogether.

I reminded myself that when I'd first agreed to come along on this little adventure, it was with the full understanding that it was either going to be an epic triumph or an absolute dumpster fire. Plus, some wise, honorary doctor of life coaching once said something about missing 100% of the shots you don't take. Honorary doctors knew everything.

So, swing for the fences, baby!

(Also, stop mixing up your sports metaphors.)

I had no idea what key "Desperado" was in, what with never having played it before. But we quickly decided that the only thing that mattered was what key Gavin could sing it in since Don Henley wouldn't be joining us for a duet. Gavin took a few test runs at the highest part of the song until he found a key where he could hit the top notes without his voice cracking. Having found the upper limits of his range, we worked backward to whatever that starting chord was. Now I just had to hold that note in my head until we took the stage.[44]

The audience found its way back to their seats, politely settled in, and we waited for our cue to get this hopefully-not-a-trainwreck started.

As soon as the stage manager gave us the nod, Gavin and I walked out together. I stopped at my keys as he continued to Dean's mic stand at center stage. Then, without warning, Gavin turned and walked back offstage with no explanation, leaving me alone without a plan. I figured his nerves suddenly got the best of him, and he decided to bail before we both made fools of ourselves.

No cause for panic—I could just improvise something until the band decided to join me. I eased into something melodic and didn't get more than a couple notes in when Gavin returned to the stage. He was carrying a dilapidated old wooden chair for some reason. He walked out to the very edge of the stage—mere feet from the front row—and set the chair down, spinning it around so its back faced the audience. He pulled the mic from its stand, straddled the chair, and leaned

---

[44] Unfortunately, I was not blessed with perfect pitch. I got the next best thing, which is *relative* pitch. A person with perfect pitch can immediately identify any note on its own just by hearing it, devoid of any other context. *Relative* pitch is being able to identify a note, provided you have at least one other known note for comparison. This mean that I wouldn't be able to walk out and pinpoint the exact note on the piano that I was humming, but I'd be able to find it on the second try after hitting any random note for context. (The original Eagles version was in G. We pulled it off three steps down in E.)

forward with his forearms on the backrest. I'd already played a few notes, so I had a reference for Gavin's key. Now, if I could only recreate that beautiful piano intro I could hear in my head but had never played before . . .

I hit the opening notes.

And then something magical happened.

There was an audible gasp from the audience as they instantly recognized the familiar intro. As soon as Gavin sang that opening line, *"Desperado . . ."* they burst into applause. Not the tepid ones they'd been politely doling out between songs during the first set—a genuine, heartfelt, *sincere* applause this time. When we arrived at the same opening line to the second verse, every voice in the auditorium chimed in in unison: *"Desperado . . ."*

They were singing along with us?

I was covered in goosebumps.

I have no idea how or why "Desperado" achieved its lofty status as one of the Three Most Famous Songs in a country that didn't allow in many Western cultural influences and where only a small fraction of the populace spoke English. To this day, I don't know why *that* song was so popular, if the people who loved it so much knew what it was about, or if they even understood the words at all. Nobody sang any of the lyrics other than *Desperado*, but every time that word made an appearance, the entire audience was in lockstep with us.

I'm quite sure it would've gone over equally well had Gavin simply stood at the microphone stand and delivered his performance. But dragging the chair out to the front of the stage and spinning it around backward was a stroke of inspiration.

That tiny, subtle act of defiance was Gavin way of saying, *Fine, I'll do this one song you're insisting on, even though this is the precise opposite of an appropriate situation to be making requests of us in, but I'm going to do it* my *way.*

It was a brilliant little flourish, and it most likely saved the rest of the evening. With that one tiny shared moment, we'd managed to capture something that had eluded us the entire first half of the show—the audience was finally on our side. And we were about to have some fun with them.

Once the crowd had dipped its toes in a little bit of audience participation and nobody had reprimanded them for it, they took it as permission to loosen up. And with each additional song in the setlist, they tested the boundaries a little further.

During our "official" opener to the second set, we caught some people swaying to the beat and lightly clapping along, their hands pulled in close to their chests in case anyone was looking. By the second song, more people were joining in, and the sound of clapping from the audience around them appeared to give a sense of confidence to the holdouts. At the third song, realizing they were starting to get into it, Dean broke out the big overhead clap, encouraging everyone to join him. About a third of the audience took him up on it.

Off to stage right, I spotted two Communist officials tapping their feet and nodding along. I pointed at them in acknowledgment, gave them a big thumbs-up, and—knowing full well they couldn't understand a word of it—belted out my chorus harmonies to DC Talk's "Jesus Freak" without breaking eye contact:

What will people do if they find out I'm a Jesus freak
What will people do when they find out it's true
I don't really care if they label me a Jesus freak
There ain't no disguising the truth[45]

It was like that scene from *Indiana Jones and the Last Crusade* where Indy is running through the streets of Berlin with the Grail Diary that the Nazis are in hot pursuit of. Indy gets swept up in a crowd surging to get a glimpse of the Fuhrer's parade and eventually backs into someone in the procession line. He spins around—Diary held aloft—and finds himself face-to-face with Adolf Hitler. For an awkward, uncomfortable moment, they size each other up. Then Hitler snatches the prized Diary out of Indy's hand without realizing it's the sacred

---

[45] Interviewing Mom for this book, 24 years later, is when I found out for the first time that Mr. Wu had specifically requested they didn't play any really *hard* rock. Mellower rock or pop-rock was okay. The Newsboys had agreed to reach into their older material to fill out their setlist if they had to cut some of their current songs for being too "edgy." This was a small detail Mom had neglected to tell any of us. DC Talk's "Jesus Freak" sounded like something that could've been performed by Nirvana, which was exactly what China had asked Mom not to do.

book his entire Third Reich is searching for, opens it up, signs his autograph, hands it back, and continues on.

Sure, I was banging on the keyboards, not swinging around on a bullwhip, but it was still an Indiana Jones tie-in, which brought me great joy. We were waving the proverbial Diary directly in the faces of our unsuspecting hosts, and they were all rainbows and smiles about it.

Then it was time for Budd's song over at my keys. Initially, my plan had been to slide over and "pretend" to play the non-working keyboard from the closet so I'd have something to do. But with the crowd starting to respond like they were, I now had a better idea.

Mimicking Dean's big overhead claps, I danced my way out to the front of the stage and began throwing the prison candy I'd stuffed in my pocket during intermission out into the audience. People leaped out of their chairs to catch whatever it was I was throwing, and then Gavin joined me. I reached into my other pocket and handed him a handful to toss. When we were both empty, I suddenly remembered Mom's beachballs and ran offstage to grab them. I tossed one over to Gavin then batted the other one into the crowd.

The crowd seemed confused by the ball and politely passed it back to the front row, who gently placed it back on the stage. I picked it back up, motioned for them to hit it out into the theater, then sent it sailing again. Gavin did the same. When it appeared they had caught on, I jumped off the stage and started running up and down the aisles, occasionally stopping to grab someone's hand and pull them out of their seat, encouraging them to move and clap along. Gavin followed suit on the opposite aisle.

So it went for the duration of Budd's song. We'd run up one side of the aisle, hands outstretched to high-five everyone at the end of the row like a basketball player jogging into the tunnel at halftime. At the back of the auditorium, we'd turn around and sprint back down, doing the same thing on the other side.

Apparently, that's all it takes to win over an audience in China: some Eagles, some high-fives, some candy, and a couple beachballs. Who would've guessed?

You never know.

As Budd wrapped his song, Gavin and I climbed back up on the stage and returned to our instruments.

The two halves of the show were already night and day, but we weren't quite done. The two songs Dean had written in both languages were straight-up church worship songs. As he sang them, he invited everyone to lift their hands in the air. A good portion of the crowd took him up on it, which was quite a sight to behold. Hundreds of audience members in Communist China with their hands stretched up to the heavens while Dean sang blatant, unapologetic songs about God in Mandarin.

That was most definitely a new one.

I don't know if anyone with their hands up knew *why* they were up—or if they even understood the real meaning behind the lyrics Dean had written specifically with their country in mind. I wondered if it even mattered. If God was up there looking down at this spectacle, would He care if they knew what they were doing or not? Did He take any pleasure in people going through the motions with no understanding of what they were doing?

Did you still get missionary points for tricking people into participating in your religious activities?

Those were probably good question for philosophers and theologians.

The last song in our set wasn't an ideal closer. Bands were supposed to save their biggest hit for the end, but since nobody knew any of our songs anyway, we figured it didn't matter what we closed with. Last night at the club, we hadn't even noticed it. Now, it didn't feel like a proper send-off. Also, we were having such a good time at this point that none of us were quite ready to get off the stage. But what do you do when you're a band at the end of its set and you don't have any more songs up your sleeve?

You play one you already played, that's what.

With a little encouragement from Dean, the entire audience rose to its feet, and we closed the show with the same song we'd opened with, the Newsboys' "Not Ashamed." Only this time we played it as a five-piece.

When it ended for the second time that evening, the audience cheered and applauded and refused to stop. We took a few bows, waved, took a few more bows, waved some more, walked up to high-five those crowding the stage, took a few more bows, and then stood there awkwardly waiting for the ovation to subside. We had no idea how to handle the moment.

Mr. Wu came out on stage, took the mic, and turned to address the band. "I think everyone in the building would like to hear an encore!" Adam yelled the translation to us from offstage.

We all looked around at each other, unsure of what to do. We didn't have an encore. We had prepared exactly 20 songs, we had already played all of them, and we'd played one of them twice. We didn't have anything else.

Fresh out of ideas, Dean suggested, "'Not Ashamed' again?" with a shrug.

Why not?

So, for the third time that evening, the Newboys/Newsboys launched into "Not Ashamed," playing it with every last thing we had to give.

The encore was supposed to be the pinnacle of the evening—the jewel in the performance crown—when both the audience and the band finally get what they came here seeking. For the audience: *the epic closer.* For the band: *validation that the audience wanted more.* And here we were—standing up in front of The People's Republic of China in our ripped jeans and Goodwill shirts and broken decoy instruments, playing the same song for our opener, closer, and encore . . . and the enraptured audience couldn't have shown us more love if they'd tried.

When "Not Ashamed" ended for the third time, Mr. Wu took the mic again and said a few words about this "incredible moment in Changsha's history." Then he brought Mom out and presented her with a bouquet. Then he thanked everyone for coming out and wished them a wonderful night.

Nobody moved.

They wanted autographs.

When it was clear nobody was leaving until they'd gotten a memento proving they'd witnessed this once-in-a-lifetime event, Mr. Wu motioned for security to unblock the steps on either side of the stage. For the next hour, the five of us stood on stage in a mob of people, signing whatever they handed us to sign.

There were going to be an awful lot of disappointed people someday if they ever whipped out a napkin to prove they really met Shane Almgren once upon a time, and nobody knew who the hell that was.

When the last person had gotten the last signature of the last unknown member of the band they'd never heard of before tonight, it was finally time to go.

Outside the front entrance of the theater was a huge poster of the Newsboys that Mom wanted a picture of all of us in front of. Dean, still of the mind that we were the Newboys, not the Newsboys, declined to be in it.

One of the reporters who'd been following us since we got to Changsha stepped forward and inquired, "Okay, which one are each of you in this picture?"

Before any of us could answer, Mom jumped to the rescue, "Let's play a game! Which one do *you* think they are?"

The reporter studied the poster and looked back at us, trying hard to determine which faces standing before her matched up with which faces on a poster that didn't contain any matches.

"You," she pointed at me, "are this one?" She pointed at the second person in the photo, Newsboys bassist Phil Joel. "Am I correct?"

"Now *that* was a great guess," Mom piped in. "A truly remarkable guess!"

There are no limits to
what you can accomplish,
except the limits you
place on your own
thinking.
– Brian Tracy

If you think you are too
small to make a
difference, try sleeping
with a mosquito.
– Dalai Lama XIV

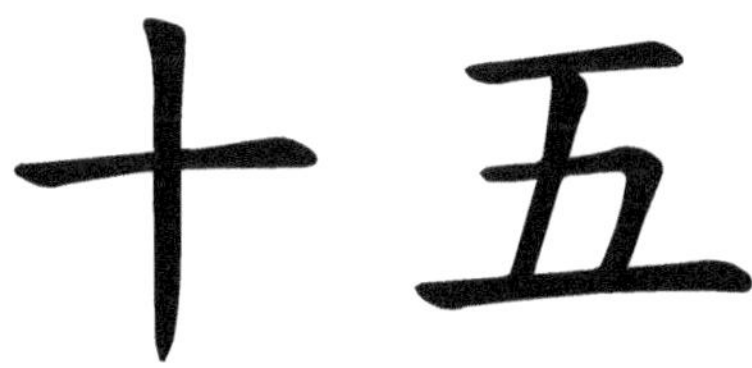

Toasted

As we walked back to the hotel, Mom sidled up to me and asked, "How did the second set go?"

Why is she asking me that?

"What do you mean, 'How did it go?'" You were filming the whole thing from the front row of the balcony. You had the best seat in the house."

"The battery in the video camera died right before intermission," Mom explained, "so I ran back to the hotel to grab a backup battery. I didn't make it back until halfway through the last set."

"Mum, the theater is a five-minute walk from our hotel. Intermission was 20 minutes. The second set was nearly 50 minutes. What took you so long?"

"I got lost going back to the hotel."

Lost.

It was exactly two turns from the hotel to the theater. Exit the hotel lobby and turn right. Walk to the end of the block, turn left, and go straight until you come to the theater. That was it. A decade in the making, and the woman responsible for the entire thing had missed the highlights because there were two turns involved.

Blame it on Changsha for not having an Atlantic Ocean handy.

Once we'd made it back to the hotel, we had about 30 minutes to relax, unwind, towel off, and change clothes—whatever we needed to do before meeting back downstairs for the elaborate, 12-course celebration banquet our hosts had arranged.

The banquet room was on the second floor of the lobby, at the top of a winding, Cinderella-style staircase. It was an intimate, private affair planned for just the six of us, our translator Adam, Mr. Wu, and four other key city officials whose names I couldn't remember but who'd been instrumental in making this whole thing happen.

The twelve of us in attendance were seated around a large circular table, the seating arrangement alternating between American guests and Chinese hosts. Mom was one person over to my left, Gavin one over to my right. Each of us had been assigned our own individual server who stood behind us at the ready to immediately attend to whatever we required throughout the evening.

First things first, Mr. Wu wanted to propose a toast. On cue, each server stepped forward and poured a toast's worth of wine into the glasses on the table in front of us.

Mom, not a drinker *at all* and not terribly fond of others indulging in it either, leaned over towards Gavin and me and whispered, "This is the *one* time you're allowed to have a little wine." Then to Jeremy, she said, "Sorry, but you do not get to partake."

Adam wanted to know why Jeremy couldn't have some wine. "Because he's only 19," Mom said. "He's not old enough."

"The drinking age in China is 18," Adam informed her.

"Well, it's 21 in America, and those are the rules I follow," replied Mom.

"When in Rome," eh, Mum? Also, since when do you follow any rules anywhere ever?

This was news to me.

Mr. Wu stood and raised his glass. The rest of us followed suit. Adam translated for the table, "To my new American friends, on behalf of China and the city of Changsha, congratulations on a successful, exceptional performance this evening!"

Each person touched glasses with as many people as they could reach, knocked back our wine, and returned to our seats. I observed that Mom hadn't actually downed hers, just faking the motion.

Optics.

Immediately, every server stepped forward and refilled the wine glasses to the same level. I looked over at Gavin.

Were they going to step up and refill the glasses every time they were emptied?

We didn't have to wait long to find out because the Chinese host sitting between us raised his glass to the two of us, clinked ours without saying a word, and tossed it back. We did the same. Once again, the servers stepped up and immediately refilled them. Mom was in deep conversation with the person to her left and hadn't seen us, which was good. As we were about to discover, the Chinese *loved* to toast.

Over the next two hours, we toasted everything under the sun. *To American friends! To Chinese friends! To America-Chinese relations! To you! To me! To him! To her! To that guy over there! To your family! To your health! To your family's health!* Toast after toast after toast, each time knocking it back, each time immediately being refilled. Mom still wasn't paying any attention.

And still, it continued. *To good luck! To the future! To much happiness! To full bellies! To peace on earth!*

"To coming back again soon!" Adam translated for Mr. Wu.

What was that?

Coming . . . *back?* That must've been the wine talking. I was feeling a pretty good buzz myself.

"Yes," Adam continued to translate, "he says you are welcome to come back any time you want. You are all family now. Changsha would be delighted for you to do more shows."

Seriously?

That had to be the wine talking. This was a one-off affair. That had always been the plan. Show up, pretend to be the Newsboys, try to pull off a couple shows without embarrassing ourselves into oblivion, hopefully not get busted for attempting to pull a fast one, hightail it home, and breathe a huge sigh of relief, never mentioning it again. They couldn't possibly want *us* to come back. We were just the stand-ins, posers.

Imposters.

Mr. Wu was definitely drunk.

Right?

The banquet room doors opened, and five beautiful young women entered, seductively dressed, each wearing a platinum blonde wig.

"One for each of you," Adam translated for Mr. Wu. "Take your pick."

Jeremy's eyes bulged, and a grin slowly crept over his face. Before he could start pointing, Dean leaned over to Adam and said, "Thank you, but we're not that kind of band. Tell them they may leave." Jeremy looked like he'd just been told an alligator ate his puppy.

When everyone had eaten all they could eat, toasted all they could toast, and posed for every possible people-combination of photos it was mathematically possible to configure, it was time to call it a night.

Gavin and I exited first, both a bit wobbly (okay, a lot wobbly), our arms draped over each other's shoulders. We stepped out of the banquet room to the top of the winding staircase, surveyed the expansive 5-star lobby that had been our temporary rock-star digs for a brief moment in time, missed the first step down, and promptly rolled in a tangled heap all the way to the bottom of the spiraled staircase, like the world's greatest stuntmen. Or the world's worst rock stars. Take your pick.

"You okay, dude?" Gavin grunted.

"Uh, I think so," I managed to croak.

"Can you take your elbow out of my crotch?"

"Yeah, gimme a second."

"I'd rather not wait if you can help it."

"Gavin, I just had a thought."

"What's that, dude?"

"We should've rappelled down the stairs."

We managed to stand up and collect ourselves, slung our arms over each other's shoulders once more, and wobbled ourselves to the elevator.

We made it up to our room and changed into our pajamas. "Let's go say goodnight to everyone and then crash, sound good?" Gavin suggested.

"Let's do it."

We walked over to the next room to knock on the door, but it was already cracked open. I peeked in to see who was there. Budd was sitting at the foot of the bed. He was staring at the TV. Jeremy was spread out behind him, sound asleep, still fully dressed.

"Guys, come in here and take look at this," Budd waved us in and motioned at the TV. We came in and plopped down on the other bed.

Budd pointed at the screen. We stared at it dumbfounded, trying to process what we were looking at.

A knock came at the door, and Mom rushed in without waiting for an answer. "Have you guys turned on the TV yet? Okay, you have, good!"

Dean entered a moment later and sat on the bed next to Budd. "Change the channel," he said.

Budd clicked the remote.

"Change it again."

Again, Budd obliged.

"Is that all of them?"

"All the ones I've got," Budd answered.

"Unbelievable," Dean whispered.

Yes, it was. It was unbelievable indeed.

Every broadcast TV station—every *Communist Party State-sponsored* channel—was broadcasting the same thing to the entire country of China.

It was the concert we had just performed that evening.

It is impossible to be a
maverick or a true original if
you're too well behaved and
don't want to break the rules.
You have to think outside the
box. That's what I believe.
After all, what is the point of
being on this earth if all you
want to do is be liked by
everyone and avoid trouble?

– Arnold Schwarzenegger

You only live once, but if you
do it right, once is enough.

– Mae West

Off the Wall

The morning after the concert, Dean and Budd flew back to the States. They'd both upended their lives for two weeks to be here and didn't have any more time to waste dillydallying around. It was the last time I saw either of them (though I'd reconnect with Dean on Facebook 20 years later, and Budd four years after that).

As for Mom, Gavin, Jeremy, and me, we were going to Beijing for a couple days to do some sightseeing. You don't come all the way to China and not stop by the Great Wall if you get the chance. Especially not when you're secretly toting rappelling gear specifically intended for that exact landmark. That would be borderline sacrilegious.

The four of us arrived in Beijing, collected the copious amounts of luggage, instruments, and rental equipment we were still lugging around, and hailed a van large enough to accommodate all our belongings. The plan was to find our hotel, settle in, and relax a bit, then meet up later to go for a casual stroll through the neighborhood in search of a place to grab dinner.

Each of us was still wired from the night before, trying to process what we'd just experienced in our own way. The reality of it still hadn't quite sunk in. For Mom and Jeremy, this was something like the proverbial holiday hangover—all the buildup, all the festivities, all the anxiety that comes with out-of-town houseguests, all the cleanup, and then the calm that sets in once the last bit of wrapping paper has been thrown away and the last guest has driven off into the night.

Gavin and I weren't quite there yet. If everything went smoothly, we'd be there the next evening. But not just yet. We still had one more impossible feat to attempt.

The next morning, the four of us got up early, grabbed breakfast in the lobby, and then piled into a taxi. It fell to me to do whatever translating needed to be done. Had I not been back here a few months ago, I would've been only marginally more useful than Mom. But her college graduation present to me had been a four-week trip backpacking around the Himalayan foothills with another missionary friend of ours. Immersed in the countryside for a month that summer had allowed enough of the Mandarin I'd lost over the previous decade to creep back in that I could now be serviceable. Barely.

According to the concierge desk, it was supposed to be a 45-minute drive to the nearest section of the Great Wall that was accessible to tourists. Twenty minutes into the trip, we hit Beijing morning rush hour gridlock. The four-lane highway we were on ground to a halt until it became a four-lane parking lot. About a mile up ahead, the road curved to the right, and we could clearly see the cars up there weren't moving either.

Beijing traffic jams were legendary, though I'd never actually experienced one myself. I'd read somewhere—*National Geographic* maybe?—that much of the capital city's notorious pollution and smog wasn't due so much to the number of vehicles on the road at all times, but the number of vehicles that were simply parked on the road with their engines running for hours on end, waiting for someone to move. The State kept encouraging people to shut off their vehicles if it was obvious traffic wasn't going to be moving for a while, but apparently, everyone here liked their air conditioning far more than they cared about being able to see more than two miles into the distance. Or breathing.

One anecdote recounted a traffic jam that was so bad a businessman got stuck in it on his way downtown and showed up two hours late for work... the *next* day. He spent 26 hours in his car making a 30-mile commute. Maybe it was an exaggeration, but very possibly not. As far as I could see in any direction, nobody was going anywhere for a very long time.

In an apparent effort to show his foreign fare what a responsible citizen he was, our driver switched off the engine. Thankfully, it was brisk enough this time of year that we were all wearing jackets and didn't mind. If it had been July, this would've been intolerable.

Since it looked like we were going to be living here for the foreseeable future, I decided to get to know our new roommate, the driver, as best I could with my now-limited Mandarin. Naturally, he had some questions about us, and I did my best to answer them.

Where were we from?

"America."

Was this our first time in Beijing?

"For two of us, yes. The lady and I had been here once before, many years ago."

Were we here on business or pleasure?

"A little of both."

What did we do for work?

"We were here to play music."

You are in a band?

"Yes, the three of us. Our other two members left yesterday."

You are a band from America, and you were playing in China?

"Yes, in Changsha. We performed two times."

No, I don't believe you. It is not possible. It is strictly forbidden!

"That's what we thought too!"

And you did not get in trouble?

"No. They even put our shows on TV."

Your band has been on the television?

"Yes, we were on TV last night—on all the . . ." I couldn't remember how to say "channels" or "stations," so I mimed turning the channel while pointing at his radio.

His eyes grew big as saucers.

So, you are very famous then, yes?

"I don't think we are fam—" I didn't get a chance to finish the thought.

The driver fired up the car, rolled down his window, pulled what looked like a hood-mounted police flasher light from under his seat, and stuck it on the roof of the taxi. Then he flipped on a siren—

Why does this taxi have a siren?

—pulled off onto the shoulder of the highway, and gunned it, speaking excitedly as he did so.

I will get you to the Great Wall in 20 minutes, my American friends!!!

I'm not sure what he was thinking. He didn't get us there in 20 minutes—more like 13. With siren blaring and removable light flashing, he flew down the shoulder, veering off into the grass whenever a pothole presented itself. We fishtailed off the exit ramp (am I allowed to say *Tokyo drifted* in Beijing?), hopped a curb, and sped down a sidewalk, swerving to avoid the pedestrians, who were flinging themselves out of the way. It was just like a car chase scene out of a movie—at least, it would've been if a second car had been involved.

Rounding a corner fast enough to send all of us flying into the passenger doors from the centrifugal force, he suddenly slammed on the brakes, bringing the cab to a whiplash-inducing, screeching halt. Directly in front of us, no more than six feet from our front bumper, two camels were slowly being led across the street by their handlers to their daily station in front of the Great Wall. They made a great photo op for tourists.

As an animal lover, I heaved a sigh of relief. But the lower-evolved, reptilian brain inside my head was slightly disappointed. "Imposter Rock Stars Obliterate Camel Pair in Great Wall Taxi Crash" would've made an epic headline.

The driver appeared unimpressed that he'd narrowly avoided a circus disaster. He was too busy grinning from ear to ear and pointing at the clock on the dash, making sure we were fully aware of the excellent time he'd just made.

We exited the cab, and Mom fished around in her ever-present fanny pack for some money to pay him. She began counting out a stack of crumpled bills, but he furiously waved her off. She tried forcing the fare into his hand, but he adamantly refused to take it. Resigned, Mom thanked him, then ordered me to tell him that God loved him and she would be praying for him.

I leaned into the window and translated, "She says that you are the best driver we have ever known. Thank you for getting here so fast!"

Beaming, the driver fished around in his console and came up with a few random scraps of paper. Beckoning Gavin and Jeremy over to his door, he asked the three of us to sign our autographs, which we happily obliged.

Now, with the rock star formalities and narrowly-averted camel murder out of the way, it was finally time to get to tourist-ing.

The walking path from the parking lot to the Great Wall entrance was a tourist trap. It was lined on both sides with makeshift shops selling T-shirts, trinkets, and various souvenirs proudly announcing "I Climbed the Great Wall of China." Jeremy wanted to shop, so Mom stayed near him while Gavin and I made our way to the main entrance. Two stalls from the end, I saw it.

A sword.

I hadn't been looking for any sword in particular—anything larger than a Rambo knife would've sufficed for my purposes—but the one hanging in the back of the stall was exactly the one I didn't know I needed. I approached the shopkeeper and pointed up at the blade.

I'll take that.

She told me the price: ¥300 yuan—about $75. That meant its fair market value was probably half that.

I was happy to pay it so we could get on with the important illegal business we'd come here to do; however, bargaining was expected here, and passing up an opportunity to haggle would've violated my morals. Since everything was pre-priced to give the vendors plenty of room to come down and still make a profit, I offered her 125.

No good. 250.

Too much. 150.

240.

160.

220.

180.

210.

190.

205.

200.

Okay, you have a deal!

Fifty bucks. A proper bargaining session.

Sword in hand, Gavin and I made our way to the ticket window and purchased two passes. Moving past the window, we climbed the two flights of stairs to the top.

The Great Wall of China is not particularly tall. When people mention the height of the wall being hundreds—or even thousands—of feet high, they're talking about the elevation of the hills or mountains it's built on, not the wall itself. The actual stone structure ranges anywhere from 20 feet to nearly 50 feet from its base to the tops of the watchtowers. Naturally, Gavin and I would've preferred the highest spot we could find, but we decided that going undetected was the higher priority.

Standing on the top of the wall, you can head off in either direction you like. There are no lines, ropes, or railings to funnel people anywhere, no modern artifacts of any kind to sully the original, pristine architecture of one of the Seven Wonders of the World. Too many (for my taste) ancient tourist attractions have been lined with red carpets or cordoned off with velvet ropes to keep visitors confined to specific locations. For me, that spoiled all the magic. Standing atop the Great Wall, you got the exact same experience as the guards who patrolled it back when construction started in the third century BC.[46]

To our right, the wall was relatively tame, gently rising and falling on low hills. That's where most of the tourists were conglomerating. That meant we were going the other way, where the steeper inclines guaranteed a quad burn within a couple hundred yards. Jazzed, we set off.

Being a tourist hotspot, another cool thing about the Great Wall is that there aren't any "This Is As Far As You Can Go" signs telling you to turn around. Once you're up there, you can keep walking until you plunge into the ocean or drop from exhaustion. No one's gonna stop you.[47]

Tourists generally confined themselves to within a few hundred yards to a quarter of a mile in either direction of the entrance. A half mile out, the tourist flow slowed to a trickle. At a mile, you'd maybe cross paths with someone walking in the opposite direction every 10 or 15 minutes. Our plan was to keep walking until we couldn't see anyone in either direction.

---

[46] The Great Wall was continuously built from 220 BCE until the 17th century CE.

[47] At a total length of nearly 22,000 km (13,000 miles), you can walk the entire thing, if you were so inclined, in about 18 months.

After 45 minutes, we spotted a watchtower in the distance at the top of an imposing, quarter-mile climb and decided that would be our first spot to scope out. Another 15 minutes, and we'd be there.

Halfway to the tower, we were startled to see a sight neither of us had noticed when we were scanning the wall. There was a seated figure 50 yards up ahead, his chair rocked back on two legs and leaning against the wall. As we approached, a middle-aged Chinese man decked out head to toe in authentic Ming Dynasty guard regalia hopped up out of the hand-carved wooden chair he'd been reclining in and formally bowed in our direction.

What is he doing here?

While certainly less common than seeing your favorite costumed characters at Disney World or Times Square, it wasn't out of the ordinary for people dressed up in traditional garb to be stationed around historical landmarks for photo ops with tourists.

But this wasn't exactly a high-traffic area. There was literally nobody else in sight but the three of us. If he was there just to take photos with the dozen or so hikers who ventured out this far each day, that was some serious commitment to his profession. It was a grueling walk to make in jeans and good hiking boots, never mind all that battle armor he was wearing. This didn't make a lot of sense.

Was he actually . . . guarding . . . *the place?*

That thought made me smile. For the second time in three days, my mind flashed to *Indiana Jones and the Last Crusade*—that scene at the end, where Indy finds an ancient Knight Templar inside the city of Petra, guarding the Holy Grail.

I wanted to chat with him to find out what he was doing way out here, but his accent (or was it a local dialect?) was so thick that I couldn't make out anything he was saying.

Observing what was strapped to his belt, I quickly determined it didn't matter whether he was just some poor guy in desperate need of a paycheck stationed out here for photo ops or a genuine 700-year-old mystic—I was going to get a photo. A very *specific* photo.

Señor Ming Dynasty had a jewel-encrusted dagger on one hip and a sword that kind of looked like mine on the other. Pointing to his sword, I gave him a thumbs-up. Then I drew my sword and motioned for him to draw his. We squared off in a mock battle stance, blades locked. I tried to scowl for the camera, to no avail. There was simply too much childlike joy in the moment, and my brain wouldn't let my face pretend like there wasn't. Trying once more anyway only made me break out into a laugh. Which made him laugh. Gavin snapped the picture.

I thanked him, tapped his sword with mine (I have no idea how congenial sword-based encounters are supposed to end), and then we continued on.

If only he'd pulled out that knife first . . .

That encounter was probably the closest I'd ever get to having an opportunity to unleash my devasting *Crocodile Dundee* retort.

A few minutes later, we were at the tower. We ran up the steps to the platform on top and looked over the side. It was maybe 40 feet to the ground. One side was in full view of anyone who happened to be coming this direction from the entrance. The back side was shielded from view, so back side it was. We unshouldered our backpacks and started to remove our harnesses when Gavin had a sudden realization.

"Dude, if we go off here, how are we gonna get back up?"

It was a very salient point.

Once you rappelled to the ground, there was absolutely no way to get back on the wall. Walking up the side of a building with just a rope to pull on worked for Batman and Robin in the old TV show and exactly nowhere else. This wasn't Gotham City—once you hit the ground, you were stuck there. If we both went down, there'd be no way to retrieve our rope, and we'd have to walk all the way back over the natural terrain. I couldn't believe none of this had dawned on me before right now.

We briefly debated that option, then decided against it. For broke college grads, the rope was too expensive to leave behind, and walking a couple miles over the mountains through the brush would probably put us back around dinnertime. We were supposed to rendezvous with Mom and Jeremy in about an hour.

There was another option, but it was risky. At irregular intervals along the Great Wall, a staircase led down to a ground-level doorway in the side of the wall. I wasn't sure what purpose these random exits served, as there was nothing to do or see once you stepped through them. You were literally stepping out into the wild in the middle of nowhere.

I had counted two of these arbitrary doorways on our way here. The one closest to the entrance was in the thick of the tourist throng. So, that was out of the question.

We could continue walking and hope we came across another one, but with their random distribution, there was no telling how far we might have to go before we found one. Timewise, it probably wasn't feasible.

That meant the only realistic option was the second doorway we'd passed—far enough from the entrance that being seen wasn't a guarantee, but still close enough that it wouldn't be a surprise either.

Option 4: Don't illegally rappel off the Great Wall at all. [48]

"Get thee behind me, Satan," I muttered under my breath.

"What was that?" Gavin asked.

"Nothing," I replied. "Just rebuking some evil temptations from the pit of hell."

"Right on, dude. We doing this?"

Yes. Yes, we were.

We walked back to the stairwell and removed our backpacks. A group of tourists was approaching from the opposite direction, so we waited a few minutes for them to pass before taking out our gear. We pulled on our harnesses and then stood there mulling over the best way to tie off. There was nothing on the walkway to anchor to, so we were going to have to find a creative way to use the battlements that lined the wall.

---

[48] As a UNESCO World Heritage site, tying a rope around a turret and climbing off the side of the Great Wall of China is about as encouraged as scaling the Great Pyramid of Giza, which is to say, it's not. While I don't actually know what the punishment is in China if you're caught, I know Egypt has a penalty of up to a month in jail and/or up to $6,300 in fines. (That's why I've planned how I'm going to climb the Great Pyramid very meticulously. Obviously, it will involve a ninja suit. The plan is to walk straight out into the desert during the day, wearing traditional nomad clothing so as not to attract attention. After nightfall, I'll change into my ninja suit and approach the Great Pyramid from the desert in the back, where no one is expecting. Scramble up, snap a pick, and scramble back down. A headlamp seems like a potential giveaway, so I'm looking into night vision goggles on Temu. Since I've never been to Cairo to case the joint and thus have no clue how feasible this plan is, I'll bring the $6,300 for the fine—just in case—and mentally prep for doing a month of jailtime in northern Africa.)

We finally settled on looping the rope around two adjacent battlements, then passing both ends of slack back through the gap between them and over the side. A rock-solid anchor with no knots involved.

The group that had passed by five minutes ago was still walking into the distance, and nobody else was coming from that way. In the other direction, a family with a stroller was slowly making their way toward us, but judging by their pace, they were 10 minutes away. This was probably as good as it was ever going to get.

We rock-paper-scissored for first honors. Gavin won. I called two out of three. Gavin won that round, too, so I called four out of seven. Gavin told me to screw off. And while I was doing that, perhaps I could snap a picture too?

That was another stellar idea that hadn't crossed my mind.

Picture or it didn't happen!

With these stairs and the doorway, whoever wasn't on the rope could run out and capture a snapshot from the perfect angle. You know, just in case we ever needed to prove our crimes to the authorities.

When I was in position, I gave Gavin the thumbs-up, and he edged backward off the wall, pausing midway down to ham it up for the camera.

As soon as he was down, I handed him the camera and ran up for my turn. I quickly tied in, kissed the wall for good measure, and backed over the edge.

The moment I touched the ground, Gavin bolted up the stairs to clean the rope. I untied myself and followed suit, wriggling out of my harness on the way. I grabbed the harnesses while Gavin stuffed the rope unceremoniously into his pack. Bad practice, but now wasn't the time to lay it out flat and wind it up properly—we could do that back at the hotel. We needed to book it out of here.

With our packs on our backs, Gavin checked the time. The whole episode had taken less than 10 minutes, start-to-finish. It was barely more than a 20-foot drop to the ground. Over in a matter of seconds and hardly worth mentioning.

Then again, the distance had never been the point.

Relieved and elated, we high-fived and started the long trek back the way we came. This had been the last item we needed to do. We'd accepted this crazy mission and turned ourselves into an actual band on 12 days' notice. Maybe not the band China thought they were getting, but we'd pulled it off, ended up on television rather than in prison, and gave a good enough accounting of ourselves to get invited back by the people we'd just duped. Now, we had topped it all off by rappelling off the Great Wall of China.

And I'd gotten my sword.

There was simply nothing else to ask for. It was time to go home.

If all difficulties were
known at the outset of the
journey, most of us would
never start out at all.
– Dan Rather

Wrap Party

The following day, Mom, Jeremy, Gavin, and I traveled to the airport together, where we parted ways for our separate flights to Pennsylvania and Florida.

Realizing this farewell was the final, riding-off-into-the-sunset existence of the Newsboys—or Newboys, or whatever the hell band we were supposed to be—I wrapped Mom in a bear hug and lifted her off in the ground. I couldn't have been prouder of her. She'd actually done it.

She had pulled off the impossible.

(She is free to give credit to whomever she wishes, but I give her every last drop of it. She can argue and protest and deflect until she's hot pink in the face, but I'm not doing any takebacks.)

Gavin and I had an overnight layover in New York City, arriving at our hotel a little after 9 p.m. The responsible thing to do now was relax, unwind, and then go to bed and get some good sleep. But I'd just slept 12 hours on the flight back and wasn't tired. I also wasn't responsible (that was still another ten years off, give or take). So, a New York City subway ride on a Saturday night that was also Halloween Eve (a.k.a. *Devil's Night*) it was gonna be.

I'd never been to New York before, but I had—let's all say it together now—*seen a lot of movies*. If the inerrant Hollywood was to be believed, the New York City subway was approximately 90% climactic showdowns and 10% breakdance battles. I found both possibilities acceptable.

We threw on our jackets and walked the couple blocks to the nearest subway station. When we got there, Gavin and I had our first disagreement of the trip.

He was of the opinion that we should pay for our passes like normal people and then board the train, also like normies, clearly not understanding how anything in this town worked. That gallant nonsense may fly in Hong Kong, but here in The Big Apple, I knew the proper way to navigate the subway was to bound down the stairs at full speed, vault over the turnstile, and then sprint to the train and dive in headfirst as the doors closed. Presumably with bullets flying overhead. Gavin was an idiot and needed to travel more. Plus, I wasn't sure when or if I'd ever be back here again, so this wasn't up for debate.

Since we couldn't come to an agreement, we found an amicable compromise: we would purchase two passes—like normal people—and then he would go wait on the platform, normally, while I went back out to the top of the stairs and ran the obligatory obstacle course. If anyone collared me for hopping the gate, I'd actually have a pass to show them.

So, that's what we did. I flew down the steps, side-vaulted the turnstile, sprinted for the train—whose doors were wide open and Gavin was now aboard—and flung myself into the car like Pete Rose sliding into third. I hit the deck hard, slamming shoulder-first into a metal pole.

Rather than the doors closing immediately behind under a hail of Uzi fire, they remained open. For an uncomfortably awkward amount of time. Gavin was cackling. I glanced up at the lightly populated car I'd just dove into and saw a few people in full costume and face paint staring at me puzzled. Then they turned their attention back to whatever they'd been doing and didn't give me a second look. Apparently, this was nothing out of the ordinary.

After what seemed like an eternity, the doors finally shut, and the train lurched off. I pulled myself to my feet. My shoulder was throbbing, and now I didn't feel like doing anything but sitting.

So, Gavin and I sat. We rode for about 30 minutes, watching people get on, get off, go about their lives, oblivious to our existence. Not 48 hours ago, we were rock stars, broadcasting to a billion people on national TV—everyone in our vicinity clamoring for interviews, asking for autographs, willing to annihilate dromedariesto get us to our next destination. Now, we were invisible—just two random guys on a train. There was something emphatically melancholic about the realization. It all felt . . . *hollow*.

Half an hour later, we got off, switched tracks, and rode back in the other direction to our station. We stopped at a convenience store on the walk back to the hotel and picked up a six-pack of Tsingtao—or was it Yuengling?[49]—for a low-key, celebratory nightcap. Neither of us was ready to let go of the whole China experience just yet, and I think we both felt that the simple act of imbibing an authentic Chinese beverage would allow us, if only for a few more moments, to cling to that fading connection before it was gone forever.

The next day we flew out of La Guardia, bound for Fort Lauderdale. We arrived in the evening, and, true to his word, Chris was waiting for us at the airport. As soon as he saw us exit baggage claim, he hopped out of the car to greet us, dressed casually in a striped T-shirt and sporting a full, painted-on Frankenstein face.

Yep, that's on-brand.

After a few different attempts at Tetris-ing all the luggage and musical gear into the car, we finally found the one configuration that fit, and away we went.

Chris wanted to hear every last detail, and Gavin and I launched in at the same time, giving no thought to chronological order, interrupting, talking over each other, and making the whole recounting nearly impossible to follow.

"Wait, wait, wait!" Chris finally interjected. "One at a time! I caught something about a radio interview for a soda commercial and someone had machine guns, and you were on television and there was a car

---

[49] Yes, I know Yuengling is originally a German beer, now produced in Pennsylvania. I know that *now*. But we didn't know it at the time, so don't judge. I bet some of you reading this are just now learning that piece of trivia for the first time. That makes me better than you.

chase, and you climbed off the Great Wall, and . . . did I hear one of you say something about running over a *camel?*"

Yeah, he'd gotten the basic gist of it.

We were about to start over and try again in a less Tarantino fashion when Chris exited off I95, nowhere close to where we were going.

"Yo, what are we doing?" Gavin asked. "Aren't you taking us home?"

"Are you kidding me?" said Chris. "It's Halloween. There's a huge party at the coffeehouse."

That would explain the face paint.

"And my mom's got a little surprise for you guys."

Gavin and I glanced at each other. At least we still had a couple fans.

We pulled up to the church, packed with cars for the Sunday evening service. Chris assured us half the cars were there for the Halloween party,[50] which was already bumping.

That was going to be a problem. I didn't have a costume. It was hard enough for me not to go out fully costumed for occasions where they were either not called for, not appropriate, or actively prohibited, so going to an actual costume party in street clothes seemed gauche. This would not do.

I remembered that I had my sword in the trunk, so at least I had a prop. That was something. I asked Chris if he had any more face paint, and he said he had plenty inside.

Great. Now we're cooking with gasoline.

Chris led us into the church through a side door so we wouldn't give away our presence until we were properly painted up. I opted for a quick rendition of Brandon Lee's makeup from *The Crow,* while Gavin settled on something halfway between mine and Chris'.

---

[50] I don't remember exactly what it was really called, but it wasn't actually a "Halloween" party. Halloween is frowned upon in Christendom because of reasons, and we're vehemently discouraged from observing the blatant pagan rituals of dressing up in costumes and engaging in candy-related activities. Instead, The Church would prefer that kids treat October 31 as a day to dress up in costumes and engage in candy-related activities, but calling it something like "Harvest Festival" or "Hallelujah Night" or something else that starts with an "H." For Jesus.

Once we were properly made up, Chris walked us back to the double doors leading to the coffeehouse. He told us to wait there while he ran and did something. He squeezed through the doors and disappeared. A minute later, his head reappeared through the doorway and said, "Alright fellas, come on out!"

Gavin and I stepped out into the coffeehouse and were instantly greeted with a thunderous ovation. I'd love to call it a *standing ovation*, but I'm pretty sure you only get to call it that if everyone starts out from a seated position. This was a room where everyone was already standing, so technically that makes it a normal ovation.

Hanging from the ceiling over the service counter area was a huge homemade banner that read, "WELCOME HOME ROCK STARS!"

There were mountains of food, snacks, and drinks to be had (non-alcoholic, of course), and Gavin and I spent the next hour gorging ourselves on the first real American fare we'd had in a week, telling and retelling bits and pieces of our story to each new person who came up wanting to know how it went.

After we'd stuffed ourselves silly, Mrs. Armfield rang a bell to get everyone's attention and called us all to gather over by the counter. The 60 or so people present crowded in, and from under the counter, Mrs. Armfield produced a large cake topped with little plastic instruments and decorated in a handwritten script welcoming Gavin and me home.

"If everyone would please raise their glasses, I'd like to make a toast," she announced.

All the glasses in the room went up.

"Here's to your successful trip, your successful concerts, and for God bringing you both back safely," she paused, smiled, "with your heads still attached to your necks! We love you, and we're thrilled to have you home. Now promise everyone here that you're never going to do anything like this ever again!"

Everyone laughed and clinked glasses. Mrs. Armfield pulled out an oversized silver cake server and began cutting up the cake, scooping the slices onto dessert plates. When she'd run out of counter space, she held out a plate and declared that the prodigal rock stars got to do the honors. She handed the first one to Gavin. She held out another for me, but I politely declined. I couldn't possibly eat another bite.

"Take it, you have to eat it," she admonished.

"I'm completely stuffed," I replied. "I don't have any room left in me."

"I made this myself specially for you two, and you are *going* to eat it, mister!" she commanded with mock seriousness.

"Dude, eat it. It's delicious," Gavin said muffledly through a mouthful of cake.

"I'll take a piece to go," I offered, "so I can fully enjoy it on an empty stomach."

"Young man, you are going to eat this piece of cake if it's the last thing you do," she chided playfully, wagging her silver cake server in my direction."

"Buddy, you better do what she says," Chris chirped in from over my shoulder, "she's holding a knife!"

Yes, she certainly was.

An enormous grin washed over my face, quickly giving way to laughter.

Had to travel halfway around the globe and come all the way back home to get a chance to use it, but better late than never.

"That's not a knife," I scoffed in the worst Australian accent I'd managed to date. From behind my back, I slowly drew out my sword, brandishing it high for everyone in the room to see.

"*This* is a knife."

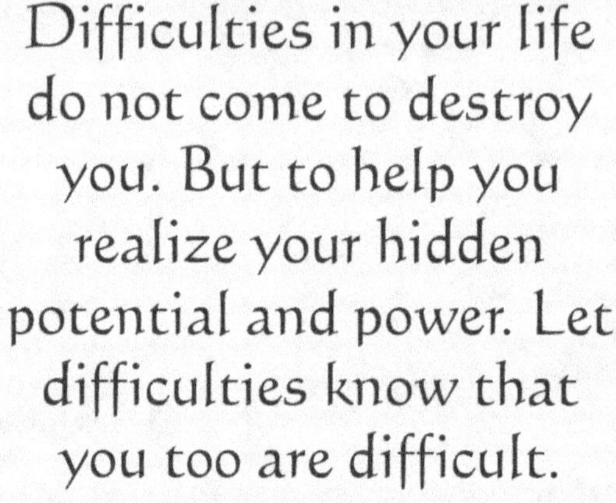

Difficulties in your life
do not come to destroy
you. But to help you
realize your hidden
potential and power. Let
difficulties know that
you too are difficult.
– A.P.J. Abdul Kalam

That's Not a Knife

t's a universal truism that the levity we bring to bear on a situation is inversely proportional to our proximity to it. The further removed, the easier the jokes fly. So, I apologize if I've given the impression that this whole endeavor was a farce. Humor makes fantastic insulation.

The other guys in the band may not have understood at the time the potential seriousness of the situation we were walking into. If not for my own childhood experiences in China, I'm sure I wouldn't have understood it either. Ignorance truly is bliss. In hindsight, it's possible that the only person in the story who acted rationally was Mrs. Armfield.

What Mom pulled off was next to impossible. There are a million reasons why it never should've worked, never even should've been attempted.

That she didn't have a clue what she was doing at any step in the process probably turned out to be the best thing she had going for her that actually made it work at all. Kind of the same way drunk drivers end up less injured in a car wreck. The sober person sees the crash coming and tenses up, making their body stiffer and more brittle at the moment of impact.

There's an excellent chance a competent entertainment industry professional would never have succeeded at this hair-brained mission, simply because there were too many red flags along the way that Mom didn't know were red flags. Or didn't care.

Let's be very clear that there were countless instances on this absurd journey that would have justified a person throwing in the towel.

There's a popular maxim in Christianity that goes: *When one door closes, God opens another.*

There's another—somewhat cheekier—expression out there that says: *When one door closes, push on it until it opens. That's how doors work.*

Finally, there's the school of thought my mom ascribes to: *If there is no door, rent a front-end bucket loader and drive it straight through the side of the building like the Kool-Aid Man, then give God all the credit for the new opening since you're not an engineer.*

It can sometimes seem confusing and arbitrary, and it's left up to each person to decipher for themselves what kind of situation they're dealing with.

We're told, on the one hand, that God closes doors we're not supposed to walk through. On the other hand, we're also not supposed to let obstacles stand in our way, to keep soldiering on until we overcome them.

So how do you know which kind of obstacle you're dealing with?

Is the barrier in front of us a closed door God placed there to divert us in a different direction? Or is it there because He's giving us an obstacle to overcome, a cosmic exercise in getting the tire over the fence?

No one, to my knowledge, has ever provided a definitive and satisfactory answer to that question. I know I don't have it. In my 47 years on the planet, all I can offer is the humble observation that humans have a tendency to do whatever it is they feel like doing and then formulate a retroactive justification for it after the fact.

Everybody has their own perspective on why things happen. Mom saw this entire exercise as one giant series of divine interventions. I can see why she would think that, as several key players in the story were random strangers she just happened to bump into.

But there's always more than one way of looking at any situation. With no manual or guidebook telling you which interpretation is correct, most people tend to just interpret events in the manner that best confirms whatever they already believe about the world. One person's lucky coincidence or happy accident is another's divine appointment; one person's random stranger is another's guardian angel.

As Mom tells it, she could name a handful of people she thought had more connections and were better qualified to pull some strings in China, and she didn't know why God hadn't given one of *them* this mission instead of her. Because she never saw herself as a competent vessel in this endeavor, she has no problem giving God all the credit.

I find it admirable that she's content to deflect from the pugnacious part she played and give all the glory and credit to her God, but, c'*mon, Mum,* God wasn't the one whizzing around in that bucket loader!

I have no idea if Mom actually heard God's voice or not. Maybe He gave her the message quietly and she imagined the voice. Maybe she made up the mission herself and convinced herself it was God. Either way, it doesn't matter. What matters is that her faith never wavered. Just because God calls someone to do something doesn't necessarily mean it's going to get done. The Bible is full of stories of God giving people missions and them failing to see it through to completion. Peter didn't sink beneath the waves because God retracted the calling—he sank because *he* stopped believing in the mission. Just because God issued the call doesn't mean you don't have to hold up your end.

The fact is, even after 25 years working in the entertainment industry, my mother—the Erin Brockovich for Jesus—is probably the only human I know who could conceive of such a preposterous proposition and then barrel through it with reckless abandon despite every warning sign and against all sound advice.

In Robert Rodriguez's comedy-horror schlockfest *Planet Terror,* a ragtag band of survivors have to battle their way to freedom during a zombie apocalypse. The main protagonist, former go-go dancer Cherry Darling, wakes up in the hospital, horrified to discover her leg's been amputated. Later, she's complaining to Dr. Dakota Black about being a one-legged survivor in a zombie outbreak—and showing off an acrobatic backbend to drive home the point that it's her "useless talent number 66." Dr. Block tells her in response, "You know, my girlfriend had a theory. She said at some point in your life, you find a use for every useless talent you ever had. It's like connecting the dots."

The film's climax features Cherry saving the day after affixing a machine gun to her stump leg and mowing down waves of zombies while dodging rocket-launched missiles via backbend.

That's the problem with humans. We don't always see the larger picture. All we see is a hoard of zombies and convince ourselves we're the wrong person for the job. But not every zombie apocalypse situation calls for mercenaries with heavy artillery. Sometimes, a one-legged go-go dancer who can do backbends with a machine-gun leg is humanity's only hope.

This particular mission didn't call for a professional concert promoter, a foreign diplomat, international entertainment attorneys, or even an actual band. It called for someone who couldn't read a room to save her life, existed in perpetual obliviousness to actual peril around her, viewed copyright laws as polite suggestions, had no qualms about "gently shading the truth" and justifying in her head whatever illegal/unethical/dangerous things she was doing, and had zero time or interest for anyone's excuses, no matter how valid.

The same could probably be said for the five of us "Newboys." How many megastar bands out there would've agreed to an intermission and then entertained song requests from the '70s? Would the real Newsboys have rolled the dice with "Desperado," or would they have laughed off the suggestion with disdain and played their regularly scheduled tour set? Would they have met the same fate as George Michael and Wham! all those years ago—giving it their all and failing to make a connection? Maybe complete amateurs with no egos who were willing to do whatever was asked were exactly what this situation called for. Maybe this concert didn't work in *spite* of us; maybe it worked *because* of us.

This world is chock-full of people doing impossible things. It's even more full of people who are capable of impossible things and just haven't realized it yet. The fact is, every single one of us is capable of infinitely more than we think we are. Most of the limits we imagine we've got are arbitrary ones we made up for ourselves. As humans, we're always looking for ways to shortchange ourselves, discount ourselves. And as much as we may recognize that's not the way we ought to approach life (when we see it spelled out like that on paper), we all have a self-preservation mode that kicks into high gear when we see the challenges life throws at us.

Our experiences have taught us that obstacles are formidable and can be as painful to us as a weapon. We see problems as a mountain full of jagged, razor-sharp rocks that we've somehow got to scale. They can bruise us, wound us, shock us, damage us, slice and dice us up like a knife. Self-preservation tells us to turn around and avoid the pain.

But self-actualization is realizing that we are formidable too. We are greater than we imagine. We're capable of inflicting just as much damage on those obstacles as they are on us, maybe more. That's why you don't run away. When you're confronted with one of those seemingly insurmountable challenges, take it all in, size it up . . . and then remember that the worst it can throw at you isn't greater than what's inside of you:

Figure it out.

There is always a way.

Never quit.

Get the tire over the fence.

Yeah, that mountain has rocks that cut like a knife. So what? That's when you look that mountain dead in the eye—not with fear, but with pity—and tell it, "That's not a knife."

"This . . ."

Well, you know the rest.

I may not have gone
where I intended to go,
but I think I have ended
up where I intended to be.
– Douglas Adams

Afterwards

Each member of our trip had a radically different reason for being there. Mom was obviously on a divine mission from God and wouldn't be stopped. I was on board because it sounded adventurous, ludicrous, and came with a high probability of movie-esque danger (which was Chris' specific reason for *not* coming). The fact that it was an opportunity to play music was a plus, and the fact that it entailed impersonating real celebrities was an added bonus. The fact that there was an actual threat of danger, possible imprisonment, or worse, was a feature, not a bug, in my estimation. If Mom had said we were going to the bottom of the Mariana Trench, I would've immediately gone shopping for a speargun.

Gavin came along because he literally had nothing else to do that week. Dean was there because he'd had it on his heart for years to play Christian music in China, and the Newsboys backing out dropped the opportunity in his lap. Jeremy was just there to play drums and see something outside of Pennsylvania. Budd's personal ethos is just to find ways where he can be of service with his "particular set of skills."

After parting ways with Dean, Jeremy, and Budd in China, I never saw or spoke to any of them again until I started putting this book together and tracked them all down. I interviewed each of them for hours and learned more about their perspectives in that short amount of time than anything I was privy to on the trip itself.

Given all our different rationales for signing on, it was fascinating what a divergent yet equally life-changing impact the trip had on each of our lives.

As it turned out, Mr. Wu's invitation to "come back any time" wasn't just the wine talking. Dean wanted to take him up on the offer, but he was as much a cog in the wheel as the rest of us in the band.

Mom was the linchpin to the whole operation, and she was done, finished, *finito*. She had completed her mission for God and was ready to wash her hands of the whole thing. If Dean wanted to run with it, he was welcome to have at it, but he'd have to do it without her. She passed all her contacts and connections to him. He used them to add a few more intriguing chapters to the saga.

In 2002, Dean returned to China with a new band—this one called Regeneration—for a 10-concert tour. Once again, China footed the bill for the entire thing, this time even throwing in a full-fledged tour bus. Jeremy was again on the drums, and he promises me they actually rehearsed for several months this time. Budd was also supposed to go on that trip, but he and Dean butted heads over something, and he decided to bow out.

Regeneration went back for one final tour in 2007, playing another 8-10 shows over a three-week span. Dean was the lone holdover from the original "Newboys."

Jeremy had one of the most interesting and complex perspectives of the bunch. He admitted to me that he'd initially wrestled with going on moral grounds. As he put it, his parents had "conscripted him into the church," which he hated and was thus conflicted about taking part in spreading a message he didn't really believe in.[51] He was fully against the purpose of the trip, but he really wanted to play drums.

Ultimately, the musician in him, not the believer, won out.

---

[51] I didn't disagree with Jeremy's take on this. As the years went by and I had time to reflect on our adventure, I could never quite square the ethical implications of what we'd done with the way Mom had raised me. She'd used homeschool lessons—and our upbringing in general—to decry and rail against the Machiavellian idea that "the ends justify the means." But Mom also had a tendency to be a "do as I say, not as I do" authority figure, and she could justify anything in her mind. So, I guess the ultimate lesson here was: The ends never justify the means, except when they do, which is whenever Mom felt like making an exception.

For love of the game.

That, and he'd grown up poor. This was an all-expenses-paid trip. His flight over was the first time he'd ever set foot inside an airplane.

China opened up Jeremy's eyes to a big, wide world he didn't know existed. Once he'd finally seen a little glimpse of what was out there, he wanted to see the whole thing. He'd caught the travel bug. He listed Spain, Portugal, Morocco, Germany, Croatia, Japan, Thailand, the Philippines, Ecuador, and El Salvador before trailing off and saying he couldn't remember all the other countries he'd visited.

Exactly three months after getting home, Gavin and I packed up our stuff and moved to Nashville, Tennessee. Gavin had a twin brother, Trevor, who'd just graduated from Belmont University that December with a music business degree. While home in West Palm Beach that Christmas, Trevor tried convincing us to move up there with him. He was looking for roommates and wanted someone to write songs with. It was an intriguing proposition. I still hadn't gotten over the rock star high. Then again, completely uprooting yourself—particularly from the beach—to go chase a pipe dream merited some serious consideration and deliberation, not the kind of snap decisions I was known for. So, I took five minutes.

Let's go chase the dream.

It was the first time I'd ever felt a clear direction in life.

And that's perhaps the most inexplicable, extraordinary aspect of this insane journey, requiring the kind of reflection that makes your brain spin like when you try to contemplate infinity. At a collegiate track-and-field meet in a Chinese soccer stadium in 1988, Mom heard a voice from God giving her a divine mission. That voice may or may not have been real, but the mission that came with it was.

Mom completed her mission.

In doing so, the rest of us discovered ours.

October 21, 1999

Dear Mr. █████

This letter is to apologize for our pulling out of the Newsboys China concerts at such a late date. Susie Almgren worked exceptionally hard to make this happen, as did we, and unfortunately due to numerous extenuating circumstances, it just could not work out.

The business of music is a very unpredictable and constantly changing entity, and it is always a challenge to schedule anything, but especially international trips. Newsboys have quite an intense touring schedule, which alone keeps them busy, but we were also recently given numerous deadlines and demands from the record company that we weren't expecting, but yet still have to meet.

In the midst of all of this, Newsboys have to find time for their families as well, and we have to make that a priority when we are asked to take even more time out of their lives.

All in all, we definitely appreciate Susie's wonderful attitude and hard work on behalf of this opportunity to bring Newsboys to China, and regret that it wasn't able to come to fruition.

Thank you for your patience and understanding as well.

Sincerely,

Velvet Rousseau
First Company Management

The Newsboys' Management composed a sincere apology letter for Mom to pass along to China. Mom did not pass it along.

The Newsboys promo poster that was conveniently plastered all over Changsha.

(L to R) A random news reporter, Jeremy Diehl, Shane Almgren, Dean Baktay, Gavin McLaughlin, Budd Kelly, Susie Almgren

Navigating the Changsha airport with piles of gear.

Hollywood East *Discoteque:* interrupting our one and only rehearsal to fumble our way through a radio interview.

(L to R) Gavin McLaughlin, Shane Almgren, Jeremy Diehl.

Gavin McLaughlin covers up the "s" in Newsboys while the author points at a picture neither of them is in.

The author's 2 working keyboards and a non-functioning decoy off to the side.

Receiving bouquets from our hosts after our final performance.

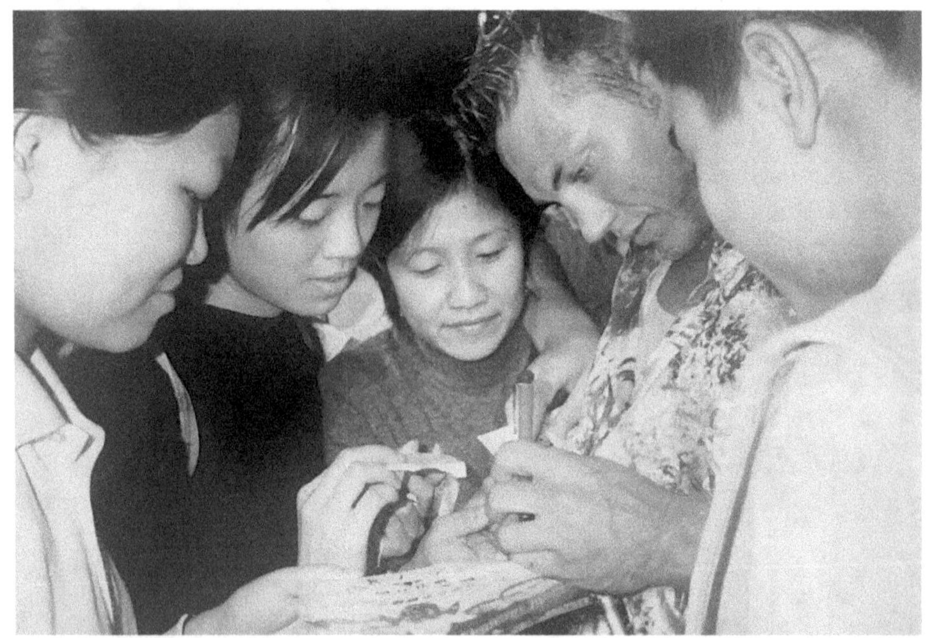

Signing autographs for a bunch of adoring fans who are going to be super disappointed one day when they find out nobody's ever heard of "Shane Almgren."

Ditto for Gavin McLaughlin.

Dean Baktay signs an autograph while Budd Kelly photobombs in the background.

Jeremy Diehl and Budd Kelly strike a pose while Mom converts a marquis from Newsboys to Newboys.

Mom and "Mr. Wu."

The author encounters and locks blades with either a paid actor out in the middle of absolutely nowhere or a 600-year-old Guardian of the Wall.

The author [incredibly illegally] rappelling of the Great Wall.

Gavin McLaughlin, Shane Almgren, Jeremy Diehl in the middle of our hotel lobby.

Shane Almgren, Chris Armfield, Gavin McLaughlin at church Halloween party after getting picked up at airport.

I, Shane Almgren, on March 11, 1997 do sell all my possessions located at 35½ Mango Promenade Apt. 1 (WPB FL 33401) to Joseph Robert Dellinger at the amount of one dollar and no cents.

This includes, but is not limited to, clothes, stereo, tapes and CD's, furniture, decorations, appliances, sporting equiptment, jewelry, safety box, books, and all other personal items. Joseph Dellinger is now the sole owner of all the above named possessions.

Shane Almgren 3/4/97

Shane Almgren 3-4-97

State of Fla.
County of Palm Beach

Personally appeared Shane M. Almgren presenting Pennsylvania D/L as Identification this 4th day of Mar. 1997.

Jeanette J Williams

OFFICIAL NOTARY SEAL
JEANETTE J WILLIAMS
NOTARY PUBLIC STATE OF FLORIDA
COMMISSION NO. CC618572
MY COMMISSION EXP. FEB. 16, 2001

The author narrowly avoids expulsion from college by selling everything he owns for $1.

You don't reach points in
life at which everything
is sorted out for us. I
believe in endings that
should suggest our
stories always continue.

– Lauren Oliver

Dean Baktay currently resides in Riyadh, Saudi Arabia, where he teaches English full-time. He just finished sound-proofing a home studio so he could start recording again.

Jeremy Diehl got a degree in engineering and became a serial entrepreneur in the CO2 extraction industry. He has played in a couple bands over the years and still loves to record when he can find the time. He currently lives in Dallas, Texas.

Gavin McLaughlin met the love of his life, got married and left Nashville in 2003 for Greenville, South Carolina, where he lives with his wife and two kids. He manages several restaurants.

Budd Kelley remained in Pittsburgh and claims he's retired now, but I don't believe him. Musicians never "retire"—they just move on to other projects. His basement looks like a music store, and he's been playing, recording, and making music to his heart's content.

Shane Almgren is still in Nashville, living the dream. He is a part-time professional musician and recording artist, and he started his own creative studio in 2011. He has been banned for life from the Nashville Zoo, though that is a story for another book.

Susan Almgren retired from teaching in 2021. She has no free time because she's constantly babysitting, or zip-lining, or teaching herself origami, or feeding elephants in Thailand, or staying up all night to finish some elaborate arts-and-crafts project for someone's birthday she knew about for two months but waited until the last second to start, or driving to Florida to run in Disney 5K races—even though she despises running—because it gives her an excuse to sew her own Disney princess costumes.

The last time I spoke to her, she was lost on her way home from Ohio.

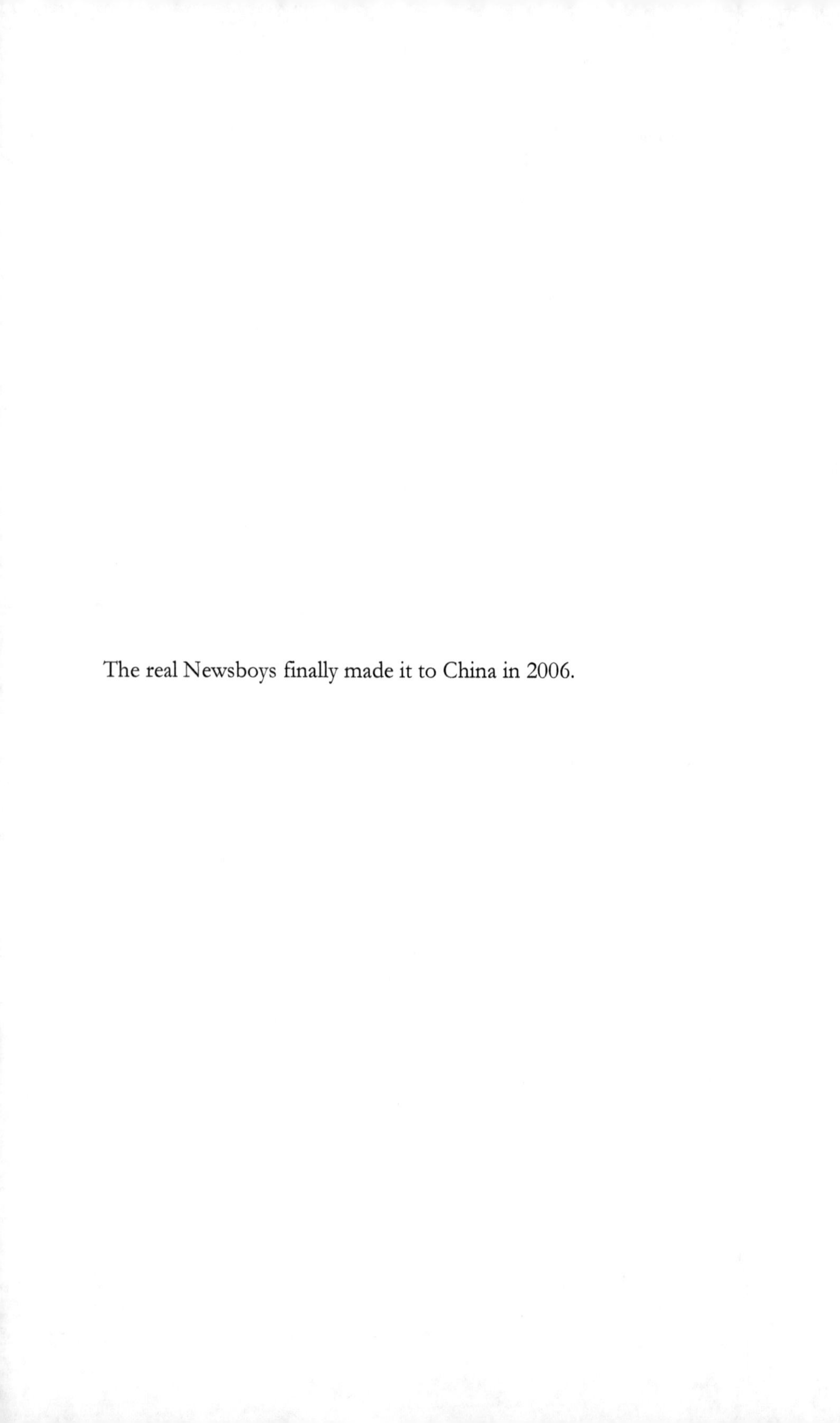

The real Newsboys finally made it to China in 2006.

Timeline of Western Music in China

1985	Wham!
1999	**Newboys/"Newsboys"**
2002	Kenny G*
2003	Mariah Carey
2006	Black Eyed Peas
	The Newsboys
	Rolling Stones
2007	Christina Aguilera
	Eric Clapton
	Linkin Park
	Nine Inch Nails
	Sonic Youth
	Yeah Yeah Yeahs
2008	Avril Lavigne
	Björk
	Celine Dion
2009	Beyoncé
2010	Usher
2011	Bob Dylan
	The Eagles
2012	Elton John
	Jason Mraz
2013	Taylor Swift
	Metallica
2023	Pharrell Williams

*As mentioned in the Introduction, China had an odd fixation on Muzak, most likely due to its censor-friendly, harmless nature. Released in 1990, saxophonist Kenny G's instrumental song "Going Home" became a smash hit in China and inexplicably became the *de facto* closing time song for business establishments throughout the country. Over the next decade, it was adopted by shopping centers, grocery stores, malls, restaurants, bars, nightclubs—anywhere that customers needed to be told that it was time to start making their way to the exits. The song had such a Pavlovian-conditioned response among China's citizens that it nearly derailed Kenny G's concert when he finally performed there for the first time in 2002. Situated midway through the evening's setlist, when Kenny G began playing the familiar tune, the audience got up and left.

Notable Western Acts Banned or Censored in China

- **Backstreet Boys** – censored for "seductive lyrics"
- **Björk** – banned for yelling "Tibet! Tibet!" during a song about independence at her 2008 concert in China
- **Bob Dylan** – banned in 2010 after authorities raised concerns about his anti-establishment lyrics (how they didn't know this in advance is puzzling), but allowed him in 2011 when Dylan gave them permission to pre-approve his setlist.
- **Britney Spears** – censored for lyrics and modesty. Was approved to come in 2004 if she modified her stage costumes, but declined to do so.
- **Harry Connick Jr.** – censored when he accidentally submitted the wrong setlist in 2008. The Chinese authorities forced him to perform the set he submitted rather than the one he had planned. Since his band didn't have the old music, Connick was forced to perform solo while his band sat on the stage mostly doing nothing.
- **Jay-Z** – banned for vulgar language
- **Jon Bon Jovi** – banned for showing an image of Dalai Lama at a concert
- **Justin Bieber** – banned for "bad behavior"
- **Katy Perry** – banned for wearing a sunflower dress, which is an anti-China symbol, at a performance in Taiwan
- **Lady Gaga** – banned for "vulgar music" and meeting with Dalai Lama
- **Linkin Park** – banned for appearing in a photo with the Dalai Lama
- **Maroon 5** – banned for tweeting Happy Birthday to Dalai Lama
- **Miley Cyrus** – banned for making faces construed as racist towards Asians

- **Oasis** – banned for performing at the Tibetan Freedom Concert in New York in 1997; deemed an "enemy of the people"
- **Rolling Stones** – censored 6 of their biggest hits for "suggestive" lyrics when they performed in 2006 . . . after 30 years trying to get in
- **Selena Gomez** – banned for sharing a photo of her and Dalai Lama on social media
- **U2** – banned for performing at Tibetan Freedom Concert, photographed with Dalai Lama, "anti-establishment" lyrics

Taylor Swift inadvertently ignited a controversy that nearly led to a ban as well. When her 2014 album, *1989*, was released (named after the year she was born), a lot of the tour merchandise for sale had her initials emblazoned next to the name of the tour. China's censors were concerned that "T.S. 1989" was a reference to Tiananmen Square, 1989—the infamous student massacre that got us kicked out of China, and that the Communist Party still denies to this day.

Acknowledgments

To all of my fabulous piano teachers growing up: Pat Birch, Jan Crews, Ricky Tims, Jan McDaniel, So Mei and Mr. So, "Grandma" Anna, and Bill Tobin. Words will never do adequate justice to your profound influences on my life. Each of you deserves your own book for the monumental contributions you made to my journey. Every one of you was instrumental in creating this monster, so I take no personal responsibility for my actions. If the Communists ever come looking for me, I'm blaming everything on you guys.

To Steve Feldman: Thank you for believing in this story so passionately and insisting that I go write it down. (Even if it was only because you selfishly wanted to turn it into a movie.) Whatever your reasons, I listened to you. And now here we are.

To Kyle & Kenny Saylors: This story might be mine, but the book is entirely your fault. (Well, yours and Steve's). Thanks for the opportunity to share this story at Dinner with Dreamers. Who would've guessed that a low-key New Year's Eve get-together would spark the coolest creative networking group on the globe and launch a thousand creative ventures? It's almost like you two were on to something.

To my Mastermind group: Justin Kraus, Michelle Froedge, Sherri Bashore, and Tim Wilhoit: thank you all for your invaluable feedback and notes on everything from the synopsis to the quotes to the messaging and lessons. Without your input, this would've been 300+ pages of nothing but a bunch of stupid, asinine stuff I did once upon a time. You all gave it some much-needed direction and helped me turn an otherwise absurdist farce into something a little deeper and more thoughtful that hopefully has some lasting value.

To Paul Stewart and family—my beta readers: thanks for the terrific feedback, the constructive criticism, and for helping me understand the potential of this material.

To my fellow "Newsboys," or Newboys, or whatever the hell we were calling ourselves: Budd Kelley, Dean Baktay, Gavin McLaughlin, and Jeremy Diehl. We done gone and made some history, huh, fellas? Thanks for answering the call and choosing to accept this Impossible Mission with me (even if you didn't quite grasp what you were actually signing up for). I'd call you all rockstars, but you lovable bunch of misfits are a few notches above that.

You boys will forever be Desperados.

(Acknowledgments continued)

To my breathtaking and amazing wife and editor, Amy: I'm sure you're probably not even reading this right now after noticing you weren't included on the Acknowledgments page—after working nearly as hard on this book as I did—and probably threw the book against the wall and immediately jumped on Craigslist looking for a hitman to take me out for being such a thoughtless husband instead of simply turning the page to see that I didn't forget you, I just thought you deserved an entire page all to yourself for the mountains of hours you poured into this (and also I maybe wanted to drive home a point about a certain someone always jumping to conclusions without all the facts). I couldn't do anything I do without you doing everything you do. I've got ideas for the next dozen books and I wouldn't want to do a single one of them without you.

Just one small piece of advice: Get comfortable with editing on a boat.

About the Author

Shane Almgren was born in the wrong century. He should be a pirate on a ship that doesn't rape and pillage, but instead sails the high seas throwing 24-hour raves in the middle of the ocean. (Arggh, matey, might I borrow thy glow sticks?) He is an endless purveyor of nonsense and practical jokes with a propensity for incarceration. He's written some books, done some comedy, been in some movies, he'll never stop playing music, and he still doesn't know what he wants to be when he grows up.

He lives in Nashville with his wife and the fiercest pack of guard dogs in North America: Se7en the white German Shepherd, Finn the chihuahua, and Ollie the one-eyed/blind Shih Tzu. That fearsome trio is the only thing standing between your liberty and a Vladimir Putin invasion of middle Tennessee. They also have a pet frog named Freddy who shows up on the back patio every spring. But it's possible it's not the same frog every year.